THE UNNECESSARY PASTOR

THE UNNECESSARY PASTOR

Rediscovering the Call

by

Marva J. Dawn and Eugene H. Peterson

Edited by

Peter Santucci

William B. Eerdmans Publishing Company

Grand Rapids, Michigan / Cambridge, U.K.

Regent College Publishing

Vancouver

© 2000 by Wm. B. Eerdmans Publishing Co.

Published jointly 2000 by
Wm. B. Eerdmans Publishing Co.
255 Jefferson Ave. S.E., Grand Rapids, Michigan 49503 /
P.O. Box 163, Cambridge CB3 9PU U.K.
and by
Regent College Publishing
an imprint of Regent College Bookstore
5800 University Boulevard, Vancouver, B.C. V6T 2E4

Printed in the United States of America

05 04 03 02   7 6 5 4

Library of Congress Cataloging-in-Publication Data

Dawn, Marva J.
The unnecessary pastor: rediscovering the call / by Marva J. Dawn and
Eugene H. Peterson; edited by Peter Santucci.
p.   cm.
Includes bibliographical references.
Eerdmans ISBN 0-8028-4678-5 (pbk.: alk. paper)
1. Clergy — Office — Biblical teaching.
2. Bible. N.T. Pastoral Epistles — Criticism, interpretation, etc.
3. Bible. N.T. Ephesians — Criticism, interpretation, etc.
I. Peterson, Eugene H., 1932-   II. Santucci, Peter.   III. Title.
BS2735.6.C56 D38   2000
253 — dc21   99-053079

Regent College Publishing ISBN 1-57383-148-4

Audio and video recordings of the "Unnecessary Pastor" conference from
which this book is derived are available from the Regent College bookstore
(1-800-334-3279; www.regent-bookstore.com).

Contents

v

Contents

Introduction

I am always a bit nervous putting together a book like this. Books are wonderful. I like to read them; I like to write them. But there is a sort of built-in falsehood in what Marva and I are doing here because a book is an inevitably misleading object. All of the sentences end with a period. All of the semicolons are in the right place. All of the sentences parse. All of the pages are numbered in sequence; you don't have to skip over anything. All of the chapter titles unfold before you in an orderly fashion. Books have covers, which give a false sense of completeness. It's all there, laid out nice and tidy for you.

But life is not that way. Neither ministry nor spirituality is that way. I'm not like that, and neither is Marva. Life is full of starts and stops, blind alleys, disappointing detours, and bad guesses. Eventually, by God's grace, we find our way into acts of obedience, acts of praise. But along the way we spend considerable time extricating ourselves from brambles and scratching our heads. I think it will be useful to stop and read and pray through this — and, even better yet, do it with a colleague or spouse or friend. But you mustn't suppose that Marva and I are working at a higher level than you are. There are no higher levels in the life of Christ — there is simply following Jesus and obeying him, day after day, struggling with sin and sinners, and being surprised by grace and resurrection.

What I'm getting at is this: *spirituality and ministry are always local and specific, always taking place in conditions.* We aren't working with a set of truths, abstractions, and generalities, but rather with a cultivated habit of the heart and a determination to immerse ourselves in our place, our town, our congregation after the manner of Jesus in Galilee and Jerusalem, Paul in Rome, Timothy in Ephesus, and Titus in Crete.

So, when it comes to putting together a book on ministry, I feel like someone who has been working in a garage for most of my life, underneath the cars with grease on my face and under my fingernails. And then, someone puts me in a shower, has me scrub off the mess, dresses me up, and puts me in front of a group of people and says, "Tell them what you do."

"Well, I work on cars."

"Oh, really, you don't look like someone who works on cars. What do you do on them?"

"Well, it depends. Is it a Pontiac, a Chrysler, a BMW? What's wrong: the transmission, the carburetor, the spark plugs? Do I need a crescent wrench or a $\frac{3}{16}$ socket wrench? Ask me a question." And then you do, and I say, "I have no idea about that."

There is a wonderful radio program called *Car Talk* that I love listening to, even though I don't know all that much about cars. On it, two brothers, Click and Clack, field questions from listeners about car problems. These two brothers banter back and forth — they're witty and irreverent — but they know everything about cars. Even if you have an old car from 1932, they know exactly what you're talking about. And within thirty or forty or fifty seconds on the radio, they have diagnosed the problem with your car. They don't theorize, don't make any big pronouncements, say nothing of a general nature. They revel in the details. You never know whether they were right or not. But they act confident, and the people who call in seem to be satisfied.

Whenever I hear them, I think, I'd like to be a pastor like that. I'd like to know so much about souls that I could diagnose them that quickly and figure them out that accurately and know what I'm doing. Then I think, there are a lot of different makes of cars, but there are a lot more makes of souls. All that can go wrong with a car is something mechanical. And given physics and materiality, there are only a certain number of ways that problems can occur and be fixed. But sin is exponential. You can't imagine all the ways that sin can destroy a life. So, I give up on that and am content with being a pastor who doesn't know a lot and has to figure things out as I go along. But at least Click and Clack tell me this: don't bluff your way with big ideas, grand visions, sweeping eternal truths — immerse yourself in the details. You can't do pastoral work in general or objectively — you are *in* it.

As a schoolboy, I remember being told about the "scientific method," by which scientists in laboratories would make exacting efforts to carry out experiments that are totally objective, with no subjective human contamination. The aim was to create an absolutely sterile environment, insuring results that are pure fact, which then can be precisely duplicated anywhere, at any time. And then they found that the very presence of the observer affected the experiment. Just being there changed things.

If the scientists in controlled conditions can't come up with pure objectivity that translates into precise predictability, we're certainly not going to. For we work at the other end of the control spectrum: put a pastor and a congregation together and mostly what you have is some kind of chaos, what Genesis 1:2 names *tohu wabohu,* "without form and void." This may not seem very promising, but you also have the Spirit of God, hovering over this chaos, and God's Word being spoken, bringing a world of creation and salvation into being. All ministry takes place in conditions of sin, over which the Spirit of God hovers and into which the world-making, life-changing Word of God is spoken.

And then I sit down to write a book or give a series of lectures, and I feel like Click and Clack again — or, in this case, Marva and Eugene — full of clean, objective answers. Marva and I will probably come across as if we know more than we really do. But, hopefully, that's not what ends up happening. Our aim is to put some biblical texts before you — the Pastoral Epistles and Ephesians — in such a way that they shape your understanding of what you have been called to be as pastors and lay ministers. We want to aid you in the shaping of a biblical, pastoral identity out of which you can minister in the complex and messy details of the souls entrusted to your care by God.

Introduction

As much as we would love to mimic the ease and wit and specific solutions of Click and Clack, Marva and I have contented ourselves with painting the big picture as accurately as we can so that you can fill in the details of your life in ministry. If we have succeeded in doing that, then we will be glad.

Eugene H. Peterson

Chapter 1

On Being Unnecessary

EUGENE H. PETERSON

Introduction

We begin with the obvious: the gospel of Jesus Christ is profoundly countercultural. "I came to cast fire upon the earth," said Jesus; "and would that it were already kindled!" (Luke 12:49).

There are powerful cultural forces determined to turn Jesus into a kindly, wandering peasant sage, teaching us how to live well, dispensing homespun wisdom, arousing our desire for God, whetting our appetite for higher truths — all of which are good things. These same forces are similarly determined to turn us, the church's pastors and leaders, into kindly religious figures, men and women who provide guidance through difficult times, who dole out inspiration and good cheer on a weekly schedule, who provide smiling reassurance that "God's in his heaven . . . ," and keep our congregations busy at tasks that bolster their self-esteem — also good things.

And if they don't turn us into merely nice people, they turn us into replicas of our cultural leaders, seeking after power and influence and prestige. These insistent voices drum away at us, telling us pastors to go out and compete against the successful executives and entertainers who have made it to the top, so that we can put our churches on the map and make it big in the world.

In such a culture, it is continuously difficult to cultivate an everyday identity that derives from the crucified and risen Jesus Christ. No matter how many crosses we hang around our necks, paste on our bumpers, and place on our churches, the radical life of repentance and baptism is mighty hard to sustain.

But the Christian is a witness to a new reality that is entirely counter to the culture. The Christian faith is a proclamation that God's kingdom has arrived in Jesus, a proclamation that puts the world at risk. What Jesus himself proclaimed and we bear witness to is the truth that the sin-soaked, self-centered world is doomed.

Pastors are in charge of keeping the distinction between the world's lies and the gospel's truth clear. Not only pastors, of course — every baptized Christian is part of this — but pastors are placed in a strategic, countercultural position. Our place in society is, in some ways, unique: no one else occupies this exact niche that looks so inoffensive but is in fact so dangerous to the status quo. We are committed to keeping the proclamation alive and to looking after *souls* in a soul-denying, soul-trivializing age.

But it isn't easy. Powerful forces, both subtle and obvious, attempt either to domesticate pastors to serve the culture as it is or to seduce us into using our position to become powerful and important on the world's terms. And so we need all the help we can get to maintain our gospel identity.

A Few Words about This Book and Its Title

The purpose of this book, then, is to reconnect pastors with the authoritative biblical and theological texts that train us as countercultural servants of Jesus Christ. We want to be free of the Egyptian slavery to the culture and free to serve our wilderness world in Jesus' name.

The leading premise is that pastors are "unnecessary," but unnecessary in a defined sense. I don't mean worthless or irrelevant or shiftless. I mean unnecessary in three ways in which we often are assumed to be necessary:

1. We are unnecessary to what the *culture* presumes is important:

2

as paragons of goodness and niceness. Culture has a fairly high regard for pastors as custodians of moral order. We are viewed as persons who provide a background of social stability, who are useful in times of crisis and serve as symbols of meaning and purpose. But we are not necessary in any of those ways.

Several years ago, I was invited to the Pentagon to meet with the chaplains of the various services — Army, Navy, Air Force, Marines — to talk about their difficult position. We'd been in a peacetime mode for a number of years, and the Pentagon was trying to cut back on budgeting for chaplains. Chaplains weren't high-profile, necessary figures. And these chaplains had called on me to come and try to convince their superiors that they were necessary, that they had to be there. They were being used in all sorts of programs — drug counseling, marriage counseling. They were finding all sorts of ways to keep their jobs, and none of them had to do with anything they thought they had signed up to be chaplains for. In the middle of all this — and I wasn't much help to them, for I was thinking about what I'm talking to you about — they told me that in wartime, on the front, every captain, every colonel, every leader of a force *demands* to have a chaplain. When the bullets are flying and the bombs are exploding, they want a chaplain right there. Chaplains are important, everybody knows they are important. They are life-and-death people. But in peacetime, who needs a chaplain? And in the course of all this, one of the men slammed down his fist and said, "What we need is a war!"

Three weeks later, the Gulf War broke out and their jobs were assured.

(2) We are also unnecessary to what *we ourselves* feel is essential: as the linchpin holding a congregation together. Some of us have been reared with an idea that being a pastor is the apex of ministry — we hold the highest position in the hierarchy of those who serve in Jesus' name. We are entrusted with the Word of God and the souls of men and women — no one else occupies this privileged position quite like we do. We come to take ourselves very seriously indeed. But we are not necessary in these self-important ways. None of us is indispensable. Mordecai's message to Esther puts us in our place: "if you keep silence at such a time as this, relief and deliverance will rise for the

Jews from another quarter . . ." (Esther 4:14). We have important work to do, but if we don't do it God can always find someone else — and probably not a pastor.

3. And we are unnecessary to what *congregations* insist that we must do and be: as the experts who help them stay ahead of the competition. Congregations want pastors who will lead them in the world of religious competition and provide a safe alternative to the world's ways. They want pastors who *lead*. They want pastors the way the Israelites wanted a king — to make hash of the Philistines. Congregations get their ideas of what makes a pastor from the culture, not from the Scriptures: they want a winner; they want their needs met; they want to be part of something zesty and glamorous.

I am in conversation right now with a dozen or so men and women who are prepared to be pastors and who are waiting to be called by a congregation. And I am having the depressing experience of reading congregational descriptions of what these churches want in a pastor. With hardly an exception they don't want pastors at all — they want managers of their religious company. They want a pastor they can follow so they won't have to bother with following Jesus anymore.

Marva and I . . .

Marva Dawn and I, between us, are going to work at building an identity of unnecessariness to counter these expectations from culture, ego, and congregation. It is our conviction that only when we realize how unnecessary we are will we be free to do the "one thing needful" — the gospel necessity laid upon the glorious but battered life of the pastor.

Marva and I have never put our heads and hearts together like this before, but for several years we have enjoyed a friendship that has prepared us for it. Every year, Marva comes to a Lutheran camp in Montana to train their summer staff. The camp is not far from where Jan and I live. For years Marva and I had been reading each other's books, and then we found that we were annual one-week neighbors. So it is now our habit in early June to enjoy a meal together and some rich conversation. Through our reading and conversing, it didn't take us long to realize that somehow or other, from our quite different backgrounds, we had arrived at similar convictions and understandings of the gospel. Maybe it was the Montana connection. . . .

The understanding and conviction that bring us together in this book are that pastoral work originates in and is shaped by the revelation of God in Jesus Christ. It takes place in the world's culture, but it is not caused by it. It is intimately involved in the world, but it is not defined by it. The gospel is free, not only in the sense that we don't have to pay for it, but also in the more fundamental sense that it is an expression of God's freedom — it is not caused by our needs but by God's grace. The Trinity — not the culture, not the congregation — is the primary context for acquiring training and understanding in the pastoral vocation.

There are extensive theological discussions in our tradition about the freedom of God. God is absolutely free. He doesn't do anything because he has to do it. There is no *necessitas* in God. He is not a part of the cause-effect sequence of things. He operates out of free love — no constraints. And there are subsequent reflections that, though none of us are free in that way, as we worship and obey God in his freedom we come to participate in his freedom and minister out of it, living not by constraints or impulses or necessities, but out of grace and love — two elemental aspects of freedom. This kind of theological reflection hovers in the background of the following pages.

A Word to Non-Pastors

But before going on, I want to say something to those who are not pastors, for most of those who work in the gospel vineyard are ministering in ways that don't fall under the label "pastor."

I have friends who think that it is virtually impossible to be an honest, God-honoring pastor in our present culture. They are convinced that the role itself, formed as it has been now in a century of buy-it consumerism and fix-it psychologism, has become so powerful that it defeats all individual efforts to work within it. The role of pastor is now so secularized and so politicized by the culture that, even with the best of intentions, it is no longer available as a venue for a genuinely Christian ministry.

Sometimes the sixteenth century is cited as precedent, following some of the Reformers who were convinced that it was impossible to give leadership to Christ's church as a monk or nun or priest. George Fox, who a hundred years later hurled anathemas on clergy of any stripe or vintage, is another sometimes alleged precedent. The only authentic leadership at such times as these, then, must come from the laity, the people of God undefined by professional considerations.

There is certainly a case to be made for this position, and I don't dismiss it lightly. In an age like ours, when we characteristically hand over the management of our lives to experts, our only link with what is truly human is the amateur, the layperson. We do live in a time when knowledge has been so computerized and institutionalized that all the wisdom has been squeezed out of it, leaving us in a condition where actual wisdom can almost only be found outside the ranks of schools and those trained by the schools.

Many of the renewal movements in our two thousand years of Christian history originated among the laity. The Christian faith has formed and reformed itself, not infrequently, over against the religious establishment. The so-called laity, God's people undefined by job or status or certification, is a pool from which leaders continue to surface at critical times and often in unexpected ways, to give urgency and clarity to the gospel of Jesus Christ in this old world. Jesus himself, along with Peter and the rest of the Twelve, was a layperson, functioning outside the clerical parameters of the culture. Neither he nor they came from an educated or professional caste.

All the same, I am not convinced. I am not pessimistic about the possibility of pastors living and working as servants of Jesus Christ. But we do need all the help we can get, and much of the help is going to come from you who are not pastors, who find yourselves called to serve Jesus in other work forms.

And the fact remains that we do have pastors, and we are probably going to continue to have them. My approach in all of this is to do what I can to give dignity to all lay, workplace ministries that are done in Jesus' name, and at the same time to cultivate humility among the clerical, churchplace ministries. Ministry is ministry, no matter who does it, when it is done in Jesus' name. But pastors have distinctive conditions in which to work, and distinctive responsibilities. I think we understand and practice our respective ministries, lay and clergy, best when we do it together, lay and clergy, in the same room.

When I was a boy, I remember sitting through the mandatory sex talk at summer camp. Boys and girls were segregated for this solemn occasion. Mostly what occupied our minds was what was being said to the other sex, in the other room. Sex is not something that makes much sense without the presence of the other, knowledge of the other. Similarly we have pursued a parallel strategy in talking about ministry, segregating professionals and non-professionals, clergy and laity, and have ended up with a lot of misinformation about the other. But hopefully not here. Most of what follows is as relevant to the lives of non-pastors as to those of pastors; and the little bit that isn't will give you insight for prayer and encouragement to the pastors.

My main thrust is toward cultivating humility among pastors, but the same words, with a shift in vocabulary, can be used to give dignity to all who join God in his work of ministry.

The Pastoral Epistles

When I became a pastor, I found that most of the counsel and direction I was given came not from Scripture but from the culture. It was, most of it, good counsel — it made sense, it was responsible. If I had followed it, I probably would not have done any harm. But I didn't follow it; I wanted not only my life but my ministry to be shaped by the Christian gospel revealed in Jesus. None of my learned advisors ever suggested that I give up my Christian faith so that I could be successful at this pastor business; but what they did do by implication was suggest that I give up on Scripture as having anything definitive to do with the pastoral vocation in contemporary North America. Scripture was good for preaching, but when it came to running a church, organizing a congregation, managing conflict, training church school teachers, and getting out the publicity on the new missions emphasis, the Holy Scriptures didn't offer much. Isaiah, after all, never had to run a stewardship campaign; Jeremiah didn't know the first thing about conflict management — in fact, he was in trouble most of his life with his religious colleagues in Jerusalem. My advisors were happy to supply me with up-to-date texts written by various experts in the field, showing me how to be relevant to the culture.

But I knew that there were men and women who had had their pastor work shaped by Holy Scripture. Admiring them, I wanted that for myself. Most of these people I admired were in the cemeteries, but they had left books behind them, and their books gave me enough to go on, enough to convince me that Scripture, not the culture, was the place to start. Between Sundays, I rummaged through my Bible, looking for the help I needed. I wasn't long finding it, and many of my books came directly from this successful search. First, I discovered the Psalms and Jeremiah, then the five little Hebrew scrolls — Song of Songs, Ruth, Lamentations, Ecclesiastes, and Esther — and then, a few years ago, I was surprised by Jonah. But an interest in the Pastoral Epistles predated all of these. Early on, I resolved that if anyone ever asked me to teach a course in a seminary on pastoral work, I would use the Pastoral Epistles for my text. Nobody ever asked, and so these three Pastoral Epistles, 1 and 2 Timothy and Titus, have been sitting there all these years just waiting for a chance.

And then I was asked, asked to speak at the pastors' conference at Regent College (from which this book springs); within minutes of being asked, I knew that I wanted to use the Pastorals. I talked it over with Marva, who had also been asked, and she thought Ephesians would provide just the right voice to make a dialogue out of this. The topic, the unnecessary pastor, emerged from our conversations. And here we are.

Therefore, the Pastoral Epistles will be our orienting text, taking three early church pastors, working in three quite different settings, but in each case working prayerfully, intelligently, and insistently *against* the prevailing culture. Marva's exposition of Ephesians will set the larger context in which all Christian living and ministry take place.

Here's the background to my interest in the Pastoral Epistles in relation to contemporary pastoral work. When I became a pastor, I was determined to be a radical pastor. I wanted to do things the first-century way — none of the twenty centuries of landfill in between, it's back to rock bottom for me; none of this accommodating to the culture, going along with traditions, fitting into institutional religion stuff for me. Nobody was going to go to sleep in my congregation. Nobody to whom I was pastor was going to serve two masters.

And then, after a few months on the job, I realized that there were heating and electricity bills to pay, a nursery for small children and infants to get in place. One Sunday, I woke to a foot of snow and realized that I hadn't anticipated snow in my planning and hadn't arranged for anyone to be responsible for this kind of gospel work. On that Sunday, I spent three hours preparing for worship by shoveling snow. And then there were the people who wanted help in raising their children, dealing with their spouses. We had committee meetings to work out what kind of carpeting to put in the nursery.

How do you spend three days exegeting the text, "I am crucified with Christ," stay up half of Friday night on retreat with the youth listening to their rock music, attend a Saturday meeting with your deacons trying to decide how much money to budget for janitorial services, and step into the pulpit on Sunday morning as a radical pastor?

If I was going to be a pastor, I was going to have to deal with the responsibilities that went with living in community with people who took their jobs seriously, took their kids to the dentist faithfully, and balanced their check books every month. Could I also be a radical pastor? Did I have to give up "radical" the moment I agreed to share the responsibilities of a moral and just community life?

That's when I discovered the Pastoral Epistles.

But these three letters were bruised and tattered, having been treated with considerable condescension by New Testament scholars for the past 150 years. The prevailing view until quite recently was that they are second-rate Paul, warmed-over Paul. Paul could not have written them: Paul was radical, fiery, an uncompromising evangelist/missionary, in and out of prison, a disturber of the peace, an agitator — unsettling people and provoking opposition left and right — and on the move, restlessly going from city to city. The only way to keep him quiet for very long was to put him in prison. But the Pastoral Epistles, though claiming to have been written by Paul and having some Pauline phrases and ideas in them, have none of the passion of Paul. The Pauline lion had been turned into a house cat. The real Paul expected the coming of Christ at any moment — life was lived on the sharp edge of expectancy — but the Pastoral Epistles had settled down for the long haul, working out ways to keep order and maintain continuity. They reflect a church that has come to terms with its relation to the world. That couldn't be Paul.

To describe these three letters, German scholars used the term *christliche Burgerlichkeit:* bourgeois Christianity, middle-class Christianity, respectable Christianity. The tension between church and world is gone. The church has settled in. The phrase "the quiet and peaceful life" (1 Timothy 2:2) is representative of the Pastorals. Don't rock the boat; don't make waves. Philip Towner writes, "Life in Christ had merged with life in the world."[1] And then there's Titus 2:11-14: "For the grace of God has appeared for the salvation of all men, training us to renounce irreligion and worldly passions, and to live sober, upright, and godly lives in this world, awaiting our blessed hope, the appearing of the glory of our great God and Savior Jesus Christ, who gave himself for us to redeem us from all iniquity and to purify for himself a people of his own who are zealous for good deeds." And Titus 3:1: "Remind them to be submissive to rulers and authorities, to be obedient, to be ready for any honest work. . . ."

But more recent studies find that this is no tamed Paul; this is the same gospel as always — expectant, radical, fervent — but now worked out in pastoral conditions, conditions that involve dealing with family and community over the long haul. This is the same Pauline passion, a pastoral passion. Fresh and new and intense — but in the world, and dealing with the conditions of the world. And that is the perspective I will be working from.

One Regent student recently told me that when she and her husband got married, they decided that they would be "gypsies for

---

1. Philip Towner, *The Goal of Our Instruction* (Sheffield, Eng.: JSOT Press, 1989), p. 10.

Jesus" — no ties, loose, free, and just talk about Jesus. But now that she's graduating, she said, "What I really want now is to be a pastor. I just want to get rooted in a community and get to know them, care for them, serve them. I don't think Matt and I are any less radical than before, but we don't want to be gypsies anymore. We want to be a part of the household of God." That's what we're after. Not a bourgeois Christianity, but somehow working within the world of the bourgeois, the comfortable, the settled, and somehow bringing this passion for Christ into it. And that is what Paul is after in the Pastorals.

Vows — Putting in Protection

I just recently celebrated the fortieth year of my ordination into the gospel ministry. Through these forty years, I have spent much time trying to stay honest, prayerful, and biblical as I have served Jesus in this role. I have been dismayed by the widespread defection of many of my friends into officiating over Baal shrines and Ashteroth groves — this incredible revival of old Canaanite religion on the North American continent. You would have thought that men and women who had their heads full of Elijah and Isaiah and Jeremiah would have been proof against a religion that was designed to meet the needs of people as the people understood them, appealing to their pride, nurturing their greed, and providing escapist fantasies that incapacitate them from faithful and committed relationships and work. But we look around us — yes, and within us — and realize that there is not much correspondence between those fierce prophets and what is being put on display these days as the successful pastor. (When I first proposed the phrase "The Unnecessary Pastor" as the heading for the conference at Regent College, I was told, "You can't call it that; nobody will come. No pastor in North America wants to be told that he or she is unnecessary. Get a phrase that is more positive, more encouraging." But then it sold out, filled with men and women seeking to strip away the cultural plaque and get on with biblical ministry.)

As I approached this fortieth anniversary of my ordination, I had occasion to go back and revisit the eight vows I took at the time. One of them, the sixth vow, struck me as being generic to all pastors, and I want to use it now to give focus to the spirit that infuses these Pastoral Epistles, and what we are doing here. Here's the vow: *Will you, in your own life, seek to follow the Lord Jesus Christ, love your neighbors, and work for the reconciliation of the world?*

Sixty miles or so from Vancouver, up the sunshine coast, there is a mountain popular among rock climbers — the Stalamus Chief. It presents itself as a vertical slab of smooth granite, two thousand feet high. It looks like a sheet of glass. On summer days, rock climbers are spread out in varying levels of ascent up and down its face. Occasionally, climbers spend the night in hammocks (they call it bivouacking), hanging like cocoons attached to barn siding. It always strikes me as a mighty dangerous way to have fun.

I am fascinated by the sight and, when in the vicinity, pull off the road and watch for awhile with my binoculars. It is not the action that holds my attention, for there is certainly not much in the way of action up there. The climbers move slowly, cautiously, every move tested, calculated. There is no spontaneity in this sport, no thrills. Except perhaps the ultimate thrill of not falling — not dying. Maybe what grips my attention is death, the risk of death — life dangling by a thread.

Still, dangerous as it is, I know that it is not as dangerous as it looks. Looking from the valley floor with my naked eye the climbers appear to be improbably exempt from gravity. But with my binoculars, I can see that each climber is equipped with ropes and carabiners and pitons (or chocks, wedges, and camming devices). The pitons, sturdy pegs constructed from a light metal, are basic. My two sons are both rock climbers, and I have listened to them plan their ascents. They spend as much or more time planning their climbs as in the actual climbing. They meticulously plot their route and then, as they climb, put in what they call "protection" — pitons hammered into small crevices in the rock face, with attached ropes that will arrest a quick descent to death. Rock climbers who fail to put in protection have short climbing careers.

Recently, while watching several of these climbers, it suddenly struck me that my ordination vows had functioned for the past forty years as pitons, pegs driven firmly into the vertical rock face (stretching between heaven and earth) on which Christian ministry is played out. Vows are pegs, protection against moods and weather, miscalculation and fatigue. Vision and call, risk and inspiration are what we are most aware of and what others see when we become pastors or take up leadership positions in the church, but if there is no "protection" the chances of survival are slim. And so we take vows. Various churches and denominations have different ways of wording them, but they all amount to about the same thing: protection.

Here again is the one that I want to hold up for examination: *Will you, in your own life, seek to follow the Lord Jesus Christ, love your neighbors, and work for the reconciliation of the world?*

It seems odd to include a question like this in *ordination* vows. This is a question to ask someone entering the Christian life, getting ready for baptism. This is a beginning question, a vow that gets us started on the right foot. But here I was, getting ready to be a pastor, and this vow — number six in a sequence of eight ordination questions — which has nothing to do with pastoring, comes up. The ground has already been covered pretty thoroughly, making sure that the ordinand is a confessing Christian (#1), submissive to the authority of Scripture (#2), agreeable to the traditions of my church (#3), knowledgeable concerning the office to which I am being ordained (#4), and willing to be a member of a community of peers (#5). Two more vows follow the sixth, making clear that the ordinand knows that people are to be served as well as Jesus (#7), and that this is ordination not to a place of privilege but to one of diligent service, requiring a lifetime of energy and resolve (#8).

Embedded in the eight-vow sequence is this sixth, which doesn't quite seem to fit the context of ordination. Isn't the ordination ground amply covered in the first five and the last two? Isn't a basic Christian commitment assumed? Isn't this redundant?

Yes. But. *Yes,* it's all there already. *But,* long experience in this business makes us alert in detecting loopholes. The loophole, in this case, has to do with becoming so diligent in being a pastor, *working* for Jesus, that it crowds out the personal life of *living* for Jesus. The operative phrase in the sixth vow is "in your own life."

The constant danger for those of us who enter the ranks of the ordained is that we take on a role, a professional religious role, that gradually obliterates the life of the soul.

The sixth vow specifies three areas of protection against this: (1) following the Lord Jesus Christ; (2) loving neighbors; (3) working for the reconciliation of the world. This sixth ordination vow, it seems, has nothing to do with being a pastor as such; it is a vow to diligently guard and nurture our basic commitment as a Christian. Many a Christian has lost his or her soul in the act of being ordained. This vow returns us to the basic vocation of being a Christian, a mere Christian.

For, in ordination, we do not graduate into an advanced level of religion that sets us apart from or above our earlier status as Christian. But it is not easy to maintain that awareness. Karl Barth was eloquent in his insistence that we are always and ever beginners in this Christian life. No matter how well we preach, are knowledgeable in theology, competent in polity, and diligent in carrying out the duties assigned us, we are always novices; we never graduate from "Christian" and go on to advanced work in "ministry." Neither Christian living nor Christian ministry can ever "be anything but the work of beginners. . . . What Christians do becomes a self-contradiction when it takes the form of a trained and mastered routine, of a learned and practiced art. They may and can be masters and even virtuosos in many things, but never in what makes them Christians, God's children."[2]

The sixth vow lays down protection against taking on the role of expert and then taking over the work of leadership from the Christ in whose name we are ordained.

---

2. Karl Barth, *The Christian Life: Church Dogmatics IV, 4 Lecture Fragments,* trans. Geoffrey W. Bromiley (Grand Rapids: Wm. B. Eerdmans Publishing Co., 1981), p. 79.

"Will you, in your own life, seek to follow the Lord Jesus Christ . . . ?"

Ordination puts us in a place of leadership. As we become good at leadership, we become used to people following us. They look to us for direction, expect initiative from us, and not infrequently turn over responsibility for their lives to us, expecting us to take up the slack that results from their indolence and passivity. Leaders usually work harder than followers. Leaders characteristically accept more responsibility than followers. Sometimes the followers admire us, other times they criticize us, but in either case we are made aware that we are being treated as a class apart; we are leaders.

Jesus' words "Except you become as little children . . . " (Matthew 18:3) do not lose pertinence in the act of ordination. But the act of ordination does make it easy to use them primarily on behalf of other people, the people we are leading. Being childlike is a wonderful quality in a follower; it makes it much easier to be a leader when we are followed trustfully and unquestioningly. But a few years of being in charge of God's children makes it astonishingly difficult to be a child ourselves. Humility recedes as leadership advances.

It is a subtle thing and usually takes years to accomplish, but without "protection" — without that piton hammered into the rock face — the role of leader almost inevitably replaces the role of follower. Instead of continuing as followers of the Lord Jesus Christ, we become bosses on behalf of the Lord Jesus Christ. Sometimes we are very good bosses, looking out for the welfare of our employees; other times, barely disguised pious bullies.

"Will you, in your own life . . . love your neighbor . . . ?"

It is a strange thing: the first casualty on the fields of ordained leadership is usually the neighbor. The men and women with whom we live and work become objectified in the course of our work; instead of being primarily persons whom we love, whether through natural affection (spouse, children, friends) or by Christ's command (love your neighbor as yourself) they gradually become functionalized. Under the pressure of "working for Jesus" or "carrying out the church's mission," these former neighbors get treated in functional terms: they become viewed as "resources" or as "deadweight," as "assets" or as "liabilities," as "point man or woman" or as "dysfunctional." In recent years I have developed a strong allergy to the word "dysfunctional" when applied to persons, especially baptized persons. It's a word useful for describing machines, not persons. Love, the commanded relation, gives way to considerations of efficiency and begins to be interpreted by the abstractions of plans and programs, goals and visions, evangelism statistics and mission strategies. After all, we are ordained to something beyond and more intense than simply "Christian" — we have work to do. These people, with whom we find ourselves placed in a responsible position of leadership, need to be put to kingdom work, or at least church work. Loving neighbors recedes to the background as we go about making recruits, lining up allies, arguing the opposition into compliance, motivating the lethargic, and signing up participants to insure the success of a project or program. And if they don't do it, they are dysfunctional.

Do you see what happens when we replace a biblical word like "sinner" with a secular word like "dysfunctional"? What is wrong with the sinner is something that has to do with his or her relationship with God; what is wrong with the dysfunctional person has to do with not fitting into my projects. We can't be too careful in the words we use, for they betray the way we see and live our lives.

Martin Buber, in one of the most important books of the century for people like us, *I and Thou,* showed how easy and common it is to treat people as "It" instead of as "Thou." He also showed how awful it is, turning what God created as a human community of men and women whose glory it is to love one another into a depersonalized wasteland of important roles and efficient functions. Buber also conceded that we cannot continuously maintain the open intimacy of "I/Thou" in our relationships — it would be totally exhausting; we need to be able to escape from time to time into the less demanding region of role and function to carry out some of our basic routines. But the moment the functional region becomes our permanent residence and the neighbor becomes an object, an It to be used, no matter how righteous and glorious the use, sacrilege has been committed.

The sixth vow puts in protection against letting ordination develop into a subtle depersonalizing (and damning) into functions and projects of the very people Christ commanded us to love.

"Will you, in your own life, . . . work for the reconciliation of the world?"

The Johannine phrase "For God so loved the world . . . " (John 3:16) sets the context for the work in which we take up particular responsibilities when we are ordained. It is a staggeringly large, encompassing context: *world.* "World," in this phrase, means the whole thing — continents and oceans, city tenements and country barnyards, souls and societies, babies in the womb and men and women vigorously pursuing every imaginable venue for making money, helping the needy, grasping for power, exploiting the weak, discovering truth, growing food, making art, singing and playing. "World" is teeming with good and evil. It is this world for which Christ came and died, into which we are sent to baptize and make disciples and be "ministers of reconciliation."

But how does it happen, then, that being made a pastor so often has the effect of pulling us out of this immense world and putting us to work in a religious institution that carries on its business pretty much on its own terms and with its own agenda? From within the ordaining institution, it is easy to look out on the world that God loves and redesignate it as enemy, as competitor, as distraction. We who are ordained are then put to work on committees and projects that leave us with neither time nor energy for the world and diminishing interest in it. Ecclesiastical affairs require armies of ordained men and women to keep the wheels turning, and it isn't long before ordination, instead of putting us on the front lines of reconciling love for the world, has conscripted us into jobs and agendas that effectively remove us from the very world whose plight is the reason for our ordination in the first place. It's the devil's own work to get us so busy in attacking or avoiding or competing with the world that we no longer are available for the critical and key work of reconciliation, the work of Christ to which we have been ordained.

That doesn't mean that our ordained life needs to be conspicuously on display in the world, holding press conferences and marching with protesters. Much, maybe most, of the work of reconciliation takes place in ways and places that the world itself never notices: in solitary prayer, in quiet study, in energy-renewing retreats, in vision-clarifying committees. Still, at some level, everything we do and say, think and pray, requires a believing and obedient relation with God's love for the world, with Christ's reconciling work in the world. When our work for Jesus as pastors and witnesses blunts our awareness of the world, distracts us from the world, puts us into competition with the world, or is simply an avoidance of the world, our ordination is falsified.

The sixth vow lays down essential protection against losing touch with the primary work in which Christ himself is engaged and to which we are ordained. We get considerable counsel and direction for keeping us responsible in our ministries; this vow keeps us alive.

My task is to set before you three New Testament "unnecessary" pastors — pastors who responded to, but were not defined by, culture or ego or congregation, the three pastors whose names are clustered in the company of the Pastoral Epistles: Paul, Timothy, and Titus. Alternating chapters by Marva Dawn will provide the largest possible gospel context for understanding these three "unnecessary pastors."

First, Paul, finishing up in Rome. Paul, nearing the end of his pastoral vocation, willingly and graciously lets go of his authority and position. Pastoral vocation is not located in him. He demonstrates a leadership of humility.

Then, Timothy, taking over in Ephesus. Timothy enters into a congregational mess with the mandate to straighten it out. He inherits both the legacy (of Paul) and the problems (of Hymeneaus and Alexander) for which others were responsible. Pastoral vocation doesn't begin with a clean slate. Suffering is inherent in the work. Timothy reforms a corrupt church.

Finally, Titus, starting out in Crete. Titus, in the newly evangelized island of Crete, lays the foundations for Christian community in
a culture that doesn't know much about spiritual community or a life
of discipleship. Titus is sent to establish a firm foundation.

These three are good representatives of people who have done
pastoral ministry before us. They didn't do it perfectly, but they did it
in such a way that God's truth is revealed in what they've done.

Chapter 2

Preludes to Rediscovery

MARVA J. DAWN

Let us begin by thinking of a pair of phrases that the Church[1] has been saying in its worship services for hundreds of years. I find these invaluable for connecting with the community when I speak for groups in which I don't know very many participants. I say to the people, "The Lord be with you," and those gathered respond, "And also with you." We say these phrases to remember that we are a community listening to God together. I can't teach well if those present don't work on the topic with me side by side.

If you and I were in the same room together your participation with me would be as important as whatever I offered because you would evoke in me new possibilities for being open to the Spirit working through me. Since the contents of this book were first presented to a live conference audience, I will imagine you, the reader, with me as I write — and I pray that you will also imagine yourself in a lively interactive process with me in my portion of this book as you read.

When doing children's sermons on the Church's liturgical phrases, I ask the children, "What does the pastor do when saying, 'The Lord be with you'?" and they all know that the clergyperson holds out both

---

1. I capitalize the word *Church* when it signifies all the members of God's true "one, holy, catholic, apostolic Church" throughout time and space. I leave it lowercased when it refers to a single local congregation, which might include people who are not really committed to "being Church."

hands in blessing. Then I ask them, "And what do you do back?" They certainly give very interesting answers, but in general they do not realize that they are ministers also — that the pastor needs them to give the blessing back. So I always urge them to offer it physically with their out-stretched arms. In fact, many of the people in the congregation to which I belong hold out their hands to our pastor now as we give him our blessing. By offering our response with our whole bodies we are really praying for the pastor or leader to be able to serve well, to be open to the Spirit, to know that our love and support are there with him or her. This is a long introduction in order to ask that when I write, "The Lord be with you," you will commit yourself to participating actively with this book by responding in your mind, "And also with you."

The Lord be with you. . . .

Let us pray: Triune God, Father, Son, and Holy Spirit, we are overwhelmed by the magnificence of your grace. We realize that it is only through your mercy that we can gather together in spirit, that everything we do is utterly dependent upon you. Therefore, we ask you to clear away from our minds, souls, and bodies anything that would distract us from what your Spirit wants to say today to the churches. We ask that you would fix our hearts on you and transform our lives through your Word. We trust your promise that your Word will not come back empty and so we believe that we shall be changed by what we hear and read. We also ask that you would form us to be the servants you have called us to be, for your honor and your glory and your praise into the ages of ages — and for the sake of your world. Amen.

Before launching into the brilliant music of Paul's letter to the Ephesians[2] in an attempt to see how it can shape a pastoral identity, we must do some preliminary, preparatory background work. This

---

2. The canonical tradition of the earliest Christians, in passing on to us the letter to the Ephesians, has named Paul as its author. Since these meditations on Ephesians for the life of clergypersons and other servants of the Church are not intended as commentary, but as devotional and pastoral helps, we don't have to debate the historical accuracy of this or any other canonical ascription. Rather, in this book we will recognize the deep narrative and descriptive benefits from identifying the emotions and situations of the Ephesians letter with Paul in particular. Even if you are convinced that Paul did not write it, imagine his influence over the letter's writer as I use the name *Paul* to designate literary practices.

will include some warning notes as well as some sounding forth of the *cantus firmus* on which we will build new melodies and harmonies.

Glittering Images

I must confess that in the conference which gave rise to this book it was much too awesome (in the original meaning of that word before teenagers took it over) to work together with Eugene Peterson. I have admired him for so long that I felt terribly inadequate to teach side-by-side with him, but this sense of inferiority allowed me to make my first point — one that is encapsulated well in the title of Susan Howatch's book *Glittering Images*.[3] In the middle of the novel the book's central character, Charles Ashworth — whose last name is certainly significant in titling how he feels about himself — recognizes through the skillful intervention of a wonderful spiritual director that he has been hiding behind a "glittering image." The result is that his true self has not been allowed to unfold. As the spiritual director continues to guide him, he discerns how he uses the various skills and tools of his glittering image in his attempts to win the approval of others, whereas his true self would rather be faithful in serving God without regard to others' response.

Recently I caught myself in the same temptation to hide behind a glittering image. I was speaking about worship at a denominational conference for the senior pastors of very large churches and knew that some prophetic words had to be proclaimed. However, a huge part of me wanted instead to conceal myself in a more likable figure and more ingratiating words than the pointed ones the participants didn't like, but really needed to hear. Perhaps for you, too, the pulpit or lecture stand is a remarkably easy place in which to slip into glittering images.

My apparel on the first day of the Regent College conference that led to this book was intended to offer a vivid visual illustration of our

---

3. Susan Howatch, *Glittering Images* (New York: Alfred A. Knopf, 1987). I am not necessarily recommending this book. Though its insights conveyed especially through the spiritual director, Jon Darrow, were exceptionally helpful to me and are often quite astounding in their brilliant aptness and biblical depth, the large amount of sexual immorality in the book and its sequels was quite troublesome.

common human problem — since I have one "glittering image" leg and one crippled one. The latter requires a leg brace, which is quite awkward and ugly, but keeps me from breaking that leg again and thereby requiring amputation. The leg did not heal straight when I first broke it after the rebuilding of my shattered foot, so I dare not put weight on it without wearing the brace. When I want to wear dress shoes, I need a very clumsy orthopedic shoe with a wedge on it to keep me from falling over since the leg is quite bent. On my good foot I like to wear a more attractive sandal that is the same color rather than the ponderous matching orthopedic shoe, but the problem is that the sandal is not very stable for walking.

Isn't the same often true for us in our pastoral roles? (I use the word *pastoral* for all of us in this conversation, whether we serve in a professional/ordained capacity or whether we minister for the sake of the gospel in other ways.) We are tempted to hide behind our glittering images and hope that thereby others will approve of us. We would rather not acknowledge our broken selves, our selves with problems, with secret faults we would very much prefer everybody not to know.

How much easier it is — and more beneficial for the whole Church — if we can manifest our true selves. Such honesty alone can lead to genuine growth and stability. Consequently, after the first day at the Regent conference I wore my totally unfashionable, rebuilt-with-a-wedge tennis shoes as a reminder to us all that for us to walk well as the children of God we must shed our glittering images and take our respective handicaps in stride.

Let me encourage each of you at some point to spend time in quiet reflection considering the ways in which your glittering image surfaces and the reasons why it might exist. Do we sometimes pretend to be other than what we are? Do we do this for the sake of "our" ministries? Are we then doing the "necessary" things, rather than understanding ourselves in the "unnecessary" role that Eugene Peterson set out for us in the first chapter of this book? Let us contemplate how we can instead recover our true selves.

Charles Ashworth learned, with his spiritual director's guidance, that his true self was the one who wanted to serve God — and serve God faithfully, letting the chips fall where they may. Of course this is not to advocate tactlessness, but to acknowledge that the prophetic role to which we sometimes are called might arouse anger in others rather than their approval. The only way we can have the courage to live without a glittering image is if we thoroughly recognize that everything we do well as a pastoral servant of the Church is entirely empowered by grace. Then we don't need a glittering image, for it will be the authority of God and God's mercy that works through us.

Primary Colors

My second word of introduction is to connect the warning against glittering images to the primary colors of the Ephesians music I will be exploring in this book. Since God's character and intervening work through us form the basis for our freedom to be his servants, our first major subject after these preludes will be Doxology. As we contemplate who God is and how God works through us, we won't have to hide behind a false self. Instead we will learn the glory and mystery of praise so that we can be set free from ourselves in order to do our unnecessary work.

It is not possible in this book to study in depth the whole letter to the Ephesians (which would result in a commentary, not reflections on our pastoral roles). Instead, our goal in each chapter will be to focus on a specific theme by means of a particular text for the sake of what is "unnecessary." These themes will provide the primary tonal colors of our music, from which all kinds of elaborations can be made as you reflect on your own special pastoral situation.

Baptized into the Priesthood

For us to hear the music of the letter to the Ephesians in particular — and for us to hear more generally all the music of the spheres, all that God wants to sing to our world — we need all the instruments of the orchestra. For each of us to recognize our role as a servant, let us learn what it means to be the Church and how true it is that every single one of us in the community is a priest in that Church. Whatever your employment might be — whether you serve a congregation professionally or labor in some other occupation as a vehicle for your true vocation of carrying the kingdom of God wherever you go — you are an honored member of the "priesthood of all believers."

I am not an ordained clergyperson — primarily because I have never been called to serve one local congregation since I finished my M.Div., but have instead freelanced full time to serve the larger Church by speaking for various conferences and at seminaries and colleges. However, not to be ordained has been a great advantage for my goals of teaching because, if people ask, I respond that I was ordained when I was baptized at twenty-nine days old and welcomed into the Christian community as a called servant of God. Whether or not the denomination to which you belong advocates infant baptism, all of us who are God's saints can share our baptismal days as our ordination day into the priesthood of all believers.

False Notes: Science and the Myth of Modernity

Churches and scholars erred greatly in the modernist era (to be differentiated from our current, more postmodern times) by hiding behind the glittering image of historical-critical tools. I'm not denying the usefulness of these tools, but previously they have been over-used and abused as academicians bought into the Enlightenment project's empty ambition to assess everything by scientific means. We took it upon ourselves to make faith intellectually credible to those who thought that rationalistic scientism was the only way to think and, thus, tried to prove faith on supposedly objective historical grounds. As a result, we allowed the tools to atomize the Scriptures so much that the texts were no longer able to form us! I find various critical tools very valuable, but if we misuse them, we wind up ripping Jesus apart to turn him into nothing more than a "wandering sage."[4]

---

4. For a superb response to various reductionistic attempts to define Jesus, see especially N. T. Wright, *Jesus and the Victory of God,* vol. 2 of *Christian Origins and the Question of God* (Minneapolis: Fortress Press, 1996).

A similar surgical approach has been taken with the writings of Paul in that scholars strongly assert that he couldn't possibly have written the letter to the Ephesians — without asking what might be gained by meditating on the tradition's passing on of the book with this opening: *"Paul, an apostle of Christ Jesus through the will of God, to the saints who are in Ephesus and the faithful in Christ Jesus"* (1:1). We might ask instead, How does contemplating the passion of Paul freshen our interpretation of Ephesians and deepen our heart for being the Church?

Several years ago Luke Timothy Johnson, New Testament professor at Emory University's Candler School of Theology, surprised the scholarly world by critiquing his academic colleagues in a *Christian Century* article that suggested,

> When political science students were challenged about being Republicans, they were not thereby disenfranchised from voting; when economics students were challenged on the merits of capitalism, they were not thereby excluded from purchasing notebooks. But when students were told that everything they had learned about their religion before entering this [seminary] class was wrong, did we know — or care — if their capacity to function religiously in a mature fashion was diminished?[5]

He admitted that he began to wonder about his teaching of the historical-critical tools since many of his seminary students needed far more to be first introduced to the Christian tradition before being taught to think censoriously about it. At the same time, there was increasing criticism of the tools from within the scholarly guild as professors raised questions about "the goals of the historical-critical paradigm and its capacity to accomplish those goals." Johnson acknowledged, "the supposed 'scientific' and 'disinterested' character of the historical-critical paradigm, for example, is increasingly recognized as a cover for a theologically tendentious agenda."[6]

5. Luke Timothy Johnson, "The New Testament and the Examined Life: Thoughts on Teaching," *Christian Century* 112, no. 4 (1-8 February 1995): 108-9.
6. Johnson, "The New Testament and the Examined Life," p. 109.

That was a major confession on the part of an academic theologian, but Johnson hasn't stopped there; he continues to blow this reductionistic, faith-killing trend out of the water. Next he produced a book, *The Real Jesus Is the Christ of Faith,* in which he persuasively debunked much of the historical Jesus movement and most particularly the notorious Jesus Seminar.[7] In his newest book, *Living Jesus,* he insists that we must stop dealing with a dead Jesus and recognize instead the resurrected founder of Christianity who is alive in his people, in Christian traditions, and in the Scriptures and who is "learned" in the Church's practices.[8] Jesus is alive! Therefore, we need to ask, What difference does that make?

With our society's increasing turn toward postmodern modes of thinking, the modernist questions and goals have been progressively recognized for how empty they are. We simply can't prove God. And if we rip apart texts that have been faithfully kept by God's people for generations, then we don't have any means left for knowing what it looks like to follow Christ. On the other hand, if we can trust that the Holy Spirit really has watched over the process of transmitting the Scriptures and has watched over the growth of Christ's Church, then we, as part of that Church, can trust these texts, immerse ourselves in them, and be formed by them.

Several new tools for studying the Scriptures should be mentioned here, particularly because they show us all, scholars and laypersons alike, the necessity of being unnecessary. That is, these tools enable us to be immersed in texts so that the texts can do their work on us, rather than we doing "our" work on them. Canonical criticism seeks to understand the Bible as a whole, to see its unity and the unity of various books as they have been passed on by God's people through history. Literary criticism teaches us to *read* texts, to note their structures and the characteristics of their writing so that we can be formed by the way God's people recorded their faith accounts. As we study the music of Ephesians, we will notice various colors,

7. Luke Timothy Johnson, *The Real Jesus Is the Christ of Faith* (San Francisco: HarperSanFrancisco, 1997).

8. See Luke Timothy Johnson, *Living Jesus: Learning the Heart of the Gospel* (San Francisco: HarperSanFrancisco, 1999).

themes, and the specific notes of particular words in order to pile up the tune of the song until we can sing its melodies and be formed by them. As we immerse ourselves in the biblical harmonies, we are transformed.

Improvising the Missing Act

N. T. Wright offers an especially helpful analogy for dealing with the question of how we apply the biblical texts to our lives. Frequently, the ultra-conservatives take texts and slap them on to the present situation without any concern for the original or current cultures and how the differences between them might affect how we apply the Scriptures at least two thousand years after they were written. Extreme liberals, on the other hand, often react by insisting that the Bible has nothing specific to say directly to this culture, that we can only abstract some sort of ethereal principles out of the text. As a creative and yet faithful alternative beyond both sides, Tom Wright suggests a brilliant comparison.[9]

Suppose we found an incomplete play by William Shakespeare. How could we produce it? If we discovered the first five acts and the last bit of the seventh,[10] we could try to write the missing parts — but who could ever write as well as Shakespeare? Besides, Shakespeare is no longer alive for us to check out our attempts with him.

Instead, we could go to Ashland, Oregon, which has one of the

---

9. N. T. Wright, *The New Testament and the People of God* (Minneapolis: Fortress Press, 1992), pp. 140-43. See others' use of this wonderful idea in J. Richard Middleton and Brian J. Walsh, *Truth Is Stranger Than It Used to Be* (Downers Grove, IL: InterVarsity Press, 1995), pp. 182-84, and Rodney Clapp, *A Peculiar People: The Church as Culture in a Post-Christian Society* (Downers Grove, IL: InterVarsity, 1996), pp. 138-39. See also my explication of his idea in terms of the needs of our postmodern culture in chapter 4, "Pop Spirituality or Genuine Story? The Church's Gifts for Postmodern Times," in *A Royal "Waste" of Time: The Splendor of Worshiping God and Being Church for the World* (Grand Rapids: Wm. B. Eerdmans Publishing Co., 1999).

10. Wright uses a five-act schema, but I find it more helpful to divide his fifth act in order to stress the differences in our lives (my Act VI) from those of biblical characters in immediate touch with Jesus (V) and from the end of time (VII) as an entirely new kind of drama.

finest Shakespeare festivals in the world, and there we would secure the best Shakespearean actors we could find — people who have performed lots of his plays, who know his ways, his idiosyncrasies, his twists of language. They would immerse themselves in the acts that we do have, and then we'd let them improvise the parts that are missing. Since the audience would be different every time the play was performed, it would be improvised differently every day according to who is there and what is happening. Wouldn't that be wonderful?

Similarly, the Christian community has passed on the unfinished drama of God. Act I of the play, the creation, teaches us that we are all created equally to bear the image of God, that we are responsible to care for each other and the cosmos. Act II, the fall, enables us to understand the world's brokenness and destruction. Acts III and V present the stories of Israel and of the early Christians, respectively, to offer us examples of both disobedience and trust and to demonstrate the consequences of our rebellions and our following. Act IV gives an account of the life, suffering, death, resurrection, and ascension of Jesus as the culmination of all God's promises to Israel in Act III and the foundation for all the Holy Spirit's work through the saints of Act V. Those five acts are complete, but Act VI is missing, and we have only a fragment of the drama's end (Act VII) from the book of Revelation. What we know of the grand denouement of the world, when Christ comes again and destroys evil and death forever, is only a sketch meant to encourage us in the struggles and sufferings of the present.

How do we apply the Scriptures? We immerse ourselves in the first five and partial last acts of the drama, in all the texts passed on as the grand biblical story of God and his people. By means of the commandments, speeches, narratives, poetry, warnings, promises, and songs of the entire Revelation, we are formed with the character of God's people to imitate the virtues and deeds of God himself. All over the world Christians are improvising the biblical story — differently in each place because of the surrounding audience and circumstances. And we have a great advantage over the Shakespearean actors, for, as we improvise Act VI in keeping with the spirit of the rest of the drama, we can regularly check out our attempts with the Author, who is still alive!

Faith as a Language

As we improvise the Christian life, we need to draw one other perspective different from polarities between conservatives and liberals. Conservatives have frequently misrepresented faith as simply intellectual agreement with doctrinal propositions. In reaction, liberals have misunderstood faith to be the varied expressions of common religious experiences — thus positing no differences between Christianity and other world religions. The first perspective focuses inordinately on head knowledge, while the second depends primarily on emotional expression. (This is not to be confused with what is happening these days in worship, wherein many evangelical groups overaccentuate emotional hype, while liberal denominations major in social justice.[11]) All these excesses and deficiencies can be corrected if we understand, with theologian George Lindbeck, that faith is a language, a culture, a way of living.[12]

We can truly learn a language only if we are immersed in it (see Chapter 7). We can learn to sing the music of faith only if we practice it. We need the entire Christian community in order to learn to be Christian (see Chapter 9). We need to speak the language of the saints, to sing the faithful language as the best of our hymns do, to talk with the Church throughout the ages as it expresses what it means to follow Jesus. We need a lifelong immersion in the texts of the Scriptures — soaking ourselves in the language so that when we put down our Bibles we can improvise living out that language in whatever we encounter.

---

11. For an exposé of various idolatries in churches with regard to worship, see my *Reaching Out without Dumbing Down: A Theology of Worship for the Turn-of-the-Century Culture* (Grand Rapids: Wm. B. Eerdmans Publishing Co., 1995). I will occasionally footnote my other books to encourage pursuing more thoroughly topics introduced here. Since the royalties of my Eerdmans books are given away for scholarships or to ministries that help the poor, your extended reading will also support this aid.

12. See George Lindbeck, *The Nature of Doctrine: Religion and Theology in a Postliberal Age* (Philadelphia: Westminster Press, 1984). See also Timothy R. Phillips and Dennis L. Okholm, eds., *The Nature of Confession: Evangelicals and Postliberals in Conversation* (Downers Grove, IL: InterVarsity Press, 1996).

Tuned for Doxology

Just as the letter to the Ephesians begins with a wonderful doxology, so must we. The word *doxology* comes from two Greek words meaning "glory" *(doxa)* and "word" *(logos)*. Thus, defined simply, doxology is words about the Glory, words that express praise, true praise. It is important to define praise carefully at the beginning of the twenty-first century because there exists in worshiping groups massive confusion between praise and happy songs. Praise is not merely something uplifting or upbeat. Rather, it is the naming of attributes, character, and/or actions of the one being praised. To praise God does not mean only to say, "I praise you; I love you; I adore you," but to say why, for what reasons. The psalms frequently begin with a call to praise or a declaration of praise, but they don't stop there. They continue to cite the specific interventions of God that have inspired the praise; they declare how God has related to his people and therefore how he can be perceived in the world.[13] Doxology thus is praise that names the Glory and helps those who hear to see it.

If I notice a glorious sunset, I won't merely sit there and mumble, "Nice sunset." A sunset that is magnificent pulls a response out of our depths — and prods us toward others to share it. Similarly, when we really see who God is and witness his love, mercy, faithfulness, and justice in action, we are impelled into praise. Praise is pulled out of us in a way we can hardly resist; we will *have to* exclaim about our God.

The particular doxology that begins the letter to the Ephesians (1:3-14) circles around verses 6, 12, and 14, with their phrase, "to the praise of his glory." If we look closely, we discover that the subject of verses 3-6 is the heavenly Father, that verses 7-12 are about the Son, and that verses 13-14 concern the Holy Spirit. All that we learn about the Father in the first section is such good news that we can't help but live to the praise of his glory. Everything that the next section tells us about the Son and what he has done for us thrills us so much that we can't help but live to the praise of his glory. The confident assurance

---

13. Walter Brueggemann emphasizes that the verbs are primary, followed by generalization into adjectives, and only then into metaphorical nouns. See Brueggemann, *Theology of the Old Testament: Testimony, Dispute, Advocacy* (Minneapolis: Fortress Press, 1997), pp. 145-313.

that we gain from the final section about the Holy Spirit floods us with such Joy that we can't help but live to the praise of his glory.

Part of the weakness of many churches at the beginning of the twenty-first century is that our doxology is not trinitarian enough. Is it not true that some churches specialize in the Holy Spirit and pay little attention to the Father or the Son, while others overemphasize Jesus to the exclusion of the other two members of the divine Godhead? Without an equally strong emphasis on all three persons of the Trinity, our faith gets a bit lopsided. If I think only about having a close personal relationship with Jesus, I have lost the awe that is essential to what the Scriptures call "the fear of the LORD."[14] If I think only about the Holy Spirit and his empowerment, I take for granted the immense sacrifice of Jesus Christ that made my empowerment possible and lose track of the Father's infinite love in giving his Son for the world. Since it is quite easy for us to skew (subtly or overtly) our trinities, it is vital that our Christian communities invigorate genuine trinitarian thinking so that we can understand who we are and then be continually renewed and reformed in response to the Triune God.

Laments for the Death of Depth

Part of our introductory song in this chapter must be lament as we consider why churches have lost an adequate trinitarianism and other important substantive aspects of our faith tradition. Edward Farley's book *Deep Symbols* is especially helpful in diagnosing the problem that our culture has lost its words of power. We live in a society described by the collection of sound bites and snatches called the "evening news" and driven by the billions of advertisements we receive each day — and virtually everywhere we go — through billboards, radio, television, and the Internet. Our words of power have been evacuated of weighty content. (How interesting that the Hebrew word usually translated "glory," *kabod,* also signifies "weight.")

14. Concerning the importance of knowing this biblical fear, see chapter 7, "The Cry of Transience," in my *To Walk and Not Faint: A Month of Meditations on Isaiah 40,* 2nd ed. (Grand Rapids: Wm. B. Eerdmans Publishing Co., 1997), pp. 39-44.

Correlatively, our conversations become more and more superficial. Last summer my husband and I were having a deep theological discussion with some new friends from Australia when all of a sudden one of them exclaimed, "This is the first time since I have been in the United States that I have talked about something important for so long without someone changing the subject to escape it."

Farley underscores the seriousness of the problem; he emphasizes that many of our current social problems arise partly as

> the result of a loss or diminishment at the very heart of culture — some would say the loss of culture itself — namely, a loss of the society's powerful deep symbols. Without such things a society becomes alienated from past wisdom, develops institutions that have little connection with sources of humanization, and instigates styles of everyday life whose primary function is ephemeral entertainment and trivial comforts. The diminishment and sickness of all deep symbols, that is, constraining and guiding words of power, is at least one of the things at work in the larger societal infirmity.[15]

Consequently, it is crucial that we who are spiritual leaders recognize the severity of this societal loss, the thoroughness of this evacuation of content, and not fall ourselves into the "necessariness" of being culturally relevant. Many churches who have jumped on the cultural bandwagon have thereby sacrificed their deep symbols.

The response is often given, "Yes, but those deep symbols are inaccessible." Contrarily, there is no reason why we cannot instruct and educate and form and nourish people to immerse them in the depths of the symbols. We dare not evacuate our faith and make it shallow. As has been noted by many pundits, churches in the U.S. are "a thousand miles wide and six inches deep."

Here I make an unabashed plea: reinvest in the Church's symbols. All of us — preachers, musicians, Sunday school teachers, congregational officers or leaders, or supporters of all the previous servants — are required for the serious effort it will take to reclaim our

15. Edward Farley, *Deep Symbols: Their Postmodern Effacement and Reclamation* (Valley Forge, PA: Trinity Press International, 1996), p. x.

deep symbols so that they can be taught and passed on to the next generation of believers and to those presently outside the Church's communities. The symbols need to be reinvested with all the fullness of their original and multiple meanings.

For example, take the word *tradition,* which is repeatedly bashed these days by the marketing gurus.[16] Why is our culture so hostile to tradition?

Much of the antipathy arises from a confusion between tradition and traditionalism. Historian Jaroslav Pelikan's brilliant distinction is forever apt that *traditionalism* is the dead faith of the living, whereas *tradition* is the living faith of the dead. In our churches' struggles over such issues as worship forms and styles, for example, traditionalism usually becomes an idolatry of "the way it's always been done." In contrast, to value the Church's tradition is to recognize that our forebears in the faith had many insights into what worship means, that their hymns and liturgies and symbols have carried the faith well, and that therefore those tools and forms are vital for immersing us in the presence of God. To value tradition does not mean to be closed to new expressions of faith — the Church has always (ever since Colossians 3:16 and Ephesians 5:19 anyway) used "psalms, hymns, and spiritual songs" from its entire heritage past and present. So why do churches get into fights between the "traditionalists" and the "contemporaryists"? Both sides are wrong if they fail to ask the deeper, crucial question, How best do we hear and worship God? Since God probably has widely eclectic tastes and since God is vastly more than we could ever imagine, sufficiently describe, and worthily praise, certainly we need a vast array of musical sounds and worship forms to immerse us in a more adequate sense of all that he is![17]

Tradition is essential for understanding the deep symbols of the faith. We make use of the wisdom of all the saints throughout the Church's history (including the present) to recapture and reinvest our symbols. How can we discover again the sumptuous significance of

16. See the superb critique of Philip Kenneson and James Street called *Selling Out the Church: The Dangers of Church Marketing* (Nashville: Abingdon Press, 1997).

17. Questions and reflections to guide congregational processes for developing such fullness in worship are included in my *A Royal "Waste" of Time.*

Trinity? of praise? of the name *pastor?* In the previous chapter Eugene set out so clearly why we have lost what it means to be a pastor; we intend by this book to reinvest that symbol for the sake of the Church. The following chapter is my attempt to suffuse the word *praise* with greater lavishness and richer content.

One way to uncover again the wealth of meanings in our faith symbols is through good art. Frequently in my classes or seminars I show a painting done many years ago by my student Tom Mouchet. He illustrated the Trinity with the following liturgical colors: green, the color of life and creation, exemplifies the Father; white, the color of victory and Easter, reflects the Son; pink, the liturgical color for Joy, announces the work of the Holy Spirit. Using these colors in wide bands Tom painted on a black board an intricate cross in which each one of the colors makes a cross both inside and outside the crosses of the other colors. He thereby depicts the constant relationship and interweaving of the Trinity in a strikingly suggestive way. Too often we separate out the persons of the Trinity too much and become modalists who understand Father, Son, and Holy Spirit only in terms of the methods of their functioning. Because all of our metaphors for Trinity are inadequate, our various analogies eventually break down. Tom's cross, instead, offers us an evocative way to envision the Trinity as mystery that enfolds us, that goes far beyond our ability to fathom or enunciate.

An enormous part of our pastoral role is to be astonished ourselves at the profundity of the deep symbols of the Christian faith and to help others become immersed in their substance. It is a momentously needed call — and all the more crucial as our society increasingly rejects its urgency.

The Recovery of Mind and Heart and the Submission of the Emotions

In order to recover our symbols, of course, we have to restore the biblical correlation of mind and heart — that is, the bringing together in proper proportion of mind, emotions, and will. It is essential in our churches that the members reclaim the original intentions of the biblical word *heart*. Our culture uses the word metaphorically to signify emotions, but the writers of the First Testament[18] employ the Hebrew word for "kidneys" and the Second Testament authors utilize the Greek word for "bowels" to emphasize feelings. (Both my kidneys and the nerves associated with the bowels are failing, so those words seem more appropriate to me to keep us from trusting emotions which, though important, fail us if we base our life on them.) The biblical writers, instead, understand the words for "heart" to connote a more profound convergence of mental, spiritual, and psychological processes in the will. C. S. Lewis described the importance of this understanding in his essay "Men Without Chests," in which he lamented the loss of will that results when emotions are not channeled by the mind into higher purposes.[19]

How desperate is the need in our society for more active dominance of the will over feelings! Human beings do not have to act on the basis of our lusts and skewed desires, our wrongheaded goals and vain ambitions. We can instead construct our conduct on what we know — and for those of us who are Christians, especially on what we know about God and our relationship with him.

For example, let us return to the subject of praise. When I approach the Trinity first of all by means of the "renewal of mind" originating in the Holy Spirit's transformation (Romans 12:1-2) and am thereby opened for the entire changing of my being, then I come to God intellectually and emotionally and, most of all, willfully — not in the sense of a disgruntled child, but full of will to act on what I know. Then I will praise God whether I feel like it or not, because I *know* that God is worthy to be praised. The more I learn of God's attributes and actions, the more I will praise him. Often the emotions will come along, then, also (which is, of course, wonderful and to be enjoyed), but sometimes they don't, and that is all right, too.

18. I prefer to call the first three-fourths of the Bible the "First Testament" or the "Hebrew Scriptures," to avoid our culture's negative connotations of the name *Old* Testament and to emphasize both the consistency of God's grace for all God's people and the continuity of God's covenants in the Bible, first with Israel and then in addition with Christians.

19. C. S. Lewis, *The Abolition of Man* (New York: Macmillan, 1947), pp. 13-35.

I am terribly concerned in our culture about what Neil Postman calls a "Low Information-Action Ratio," caused by our society's plethora of contextless information. The result of our bombardment with too much data is paralysis — we are not able to, or become not willing to, act on what we hear and see. In fact, television has trained us NOT to act on what we learn.[20] Thus, the ratio of action to the amount of information received spirals continually lower. Notice that the acronym spells LIAR. It makes liars of us to read the Scriptures and not act on God's commands, to hear sermons and not put them into practice. It makes liars of us to read what I am writing here and then go on in the same way, wanting to live out of our emotions or requiring that we "feel" like praising God, rather than remembering that praise is an act of the will. What would happen if all Christians developed instead a high information-action ratio and would want only to seek the HIAR things?

Exactly the Right Word

The meditations on Ephesians that follow in Chapters 3, 5, 7, and 9 involve some word studies according to semantic domains. A new Greek lexicon has been developed by the United Bible Societies to help in connection with worldwide biblical translation. This lexicon gathers together into one field all the Greek words that signify basically the same thing, so that we can see how they are different in nuances of meaning and usage. This teaches us to ask not only what a word might denote but also why a particular author might have chosen that word over another. Since it is a semantic *field,* let's illustrate the method with terms for "cow." We might suggest such designations as steer, ox, bull, heifer, beef, bovine, calf. If out of the entire semantic field I chose the word *calf,* why might I have done so? Perhaps I intended to emphasize its youth, feeble-

---

20. See Neil Postman, *Amusing Ourselves to Death: Public Discourse in the Age of Show Business* (New York: Viking Penguin, 1985). This book should be required reading for all pastors to help them understand why it is so difficult these days to get volunteers in our churches and why members do not act on what they learn about the work of the congregation and the mission of God's kingdom.

ness, helplessness, or dependence on its mother.[21] Similarly, Paul elects to use the word *beloved* at strategic places in his letters; he calls the recipients "brothers [and sisters]" for important reasons.

Some of my professors in graduate school would critique my efforts at word studies and insist that particular word choices were not that important to the biblical writers, but as a writer myself I heartily disagree. Before my book on Sabbath keeping was first published, the text included the phrase, "before the advent of the deer," but my editor (not my present one!) changed it in the galleys to "before the deer came." What a dreadful reduction! I insisted that she restore my original phrase, for I had chosen "advent" for its symbolism, to evoke more than mere coming. Coming mysteriously, coming with power perhaps, coming after much waiting — the use of "advent" can be highly suggestive.

Let us look carefully in the chapters that follow at the word choices in the letter to the Ephesians. Paul was a great case builder, a person who argued carefully, so he wouldn't choose his words lightly (especially under the influence of the Holy Spirit). Furthermore, Paul frequently does theological stacking. He piles up phrase upon phrase, precise word upon precise word in order to build a montage of reasons for praise. All his mounds of descriptions are still never large enough to proclaim God, never thorough enough to explain the mystery of the Church — so that we are always ultimately ushered into wonder. And if there is anything missing in a technicized culture, it is wonder. True?

Let us pray: Give us words, Triune God, to praise you. Form our lives, dear Lord, to reflect your glory. Call us to wonder and fill us with your Joy. Amen.

---

21. See Johannes P. Louw and Eugene A. Nida, eds., *Greek-English Lexicon of the New Testament Based on Semantic Domains* (New York: United Bible Societies, 1988), vols. 1 and 2. This lexicon's approach and methodology make use of the insights of modern linguistics, and its definitions are based upon the distinctive features of meaning of a particular term in comparison with, and in contrast to, other related words in the same semantic domain. Definitions from this lexicon will be marked throughout this book with the number of the semantic field and the particular number of the word cited — e.g., *SD* 4.17 is the reference for the word translated *calf*, since it is the 17th word *(moschos)* in the field of Animals (#4).

Chapter 3

The Call to Be a Living Doxology

MARVA J. DAWN

Let us renew our commitment to think and live in God's presence as a community together. The Lord be with you! [And also with you!]

Let us pray: Triune God, open our eyes to see your grace. Open our lives to be your praise. Amen.

I am eager to immerse myself in the text of Ephesians with you. Here we begin with Paul's salutation:

> Paul, an apostle of Christ Jesus by means of the will of God,
> To the saints who are in Ephesus, the faithful in Christ Jesus.
> Grace to you and peace from God our Father
>   and the Lord Jesus Christ.
>
> Ephesians 1:1-2[1]

Paul knows who he is and what he is about. Notice his clarity in insisting that he serves in his role as apostle by the will of God. The question of who we are will remain always in the background as we consider here our role as "unnecessary" pastors. The will of God is an unnecessary consideration according to the world's standards. For us

---

1. Throughout this book I have used my own translations of passages from Ephesians. My citations of passages from other books of the Bible are taken primarily from the New Revised Standard Version.

to seek it is to resist the traps of our consumerist culture. If we know with assurance that what we are engaged in is the will of God, then we will not need to put on a glittering image of necessariness in order to hide our irrelevance to the world's ideas.

Another aspect of Paul's opening that thrusts us toward new clarity is that Paul writes "to the saints." How many of us think of ourselves as saints? What would happen in our churches if we attained a major paradigm shift so that all the people understood themselves as saints? Of course, Paul's description is not determined by whether we act like the saints that we are. Consequently, Paul's saint-talk stirs up right away our awareness of just how unnecessary we are, for none of us became a saint by our own efforts. We became saints not by working harder, but totally by sheer, unadulterated gift. Absolutely *all* of our efforts are unnecessary.

Only when we understand this can we go on to the next phrase in verse 1 — "the saints, the ones who are faithful." Our faithfulness, too, does not arise because we work at it. It is a gift just as much as our holiness is. Most people would probably assume that "faithfulness" describes how well we are doing. Let us pause to consider, however, on what our faithfulness rests. Am I faithful to God because I am a good "faith-er," or because God is absolutely faith-worthy? God's immense and gracious faithfulness, which sets me free to be faithful, and his mercy, which forgives me when I'm not — these aspects of his character evoke whatever faithfulness I evince. I do not believe because I am a good believer or good at believing. I believe because God is believable.

This truth really helps us to understand how unnecessary we are, doesn't it? We do not manufacture our faith. We don't bulldoze up better believing, and we don't force ourselves into finer faithfulness. God gifts it in us and gifts it through us.

Of course, I'm not saying that you are irrelevant, for it is indeed *you* whom God is pulling into faithfulness. However, it puts us into our proper place to know that we are the blessed and beloved recipients of faith and faithfulness.

Verse 2 enables us to know how that is possible — namely, because of grace and peace, God's unmerited favor and forgiveness, his largess that liberates us from our sin and his *shalom* that releases us from our guilt over it. What a wonder that we can be set free both from our fallenness and from how bad we feel about its results!

Is peace a feeling or a fact? When we are concerned with the peace of God, it is a fact, of course. The Hebrew word *shalom* begins in reconciliation with God, and only because of that atonement can we come into *shalom* with ourselves and with others. Since we Christians know that God has perfected his *shalom* at the cross, we can claim it as a fact and let that empower us to work for its manifestation in human affairs.[2]

This is especially important for our unnecessary role since much of the time the world around us won't like what we are doing. Still we can claim the fact of peace, even when we don't feel it. The *shalom* of being at the center of God's will by God's willing sets us free to experience that peace. Many times, as a result, we will actually feel at peace even in the midst of turmoil. The feeling won't be necessary, however, for the key will be to remember that God has created *shalom* and has invited us into it.

Look once more at Ephesians 1:2, for it seems to contradict my emphasis in the previous chapter on being trinitarian. Grace and peace are offered only from God our Father and from the Lord Jesus Christ. Where is the Spirit? It seems to me that the Spirit lies in the communication of the grace and peace. Jesus told us that when the Father sent the Spirit in his name, that Spirit would bring to our remembrance all that Jesus taught. My understanding widens, then, when I recognize the Holy Spirit's presence in the connection created between us and the God who grants us grace and peace.

These introductory verses invite us into several questions for deeper reflection concerning our call. Who am I by the will of God? By what means can I learn more clearly who I am by the will of God? Probably you struggle continually as I do with vocational questions. No matter what confusions my life's circumstances generate, I can always come back to the one thing that I know clearly: my sainthood. Furthermore,

2. The biblical word *shalom* is defined more thoroughly in my *I'm Lonely, LORD — How Long? Meditations on the Psalms,* rev. ed. (Grand Rapids: Wm. B. Eerdmans Publishing Co., 1998).

that sainthood is to be lived out in trinitarian grace and peace. Again, I am called to find out how best I can pass grace and peace on to others. How best can I model them, teach them, share them, evoke them? All of these questions are made easier if we begin with doxology.

Doxology: The First Person of the Trinity

> Blessed be the God and Father of our Lord Jesus Christ, the one having blessed us with every spiritual blessing in the heavenlies in Christ . . .
>
> Ephesians 1:3

It is important that we begin studying this verse by thinking of the Greek word *eulogétos* ("blessed be") in terms of worthiness to be praised or commended (*SD* 33.362). Otherwise we might find it difficult to think about "blessing" God since God certainly doesn't need our blessing. Our praises absolutely won't change God. Perhaps praising him is "a royal 'waste' of time." In fact, I used that phrase as the title for my newest book on worship specifically so that we would recognize the uselessness of our praise. As soon as we can stop making worship utilitarian (primarily in the current push to make worship "attractive" in order to "appeal" to new members), then we might get back to genuine worshiping.[3] It is unproductive to bless God — God doesn't need it and, if we are selfless enough truly to worship him, it might not make us feel any better. But, in fact, what a Joy it is — Joy is not the same as happiness — to respond unpretentiously and wholeheartedly to all that God is. How much it will change us to enter forthrightly and unfeignedly into blessing God!

Could we ever get to the maturity of simply blessing God without needing to go on in verse 3 to remember how richly God has blessed us? When we consider the fullness of his gifts of "every spiritual blessing in the heavenlies in Christ," of course we have to respond with thanksgiving and adoration. But could we ever be selfless enough

3. See *A Royal "Waste" of Time: The Splendor of Worshiping God and Being Church for the World* (Grand Rapids: Wm. B. Eerdmans Publishing Co., 1999).

purely to praise God for who he is even if we received absolutely no benefit from it?

We know the answer is NO, partly because the character of God is such that he *must* bless us to be true to himself. Partly the answer is NO because we will always be our sinful selves until the end of time when God absolutely and totally delivers us from this "body of death and sin." However, it is certainly a beneficial spiritual discipline for us to contemplate pure praise for the sake of stretching our ability not to be so demanding of God's blessing. The *satan*'s (that is, the "accuser's") question to God in the book of Job perhaps ought to be asked of us: "Does Job fear God for nothing?" — or in Eugene Peterson's masterful version,

> "So do you think Job does all that out of the sheer goodness of his heart? Why, no one ever had it so good! You pamper him like a pet, make sure nothing bad ever happens to him or his family or his possessions, bless everything he does — he can't lose!
>
> "But what do you think would happen if you reached down and took away everything that is his? He'd curse you right to your face, that's what."
>
> God replied, "We'll see . . ."[4]

What would God find if we were tested?

What sets us free to pass the test is the practice of doxology, the praise of God until it becomes our habit, for it is the habit of God to be eminently worthy of our praise and thanks. Indeed, Ephesians 1:3 reminds us that every single blessing we possess has come from God.

Some people might think that "every spiritual blessing" refers only to theological or churchly things, but that is because we have made a completely unbiblical distinction between body and spirit, with the result that we assume that spiritual blessings are not material. However, instead of a line down the middle to divide intangible or heavenly/ethereal things from the tangible and earthly, imagine a great big circle of spiritual blessing, inside of which is the smaller compo-

---

4. Eugene H. Peterson, Job 1, in *The Message: The Wisdom Books* (Colorado Springs, CO: NavPress, 1996), p. 15.

nent of bodily gifts. Spiritual blessing is not outside of and peripheral to bodily blessing; it encompasses all kinds of blessings, including the material, for surely God's Spirit is resident in everything.

Knowing that spiritual blessing is the larger category, we are helped to understand better the various trials of our daily lives. I happen to have a particularly afflicted body. As I struggle with handicaps of all sorts, they are hallowed if I place them within the larger sphere of every imaginable divine benediction.

Apply the insight to your own life in ministry. No matter what is going on in your congregation, it is inside the greater realm of spiritual blessings. You can say, "Even in this conflict, God can produce spiritual gifts." "Even in this shortage of money, God can generate other assets." "Even in this time of much suffering, God can create Joy."

It is all "in the heavenlies." This doesn't mean simply "pie in the sky by and by when you die," but instead underscores the encompassing of the entire reign of God. (The original Greek simply has the adjective *heavenly* in a plural form without a noun like "places." I translate it "heavenlies" so that we don't limit God's blessings to a location someplace up above.) "The heavenlies" here connotes, I think, the presence of God, just as in Jewish literature "the kingdom of heaven" is a less direct way to say "the kingdom of God." All the blessings we receive derive their benefit by being signs of God, whose presence is made known most clearly to us, as the verse concludes, "in Christ." So we have moved from the blessings of God to the God of blessing. Paul makes a similar progression in his letter to the Philippians when he insists that "the peace of God" will keep our minds and hearts in a state of settlement or security (4:7) and then, after urging his readers to think about whatever is truthful, honorable, praiseworthy, and so forth, promises that "the God of peace" will be with them (4:9).

> . . . just as he chose us out in him before the foundation of the world,
> for us to be holy and blameless in his presence in love, . . .
>
> Ephesians 1:4

Recently I heard a woman speaker tell the story of God's call in her life. She told of a past filled with drug abuse and promiscuous sex.

46

Periodically during her account she would circle around to repeat the phrase, "and yet God chose me before the foundation of the world." She told us how eventually a business man for whom she wanted to work admonished her gently, saying, "You won't work here if you are dressed like that," and, when she cursed in response, "You won't work here if you speak like that." His rebuke woke her up; she realized she had a deep hunger for a better life. The continual caring of that Christian employer helped her understand that the hunger came from a God who had chosen her before the foundation of the world.[5]

Those of us who have been Christians all of our lives perhaps don't recognize as deeply as someone whose life has been acutely wounded the wonder of this: no matter how dreadful our past, no matter how self-centered our present, still God has chosen us out! The verb *(eklegomai)* emphasizes selection out of one or more possible alternatives *(SD* 30.86), "a special choice based upon significant preference, often implying a strongly favorable attitude toward what is chosen" *(SD* 30.92).

How amazing it is, then, that out of all the possible persons in the world, God chose you for the ministry to which he has called you, whatever that ministry might be. But he chose you *out* for much more than that — namely, to come *out* from this environment of sin into the relationship he creates in order for you to be holy and blameless in his presence in love. This is simply stunning, isn't it? We can hardly do anything but say, "Ah!"

Of course, for you to be holy and blameless is impossible — so give up all your efforts! Let God make you holy and blameless, thank him for it, and then live out of the saint that you are, with all the freedom of such a sainthood. Isn't it wonderful how this text keeps coming back to how unnecessary we are because of the immensity of the grace of God? God is the one who sanctifies us and renders us irreproachable. We are declared righteous in the blood of Jesus Christ — and the Holy Spirit continually is transforming us so that we act more

---

5. See my explication of this hunger in terms of *Sehnsucht* or "deep longing" in chapter 6 of *To Walk and Not Faint: A Month of Meditations on Isaiah 40,* 2nd ed. (Grand Rapids: Wm. B. Eerdmans Publishing Co., 1997) and throughout my *Is It a Lost Cause? Having the Heart of God for the Church's Children* (Grand Rapids: Wm. B. Eerdmans Publishing Co., 1997).

like the saints that we are. What amazing grace: you are chosen to be holy and blameless!

> . . . in love he foreordained us for adoption as his sons through Jesus Christ, according to the desire of his will, . . .
>
> Ephesians 1:5

The main verb in this fifth verse is often translated "predestined," but I prefer to avoid terminology that leads many to think of an unbiblical double predestination in which God has already designated some persons to be damned. Instead the verb emphasizes that God chooses beforehand (in our human understanding of time) and invites us to recognize God's eternal desire that all would be saved, that all would come to the knowledge of the truth (1 Timothy 2:4). God longs for everyone to be his servants in the world.

God has foreordained that through Jesus Christ we should be adopted as sons. Contemporary feminist critique would like to eliminate the word *son* here, since the Greek word for adoption can also signify a daughter. However, I prefer to use the word for the sake of another point. One of the problems in churches these days is that we have too many adolescents and not enough sons. To be an adolescent is still to clamor for instant gratification. To be a son in the sense used by the biblical writers is to be trained to fulfill the Father's mission and to know that always with the rights of sonship come attendant responsibilities. To be a son is to be the agent of the Father and to do the Father's work. This requires obligation, commitment, and accountability.

But it is also an immense privilege, so I, as a woman, am thrilled about my sonship in Christ. The early Christian Church was noticeable in its surrounding society because of its inclusion of women in all the rights and responsibilities of sonship. Ephesians 1:5 concludes that this foreordaining for adoption was "according to the desire of [God's] will," and the Greek word Paul chooses for "desire" emphasizes that it is favored on the basis of its being beneficial (*SD* 25.8). The will of God desires what is good for us.

Not only does God prefer sonship for us; his will also effects it.

We are back to grace again. Sheer, pure, undiluted gift! Doxology keeps thrusting us back into wonder at the immensity of how God enables us to become and accomplish what he has called us to be and do.

> . . . to the praise of the glory of his grace, which he graciously gave us in the beloved, . . .
>
> Ephesians 1:6

Here is that great theological stacking of Paul! Though the subject and verb are not specified here, the phrase can be understood to emphasize that God means for us to live this way: "to the praise of the glory of his grace which he graced upon us in the beloved." Our adoption as sons will be lived out in and as adoration of God for the fullness of his relationship with us.

The word *glory* will be richer for us if we think about it in First Testament terms. Remember that extraordinary story in which Moses wants to see God's glory, but the LORD responds that, though he will show Moses his character, Moses cannot see the LORD's face, for no one can see God and live through it (Exodus 33:18-20). However, the LORD condescends to hide Moses in the cleft of the rock and to cover him with his hand until he has passed by. When the LORD removes his hand, Moses will see his back, but his face will not be seen (vv. 21-23). The LORD keeps his promise, passes in front of Moses, and proclaims who he is — "the LORD, the LORD God, compassionate and gracious, slow to anger, and abounding in lovingkindness and truth . . ." (34:6, NASV) — and Moses' response is to "make haste" to bow low toward the earth to worship (34:8).

That splendid account makes me think that Moses got what he asked for — to see God's glory — but on God's terms (for the sake of protecting Moses' life) of seeing only the LORD's back. Let's be lyrical with that picture and suggest that the glory of the LORD is his back, that we can't see God's face but we can see that he has been here. Since Jesus is no longer walking on the earth, we cannot know God face to face, but we can see where he has been, what he has done, how he has intervened in — and left his mark on — the world. We know who God is by the fruits of his being. Since his character is elusively, endlessly beyond our grasp, we can only know him by the result of his having been here. If our lives are actively committed to the praise of his glory, then they will offer others the visual manifestation of God's grace at work through and in us. How can our ministries help people to notice God's back?

This has happened, of course, most specifically in Christ. Jesus has made God perfectly visible in the flesh. It is in him, "in the beloved," that God graced us with grace. (The final noun in "praise of the glory of his grace" and the verb, "which he graciously gave us," are from the same root in Greek.) Everything we have said so far — God's blessing us, choosing us, foreordaining us, adopting us — all of these grand gifts are freely poured out upon us in inextricable connection with God's own beloved Son. Thus, we turn to him now in the next verses of the Ephesians doxology.

Doxology: The Second Person of the Trinity

[the beloved], in whom we have liberation through his blood, the pardon of [our] false steps, according to the riches of his grace, which he lavished upon us using all wisdom and understanding . . .

Ephesians 1:7-8

In the beloved One of God we are liberated! How easily we take that for granted because we so readily forget all the things to which we are subjugated. But we have been bought back, set free, snatched out of inescapable slaveries! One of the great gifts of the Church that we are failing to give our culture thoroughly is this great snatch.

Let us ponder the horrible slaveries to which our neighbors — and we — become condemned. In Chapter 5 we will come back to this when we look closely at the "principalities and powers" of Ephesians 6, but at this point it is important for us all to admit our addictions, acknowledge our bondages, confess our servilities, identify what imprisons us. More momentously, let us celebrate our deliverance!

I love how we do that, with the guidance of the historic liturgy, in Sunday morning worship. We admit,

We confess that we are in bondage to sin and cannot free ourselves. We have sinned against you [God] in thought, word, and deed, by what we have done and by what we have left undone. We have not loved you with our whole heart; we have not loved our neighbors as ourselves. For the sake of your Son, Jesus Christ, have mercy on us. Forgive us, renew us, and lead us, so that we may delight in your will and walk in your ways, to the glory of your holy name. Amen.

What a colossal Joy it is each week then to hear these words of assurance:

Almighty God, in his mercy, has given his Son to die for us and, for his sake, forgives us all our sins. As a called and ordained minister of the Church of Christ, and by his authority, I therefore declare to you the entire forgiveness of all your sins, in the name of the Father, and of the Son, and of the Holy Spirit. Amen.[6]

That is the most powerful liberation one could ever receive!

We have made redemption much too small. We have turned the deep symbol of salvation into a comparatively little thing by relegating it to the future. The Hebrew literature is much more tangible. One of its nouns for salvation *(yeshuwah,* related to the name *Jesus)* comes from a verb root that accents wideness or openness. God's liberation gives us plenty of room — breathing space, deliverance from our tight anguishes and confining bondages. Moreover, God is continually doing this for us now, not only in a far distant future. Do we recognize his gracious snatching as he rescues us and delivers us from our various enslavements in life?

This emancipation happens through the blood, which is another deep symbol we could explore for a long time. Certainly as a symbol the blood of Christ represents all of his sacrifice on our behalf — not just his final surrender to death on the cross, but the sacrifices of his entire life on earth.

We have put the comma in the wrong place in the Apostles'

6. These forms for confession and absolution were both taken from the *Lutheran Book of Worship* (Minneapolis: Augsburg, 1978), p. 56.

Creed, with the result that we have reduced Christ's travail for us to only one piece (though the major one) of its entirety. We say,

> born of the virgin Mary,
> He suffered under Pontius Pilate,
> was crucified, died, and was buried.

We should say,

> born of the virgin Mary,
> He suffered,
> under Pontius Pilate was crucified,
> died, and was buried.

Do you notice the immense difference it makes? Jesus didn't suffer only under Pontius Pilate. He suffered from the very beginning — even in the womb, where his life was threatened with future marginalization and poverty if Joseph decided to "put Mary away quietly."[7] Jesus suffered when he was born and laid in a manger; in bitter contrast to our homey Christmas scenes where everything is romanticized and pictured as nicey-nice, the stable was no doubt a stinky, scratchy, mucky, wretched place. He suffered the crowds and their pushiness, the Romans and their oppressions, the impossible disciples and their phenomenal inability ever to get things right. And he suffers *you!*

Therefore, when we say that we are delivered through the blood, let us remember that God is always suffering in order to liberate us. In his superb book, *The Suffering of God,* First Testament professor Terrence Fretheim of Luther Seminary delineates all the ways that God has suffered since eternity — and continues to suffer — for us, because of us, in our stead.[8]

Because of the snatching out, the blood, and the suffering of God, all of his sacrifice, we can add to the montage of blessings God's

---

7. I owe this insight to Beverly R. Gaventa, "He Comes as One Unknown," in "The Challenge of Christmas: Two Views," *Christian Century* 110, no. 36 (15 Dec. 1993): 1270-80.

8. Terrence Fretheim, *The Suffering of God* (Minneapolis: Augsburg-Fortress, 1984).

pardoning of our false steps, his forgiveness for our wrongdoing. Whenever I read the Greek word for transgressions, *paraptōmatōn,* I remember my confirmation teacher stressing that it connotes all the ways we "miss the mark" in transgressing God's will. The very next year at high school I took archery class with several others, including one noticeably new beginner, who got her bow so cockeyed that her arrow not only missed the target entirely but flew over to the track on our right side where it went straight into the very bushy tail of a dog that was running around. The dog wasn't hurt at all, but in its confusion it sprinted all over the field, while the embedded arrow implanted itself in my mind as a graphic image of the fatal wanderings of our sinfulness. Our wrongdoing doesn't merely miss the mark; it often hits someone else.

The deep symbol of sin is one we also often trivialize by terming it merely a mistake. Many sins we euphemize; for example, we label fornication "sleeping together," which sounds so nice and cozy. We call it "fudging on our income tax" when we cheat the government or a "little white lie" when we do violence to the truth. Since in our culture we do not name sin for the despicable *sin* that it is, we rarely recognize how truly *dead* we are (see Ephesians 2:1-3).

We are enslaved to sin. There is no escaping it, as Martin Luther pointed out so unforgettably in his great treatise "The Bondage of the Will."[9] This slavery to my sinful self even makes it impossible to come to faith, Luther recognized, so in his explanation of the Third Article of the Apostles' Creed he taught "that I cannot by my own reason or strength believe in Jesus Christ my Lord or come to him. . . ." Only because God calls, delivers, enlightens, frees, and graces us can we be set free for and into faith.

We have been piling up this montage of Paul's weighty symbols so that we do not lose our wonder at the monumental measure of God's grace for us. All that the blood conveys, all that God snatches us out of, all God's absolution for our missteps and rebellions — all these graces God lavishes upon us with perfect wisdom, insight, or capacity

9. Martin Luther, "The Bondage of the Will," trans. Philip S. Watson, *The Career of the Reformer III,* ed. Philip S. Watson, vol. 33 of *Luther's Works,* Helmut T. Lehmann, gen. ed. (Philadelphia: Fortress Press, 1972), pp. 15-295.

to understand. Never does God pour out his mercy in ways that are not good for us.

> ... having made known to us the *mustērion* of his will, according to his desire which he planned beforehand in Christ ...
>
> Ephesians 1:9

Mystery! Now there is a deep symbol that has been evacuated of content. In English we have reduced the notion of mystery to figuring out whether it was the butler or the maid who killed the rich man. I often say and write this word in Greek because its biblical meaning is far different. Rather than signifying something we are trying to uncover but have failed to understand, the Greek word emphasizes the content of that which has now been revealed. Jesus tells his disciples in Matthew 13:11 that "the knowledge of the secrets of the kingdom of heaven has been given to you" (*SD* 28.77).

God's desire, planned beforehand, was that we would, in Christ, be let in on the secrets of his reign. Otherwise God is so immeasurably, unremittingly, inexpressibly beyond us that we could not possibly begin to know who he is. Yet God condescends — a major mercy — to give us these hints, to reveal what is too great for us, to become actually incarnate so that we could see and touch and hear him in the flesh. The kingdom has been brought near in the person of Jesus Christ by the power of the Holy Spirit. This is mystery made known, and, because all of us are Church together, we keep on learning more of the mystery. Of course, it will remain too stupendously enormous for us ever to secure it. God will persist in being elusive, beyond our grasp, illimitably veiled in his glorious splendor. We will need all of eternity to know him.

> ... for the economy of the fullness of time, to bring everything together in Christ — the things in the heavens and the things on the earth ...
>
> Ephesians 1:10

Having disclosed the secret of his kingdom, as he purposed, God enables us to be part of his "economy." Our English translations usually use words like *plan* or *administration* to render the Greek *oikonomia,* but I like to think about how we use the word *economy* and what that might tell us about our "unnecessary" role. When we economize, we try to get the most for our money; we try to manage as well as possible. Similarly, God's plan completely administers opportune times so that ultimately everything will be brought together into the headship of Christ. What a wonder that God's way to economize is to use us! He makes known to us the secret of his reign through Christ and lets us be part of it.

In the perfection of his timing, God will someday "recapitulate" all things (the Greek verb is *anakephalaioō*). He will, so to speak, put the head back on or "bring everything together in terms of some unifying principle or person" (*SD* 63.8) — namely, Christ. God is in the process of reclaiming it all — the entire cosmos, celestial and terrestrial — for his reign. Meanwhile, you and I are engaged, too, in this "recapitulation" through the work of reconciling the world, which Eugene mentioned in Chapter 1. God has to gather together what was ripped asunder by the entrance of sin into the world.

> . . . in him in whom also we have received an inheritance, having been foreordained according to the plan of the one working out all things according to the counsel of his will, . . .
>
> Ephesians 1:11

Once again we read a grand theological stacking to make sure that we never forget how much this is sheer gift, a royal inheritance. Translations vary widely in rendering the first verb of the verse. Some versions stress that in Christ we were "destined" (RSV), "chosen" (NIV), or "chosen to be his own people" (TEV); others emphasize that in him we have received an inheritance (NRSV, KJV, J. B. Phillips) or have been "given our share in the heritage" (NEB). The Living Bible insists that "because of what Christ has done we have become gifts to God that he delights in." I found especially insightful the Jerusalem Bible, which translates, "And it is in him that we were claimed as God's own," thereby bringing together all the ideas in the Greek root — that of choice, of appointment, and of gaining a share by lot. However we interpret that first verb, according to God's plan we were foreordained for it — and God infallibly fulfills his plan because his comprehensive counsel and absolute will are behind it. His perfect purposes and impeccable intentions are not thwarted.

Why do we ever think we are necessary for that? How is it that we get our typical pastoral messiah complexes and think that we are essential for whatever needs to happen in our congregations?[10] Why are we afraid to take a Sabbath day because our churches need us so badly?[11] The world got along just fine without us before we arrived. Ephesians 1:11 sets us free again to revel in all that God is and does. We can't help but respond with the praise of verse 12.

> . . . for the purpose that we, the first ones to hope in Christ, might exist to the praise of his glory . . .
>
> Ephesians 1:12

Recently Martin Marty gave me the gift of this wonderful sentence from theologian Romano Guardini: that worship is *"zwecklos aber doch sinnvoll"* — "pointless, however still full of meaning" or "of signs." Our praise is *"zwecklos,"* useless, unnecessary — but at the same time is full of intentionality, full of significance, full of incarnation. We live, we sing, we *ARE,* to the praise of God's glory. Our lives become a sign of what God is, where he has worked, how he graces. We demonstrate our hope by living as praise. God inhabits our praises and reveals himself to the world around us.

---

10. One insight that seems very helpful to me to keep us from messiah complexes is David Hansen's distinction between being a "symbol for God" (which puts the burden on us) and a "parable of Jesus Christ," which lets us get out of the way. See David Hansen, *The Art of Pastoring: Ministry* Without *All the Answers* (Downers Grove, IL: InterVarsity Press, 1994), especially pp. 130-33.

11. One of the very best reasons for clergy and other servants of the Church to take a Sabbath day is to learn that we are not the messiah. In the process we discover what a great Joy it is to live according to God's design for work and rest. See my *Keeping the Sabbath Wholly: Ceasing, Resting, Embracing, Feasting* (Grand Rapids: Wm. B. Eerdmans Publishing Co., 1989) and *The Sense of the Call: Kingdom* Shalom *for Those Who Serve the Church* (Grand Rapids: Wm. B. Eerdmans Publishing Co., forthcoming).

Doxology: The Third Person of the Trinity

Now we come to the third person of the Trinity, the Holy Spirit. Notice that the prelude to the Holy Spirit is that in the Beloved we have *heard* the word of truth — communicated, verse 2 might suggest, by the Spirit.

> . . . in whom you also, having heard the word of truth, the Gospel of your salvation, [and] having also come to believe in him, you were sealed with the Holy Spirit of promise, who is a down payment guaranteeing our inheritance, until the liberation of those who are God's possession, to the praise of his glory.
>
> Ephesians 1:13-14

Baptism! I love the rite of baptism in Lutheran churches because it includes a ritual of sealing. The rubric reads as follows:

> The minister marks the sign of the cross on the forehead of each of the baptized. Oil prepared for this purpose may be used. As the sign of the cross is made, the minister says: "[name of the baptized], child of God, you have been sealed by the Holy Spirit and marked with the cross of Christ forever. Amen."[12]

What a wonderful visual aid for the end of the doxology in Ephesians 1! The apostle Peter promised at Pentecost that those who are baptized receive forgiveness of sins and the gift of the Holy Spirit according to the promise given to us all — young and old, near and far, Jew and Gentile (Acts 2:38-39). Every time I witness a baptism of a child or an adult I am reminded that God graced me long before I could do anything about it and at my baptism gave me the gift of salvation and the Spirit of promise. That Spirit has been working in my life through the Word and the community ever since.

For those who came to faith as adults, the sealing took place in the hearing and believing of the Word of truth. Either way, the Spirit is the down payment, the earnest money, the deposit that assures us that God will fulfill all his promises to us.

12. *Lutheran Book of Worship*, p. 124.

Indeed, if you put a hefty down payment on a house, you certainly will not renege on any of the mortgage payments, will you? No, we wouldn't want to lose the house — or the money we already put down. If God, then, has given the Spirit as his pledge, he certainly will not renege on anything else, will he? If we have received this monumental gift of the Comforter, the Paraclete (literally, the "called-alongside One"), can't we trust that the entire inheritance will be poured out for us as well?

Also notice that the sealing and inheritance make us the possession of God. This is a compelling and comforting theme in the Scriptures, based on Exodus 19:5 and Deuteronomy 14:2 and appearing also in Titus 2:14 and 1 Peter 2:9-10. It is also a grand culmination to our unnecessariness. We are the possession of God because his Spirit possesses us — inhabits us, transforms us, creates us to be praise. The world around us thinks about possessions in an entirely different way, but God's slant on the subject sets us free from the slavery of our culture's hoarding. We are liberated from all the things that would own us to give ourselves fully into the praise of God. We are unshackled from the compulsion to be necessary and emancipated for the totally unnecessary Joy of celebrating God's glory.

Pause for a moment to consider the place of doxology in your life — privately and publicly and ecclesiologically. How can our churches deepen their engagement in doxology? How does doxology shape us, personally and corporately? If it is missing — especially if it is not adequately trinitarian — how can we repent of that and be more open to God's working of doxology in us?

Let us pray: Triune God, Father, Son, and Holy Spirit, send us forth from your Word overawed with the immensity of your grace and eager to respond — to the praise of your glory. Amen.

Chapter 4

Paul: Finishing Up in Rome

EUGENE H. PETERSON

One of the difficulties that we come up against in reading the Pastoral Epistles is trying to fit them into Paul's life as it is narrated in the Acts of the Apostles. That is one reason that some give for denying Pauline authorship. The last we see of Paul in Acts is under house arrest, waiting trial. Using this as data, some Pauline chronologies assume that that confinement was followed by a trial that ended in his execution. And since there is nothing in Luke's travel accounts of Paul of missionary work in Crete, there is no historical documentation for what is contained in the Titus letter.

And so those who on internal grounds think a Pauline authorship is plausible conjecture that Paul was released from that first Roman imprisonment, made his long-anticipated visit to Spain, came back and among other things did missionary and evangelistic work in Crete, and then was imprisoned a second time in Rome, after which he was executed. If that is what happened, then we have to rearrange the ordering of the three Pastoral Epistles, for 1 Timothy and Titus show Paul still traveling. Paul, writing to Timothy in Ephesus, says, "I hope to come to you soon, but I am writing these instructions to you so that, if I am de-

---

This chapter is a slightly altered version of an article published in *Romans and the People of God*, ed. Sven K. Soderlund and N. T. Wright (Grand Rapids: Wm. B. Eerdmans Publishing Co., 1999), pp. 283-94.

layed . . ." (1 Timothy 3:14-15). He is obviously not in prison at that time. And to Titus, he writes, ". . . do your best to come to me at Nicopolis, for I have decided to spend the winter there" (Titus 3:12). Nicopolis is in Epirus, on the western coast of the Greek mainland, across the sea from Italy, and so clearly Paul was not in a Roman jail.

But in 2 Timothy Paul is in prison in Rome. He speaks of Onesiphorus, who "was not ashamed of my chains, but when he arrived in Rome, he searched for me eagerly and found me" (2 Timothy 1:16-17). He says that he is "suffering and wearing fetters like a criminal" (2:9). He summons Timothy to come to him: "Do your best to come before winter" (4:21). He is lonely and feeling abandoned: "At my first defense no one took my part; all deserted me" (4:16). He expects the worst: "For I am already on the point of being sacrificed; the time of my departure has come. I have fought the good fight, I have finished the race, I have kept the faith" (4:6-7).

It looks then like there were two Roman imprisonments; the first mentioned at the end of Acts, the second referred to in 2 Timothy. Between the two imprisonments, Paul traveled and wrote the first letter to Timothy in Ephesus and the letter to Titus in Crete.

We then read the letters in this sequence: 1 Timothy (to Timothy in Ephesus), Titus (to Titus in Crete), and finally 2 Timothy (from his Roman prison). And then, according to tradition, Paul was executed under the emperor Nero. I am going to take, therefore, 2 Timothy as a base to work from in considering Paul as pastor — Paul, finishing up in Rome, relinquishing his leadership, looking back without regrets, getting ready to die. And because Paul is writing from Rome, I will use his letter to the Romans extensively in considering his work as a pastor.

I am interested in St. Paul's letter to the Romans as a Holy Spirit source document for pastoral theology, a piece of writing that is a working demonstration of spiritual formation in the Christian community. My interest is piqued by living in an age in which the work of much of the church's leadership is neither pastoral nor theological. The pastoral dimensions of the church's leadership are badly eroded by technologizing and managerial influences. The theological dimensions of the church's leadership have been marginalized by therapeutic and marketing preoccupations. The gospel work of giving leadership to the community of the Christian faithful has been alienated from its source. Among leaders, at least, the *rationalist* mind has taken over in the schools, and the *functionalist* attitude has prevailed in churches to the extent that pastoral theology, as such, is barely recognizable. Rationalism and functionalism, both of them reductive, have left pastoral theology thin and anemic.

Paul, the church's first and most enduringly authoritative theologian, was a pastoral theologian. All of Paul's thinking and writing, teaching and preaching in the service of God (that is, his theology) was at the same time carried out in the service of a community of souls (that is, it was pastoral).

Given the commanding eminence that Romans holds in the world as a theological document, it perhaps needs saying again that Romans is a letter written to Christians to help them live their lives Christianly; that is, it was entirely pastoral in aim. It is, as are all the documents comprised by our Scriptures, directed to living. There is nothing here that is merely intellectual. Paul's mind, one of the most vigorous intellects in the church's history, works entirely in the context of a congregation of souls, men and women who find themselves called upon to repent and believe, obey and love, pray and forgive in the sin-tangled disorder of family and culture, world and work.

Therefore, the letter to the Romans, our premier theological text, is best understood and put to use when it is read as pastoral theology. This is not theology that is abstracted from the world where people live; it is theology worked out in the world where people live — pastoral theology. For too long, pastors have not been treated as theologians; theology has been leeched from our lives. At the same time, pastors have been told that they're not pastors but counselors and people who run churches. Romans restores both the theological and pastoral aspects of our vocations.

Designating Paul (along with Timothy and Titus) as "pastor" may not be strictly accurate, at least in terms of contemporary usage of the word, for Paul was not resident among the Romans to whom he wrote. He was dealing with them from a distance, neither having been to their city and walked its streets nor having been in their homes and eaten meals with them, and he had no firsthand acquaintance with the conditions in which they did their work and raised their families. For most of us today, "pastor" connotes daily immersion in a worshiping and working community. Normally, the work of pastor is not generalized; it is specific to a particular community in a particular place. We aren't going to be able to copy Paul: we have no idea what Paul would do if he had to deal with music teams and potholes in the parking lot, figure out a budget, bury teenage suicides and marry confused young adults, run a youth program and pose as a genial man of God at the annual church picnic.

But he does provide an orientation for us, a way of going about his work. If Paul was not on site in his work with the Roman Christians, he was intensely involved in helping them live the Christian life truly and well. Everything he wrote in his famous letter to them was in the service of *life*, living immediately and believingly and obediently as disciples of Jesus Christ. Granted that Paul is a *thinking* theologian, he is simultaneously a *working* pastor: the letter to the Romans is a major source document showing Paul thinking theologically as he goes about his pastoral work. There is little danger that the significance of Romans in establishing Paul as master theologian will be missed; he is one of "the giants in the land." But the way in which Romans shows Paul at work in the care of souls, Paul in his assigned work in the Christian community, is missed most of the time, missed by both pastors and scholars.

Pastors who are pleased to sit at the feet of Paul the theologian more often than not sign up with the psychologists and management consultants for expert counsel when it comes to going about their daily work in the kingdom. This is understandable, for caring for souls is honored and demanding work; those who give their lives to it need all the help they can get. But without theology, caring for souls can easily transgress into manipulating or seducing selves, and "the last state of that man is worse than the first" (Matthew 12:45).

And scholars for whom Paul is the patron saint of the learned life frequently minimize the way in which Paul used his mind in the immediate service of God and souls, preferring thus to work in settings protected against interruption. Theological and exegetical study is honored and demanding work, but abstracted from the actual conditions of community and congregation it easily loses connection with the God who loves the world and gave himself for it. Having a mind, a glory we hold in common with the angels, is grand. Cultivating the life of the intellect is essential to the sanity of the church of Christ. But the use of the mind can as easily lead us into pride as into truth. This happens when it severs itself from the pastoral.

I want to identify four elements in Paul's writing of Romans that contribute to his formative influence in pastoral theology: his submission to Scripture, his embrace of mystery, his use of language, and his immersion in community.

Submission to Scripture

In 2 Timothy 3:16, we have Paul's well-known designation of Scripture's centrality and authority: "All scripture is inspired by God and profitable for teaching, for reproof, for correction, and for training in righteousness, that the man of God may be complete, equipped for every good work." By using Romans, we can see him writing out of that authority.

It becomes clear early on in the reading of Romans that Paul is not an independent thinker, figuring things out on his own. Nor is he a speculative thinker, playing with ideas, searching for some ultimate truth. His thinking is subordinated to all that God has revealed of himself and his purposes in Holy Scripture. Scripture for Paul is the Hebrew Bible, what we now designate as the Old Testament. At the time of his writing to the Romans, Paul's intellect is entirely harnessed to and saturated with Scripture.

"Arrogant" is the accusation often directed against the professional intellectual — prideful reveling in the powers of mind. It is an accusation easy both to understand and to substantiate. Men and women of conspicuous mental prowess easily acquire a sense of superiority over the less well endowed. That sense of superiority has a way of developing into an attitude of prideful condescension. The assumption that underlies the sin is that the ability to think is the distinctive glory of the human — this ability being a characteristic that we and the angels alone share. Therefore, the more we think well, the better humans we become. Our humanity is evaluated in terms of our minds: a man who writes excellent books is superior to an illiterate migrant worker picking fruit; a woman who manages the financial affairs of a large corporation is worth far more than the woman who cleans the toilets in a public washroom. This categorizing that we so easily slip into just doesn't register with the Paul we see in the New Testament.

Paul, one of the most competent minds in history, shows none of that intellectual hubris. And the reason is that all his mental processes are subdued and submissive to what has been handed to him by revelation in Scripture. He is not using his mind to figure things out; he is not using his mind to acquire the kind of knowledge that is power; he is not using his mind to probe the frontiers of thinking, conquering ignorance and setting himself up as a master of minds.

Not that he is incapable of rigorous reasoning. The grammatical accuracy of frequently used logical connectives such as *hina* and *hoti*, *hoste* and *oun* are evidence of a keen mind disciplined to the standards of language developed by Greek and Roman intellectuals. The careful employment of verbal moods and voices displays his skill at nuance and modulation in conveying meaning. There can be no doubt that Paul *thinks* well. But he is not using his mind as an adventurer, as a conquerer, as a master — he uses his considerable powers of mind to enter into what has already been made known, what God has "revealed through faith for faith" (Romans 1:17).

The words of the scriptural revelation are the means by which Paul thinks. It is an embarrassment to some that Paul does not exegete Scripture according to modern standards — it is amusing to watch scholars scramble for explanations of what he is doing — but he is no less an exegete for all that. Paul did not use his mind in isolation from his life — Paul's relation to the Scriptures was not as a student finding out what was there but as a disciple who is living the text. Paul, gifted with a fine intellect, had a well-trained mind and had acquired a comprehensive knowledge of the Scriptures. He spent the first part of his life as a Pharisee, *using* the Scriptures zealously but wrongly; he spent the second part of his life as a Christian, *living* these same Scriptures just as zealously but very differently. The difference between his life as Pharisee and as Christian was not in his intellectual ability nor in his knowledge of Scripture but in his relation to the Scriptures: as a Pharisee he *used* the Scriptures; as a Christian he *submitted* to them.

It is in his relation to Holy Scripture that we see a primary characteristic of his work as a pastoral theologian: the Scriptures are not so much something to use as the text that furnishes his vocabulary, shapes his imagination, and forms his life. The texts he cites are not set out merely as proofs in an argument; they are vast presences, suggesting the immense horizons within which he writes.

There are sixty-five quotations laced through his letter to the Romans, cited from sixteen of the thirty-nine Old Testament books. Isaiah (with eighteen citations) and Psalms (with thirteen) are his favorites, but he ranges widely, covering much of the territory from Genesis to Malachi inventively and casually. But it is not only that he quotes; he *inhabits* the story, he gives the impression of being on familiar terms with everything written by his prophet ancestors, totally at ease in this richly expansive narrative of God's Word. The Scriptures have become for him, in Alexander Whyte's words, "all autobiographical." For instance, he puts the imagery of the Genesis creation to fresh but very different uses: first, as he writes of culpable sin in the first chapter ("they exchanged the truth about God for a lie" [1:25]), and, later, as he writes of unavoidable suffering in the eighth chapter ("the whole creation has been groaning in travail . . ." [8:22]).

Paul doesn't so much cite texts as evoke presences. Adam and Abraham, Sarah and Rebekah, Moses and Elijah are alive in his imagination; but he doesn't use his mind to invent plausible emotional and human interest details to elaborate the story; he discerns the action and purposes and presence of God in these lives and retells the story of salvation for his readers with his ancestors alive and present in it. We see this in various ways. For example, in the process of arguing the equal status of Jews and Gentiles as sinners before God (3:10-18), he pulls six strands of Scripture text out of their contexts in the Psalms and Isaiah and weaves them into a brilliant prophetic poem, as masterful a piece of rhetorical art as we are likely to come across (Psalms 14:1-3; 5:9; 140:3; 10:7; Isaiah 59:7-8; and Psalm 36:1). And he does it without violating or distorting the meaning of any of the six. There is a sense in which nothing in Scripture is ever "out of context" for Paul. He is so at home in the entire country of Scripture that he has an intuitive sense of what fits and where. He has not used his intellect to rearrange or correct or improve upon what he has been given; he *enters* it as a guest and receives with gratitude everything set before him, trusting the Host to see to his needs.

As pastors under the authority of Scripture, it is important for us to acquire this way of living with Scripture, so that we don't use it as a source book for quotations or proofs or applications, but so that we enter it as a world of revelation. We don't want to live — and teach our congregations to live, through our example — in a small world that has Bible verses pasted on it for validation. We want to live out of the whole of revelation, so living out of it that, even if we lack citations for specific situations or questions, we know that we are still living biblically.

When he was writing to Timothy, Paul said, "continue in what you have learned and have firmly believed, knowing from whom you learned it, and how from childhood you have been acquainted with the sacred writings . . ." (2 Timothy 3:14-15). That phrase "from whom" is essential. These Scriptures have a personal voice — they are evocative, contemporary, alive. They are never just books on a shelf, they have voice. "From *whom*."

A necessary pastor seeks to control Scripture, wielding it for his or her own ends. An unnecessary pastor finds a home and a country within the Scriptures and is shaped by them.

Embrace of Mystery

Another feature of Paul's pastoral work is his sense of mystery. To Timothy he wrote, "Great indeed . . . is the mystery of our religion" (1 Timothy 3:16).

This sense of mystery is embedded in Paul's Romans, where there is an extravagant embrace of mystery. Paul is comfortable with mystery, he delights in mystery, he accepts mystery. His celebrated and joyous outburst at 11:33-36 is characteristic:

O the depth of the riches and wisdom and knowledge of God!
How unsearchable are his judgments and how inscrutable his ways!

"For who has known the mind of the Lord,
    or who has been his counselor?" [Isaiah 40:13-14]
"Or who has given a gift to him
    that he might be repaid?" [Job 35:7; 41:11]

For from him and through him and to him are all things. To him be glory for ever. Amen.

One of the things I am trying to counter is rationalism — the reduction of reality to what you can describe or account for. I'm a fierce opponent of rationalism, and Paul doesn't buy it either. It is significant that this reverent but exuberant stance before the God who cannot be figured out or diagrammed comes in the context of some of Paul's most vigorous reasoning (chapters 9–11). By it he is saying, in effect, "I want you to understand this, but you can't — it's bigger than you are." Mystery, for Paul, is not what is left over after we have done our best to reason things out on our own; it is inherent in the very nature of God and his works.

His personally expressed delight in the mystery of God's ways in 11:33, 36 sandwiches (unfootnoted!) lines from Job and Isaiah that likewise give witness to the "more" that we consistently encounter in God — more than we ever expected, more than we can ever grasp, more than we are capable of explaining. But the "more" is not some secret that is kept hidden from us, teasing our curiosity; it is not esoterica from which common people are excluded but to which privileged adepts are admitted.

Mystery, in other words, is not a fancy or spiritual word for ignorance that we can conquer by more knowledge; nor does it designate a secrecy that we can penetrate by painstaking search. A few sentences previous to his famous exclamation, Paul is explicit on this point: "I do not want you to be ignorant of this mystery" (11:25, NIV). Ignorance and mystery are not synonyms; neither are secrecy and mystery. Paul's subject is "the revelation of the mystery which was kept secret for long ages but is now disclosed . . ." (16:25-26).

There is a kind of mind, too common among us, that is impatient of mystery. Mystery, these minds assume, is what pastors and theologians are paid to get rid of. They assume, and not without evidence, that what we don't know is a breeding ground for superstition and uncertainty. If we don't have a clear and concise outline of what we must know, how can we think straight about God? And if we don't know the lay of the land, the problems that we face in our daily lives, how can we devise an effective plan or set workable goals? The task of the human mind is to *know;* if it doesn't know something, it seeks to find it out.

The ability of the intellect to move into the unknown and make it known, to penetrate areas of ignorance and map reality, is, of course, formidable. This kind of aggressive intellectual work has primarily been associated with science; its results, always impressive, fairly stagger the imagination in our modern world. Robert Frost once likened the modern acceleration of results acquired by the scientific, ignorance-conquering mind to a hundred-yard dash followed by a pole vault. So it is understandable that the modern mind accustomed to seeing the tangled undergrowth of "mystery" cleared out by the "knowledge" bulldozers would retain little appreciation for the kind of mystery that Job and Isaiah and Paul speak of, a mystery that deepens as our knowledge increases.

But the conception of mystery as a quality of the Unknown has never satisfied the deepest insights of the human spirit. Children and poets, lovers and priests have, in Jaroslav Pelikan's words, "repeatedly gone on to recognize the mysterious quality of the Known."[1]

The mystery to which Paul gives witness is not the mystery of a darkness that must be dispelled but the mystery of a light that may be entered. It is not something we don't know but something that is too much to know. God and his operations cannot be reduced to what we are capable of knowing and explaining and reproducing.

---

1. Jaroslav Pelikan, *The Christian Intellectual* (London: Collins, 1996), p. 70.

It takes considerable humility to embrace this mystery, for in the presence of mystery we are not in a position to control anything, to predict or manage, to pose as authorities, to, as we say, "master the subject." But it does leave much room for worship, for there is no worship where there is no mystery.

Gabriel Marcel distinguished between approaching life as a problem and entering it as a mystery. If we deal with life as a problem, we reduce it to what we can do something about; we are concerned with figuring out and fixing. And, while there is an important place for figuring things out and fixing them, if that's all that we do we become myopic, managers and mechanics of what is immediately before us, with no peripheral vision and no horizons. We miss most of life. But if we approach life as a mystery, we are forever coming upon meanings that exceed our definitions, energy and resources unguessed in our calculations. "Mystery is not the absence of meaning, but the presence of more meaning than we can comprehend."[2]

Scripture is not the answer book to all our problems but a doorway into the world of God's mystery. And one of the mysteries of this life is that God isn't interested in solving all of our problems in the ways we think they should be solved. Paul's letter to the Romans deals with plenty of problems, problems both of behavior and of thinking, as every pastoral theologian must. But the letter is not *about* problems. It is about *God* and God's ways, which can only be approached rightly as mystery — the "more" that keeps surprising us with fresh light and grace. This "more," this mystery, is never used by Paul as an excuse to quit thinking and never invoked as a diversion from doing what needs to be done for God. Rather, it draws Paul (and us) into ever more vigorous thinking and energetic obedience. It is a thinking that doesn't dispel mystery but deepens it. "Glory," the light of God that exceeds our capacity to take it all in, is the usual word in our Scriptures to mark this mystery; it is a word that Paul uses easily and often: "to him be glory for ever" (11:36 and often elsewhere).

Necessary pastors operate within the known and the controlled,

---

2. Denis Covington, *Salvation on Sand Mountain* (New York: Addison-Wesley, 1995), pp. 203-4.

majoring in explanations and problem solving. Unnecessary pastors need not figure everything out but live in the awe of the God of mystery, glad to know that there is more going on than they see or can get their minds around.

Use of Language

The way Paul uses language, in particular his employment of metaphor, is another element in the formation of a pastoral theology. Language is primary in gospel work. This comes as no surprise, since language is primary in the making of the gospel itself: "The word is near you, on your lips and in your heart . . ." (Romans 10:8). And Jesus, of course, is *the* Word. All words are derivative from Word, whether adoringly or blasphemously, whether in the service of God's truth or the devil's lies. Language, one of the defining characteristics of being human, is integral to the way God reveals and works. It follows that the *way* we use language, not simply *that* we use it, is significant.

Charles Williams noted that Paul produced "practically a new vocabulary. To call him a poet would be perhaps improper (besides ignoring the minor but important fact that he wrote in prose). But he used words as poets do; he regenerated them."[3] Conspicuous in this crafting of words "as poets do" is his use of metaphor. This feature in Paul's use of language requires comment, for it is a major element in filling out his identity as a pastoral theologian.

How do we use words? To make things precise and clean, or to evoke the mystery of God? The use of metaphor is not a precise use of language; in fact, it is quite the opposite. A metaphor, instead of pinning down meaning, lets it loose. The metaphor does not so much define or label as it does expand, forcing the mind into participating action. To use "rock" as a metaphor for God, as in "The LORD is my rock" (Psalm 18:1), a common practice in our Scriptures, does not define God. The statement taken literally is absurd. What it does is force

---

3. Charles Williams, *The Descent of the Dove* (Vancouver, BC: Regent Publishing, 1997), p. 8.

the mind into action to find meaning at another level, "engaging the imagination in a cognitive and affective exploration of the subject in and through relationships that seem strange but, in fact, are more illuminating than literal predication."[4]

Metaphor keeps us from being spectators of language by forcing us to be participants in it. And isn't that what we're after? We don't want our congregations to pass Bible exams but to live out of the living Word. Unfortunately, some exegetes have tried to nail down Scripture's earthy metaphors by exchanging them for abstract truths. But metaphor is not a truth; it is, taken literally, a lie — an intentional lie to shake you out of your spectator complacency and get you involved in the language itself.

Paul, no doubt, acquired both his linguistic taste for metaphor and his skill in using it from the Hebrew Scriptures, where it is used extensively. In doing so, he established metaphor at the center of pastoral theology. If the language used in pastoral work diverges too far from this center, it inevitably wanders into a desert of definition and explanation.

One of the features of metaphor is its accessibility — metaphors come from common sensory experience. If, because of Romans' formidable reputation as a theological document, we suppose that we need a heavy dictionary to find our way through Paul's sentences, an actual reading of the text is a happy surprise. Paul has embraced the language of metaphor (and its sister, metonymy) that comes out of the same world that we all grow up in and have lived in all our lives. One consequence of this accessibility by means of metaphor is that the same sentences on which scholars write learned books are also read and understood by truck drivers and waitresses in conversation over coffee. This kind of language doesn't just inform our minds, although it certainly does that; it enlists us in a believing/obeying participation. We cannot be passive before a metaphor; we have to imagine and enter into it.

Paul's down-to-earth metaphorical speech occurs in virtually ev-

4. Sandra M. Schneiders, *The Revelatory Text* (New York: HarperSanFrancisco, 1991), p. 31.

ery paragraph. When I started counting, I got up to seventy-five and quit. Here is a cursory sampling:

> reap some harvest (1:13);
> written on their hearts (2:15);
> throat is an open grave (3:13);
> sins are covered (4:7);
> love has been poured into our hearts (5:5);
> death reigned through that one man (5:17);
> old self was crucified (6:6);
> wages of sin (6:23);
> sold under sin (7:14);
> creation has been groaning in travail (8:22);
> wild olive shoot (11:17);
> grafted (11:24);
> living sacrifice (12:1);
> heap burning coals on his head (12:20);
> armor of light (13:12);
> another man's foundation (15:20);
> crush Satan under your feet (16:20).

Lovers, storytellers, children, and poets continually speak in metaphor. They are alive and enliven us. But there are both theologians and pastors who like things tidy and neat, without loose ends and devoid of ambiguity. Ivory tower intellectuals and rubber-hits-the-road pragmatists like things organized and orderly, under control whether by a system of thought or a management plan. But our first pastoral theologian was not a precise or propositional theologian and was innocent of "systematics." He used words not to define but to evoke. He was not interested in containing and preserving all of God's truth in his language, protecting it from contamination and then serving it up for examination, like a specimen in a laboratory. Paul did not use the language that way; he didn't take sentences apart, trying to pry the truth out of them. He did not, as Wordsworth put it, "murder to dissect."

Paul treats language as a living energy field. Words are not tight containers of "meaning" but evocations of discourse, proliferating nuance and implication. He doesn't develop a special and disciplined jargon for the sake of being precise about God; he takes the language of common discourse, which is always redolent of metaphor — common things and common actions — and uses it freely, at ease with the ambiguities that are necessarily inherent in it. And in using language this way he sets the style for language in pastoral theology.

Necessary pastors use language to define and dispense parcels of truth. Unnecessary pastors evoke and engage what must not be pinned down.

Immersion in Community

A fourth element in the Romans letter that makes it seminal for pastoral theology is a passionate concern for community. The concern pervades the letter, providing a comprehensive context of personal relationship. Pastoral theology, as Paul lives and writes it, is relational — people are involved as persons-in-relationship.

The gospel for Paul is never a matter of getting ideas correct; he is concerned with persons in community in Christ. In 2 Timothy, the last of his letters, he names twenty-four men and women: Timothy, of course, then Lois, Eunice, Phygelus, Hermogenes, Onesiphorus, Hymenaeus, Philetus, Demas, Crescens, Titus, Luke, Mark, Tychicus, Carpus, Alexander, Prisca and Aquila, Erastus, Trophimus, Eubulus, Pudens, Linus, and Claudia. Counting the persons mentioned in all his letters, there are over forty names. Paul knew people. He knew the people he was writing to. It doesn't matter that we don't know them ourselves. Paul did.

This immersion in community is signaled on the opening page of the letter to the Romans as Paul addresses the Roman congregation as "all God's beloved in Rome" (1:7), expresses his personal feeling toward them in the phrase "I long to see you" (1:11), and notes how he has often looked forward to being with them, "in order that I may reap some harvest among you" (1:13). This is not theology-in-general — it is personally written to a specific people, living in a particular place. Even

73

though Paul has not yet been to Rome he knows the names of many of the people who live and worship there; before the letter ends, we will read some of their names (chapter 16).

But it is easy to lose touch with this personal context when Paul launches into the main body of his text at 1:16, for at this point the rich interpersonal context apparently recedes into the shadows as large theological truths blaze up. But only apparently, for Paul's concern, while expressed in terms that refer to categories (Jew and Gentile) rather than individual persons, still has to do with the formation of community, the "communion" of saints. Paul finds himself dealing with Jews who feel superior to Gentiles and Gentiles who feel superior to Israel. But Paul refuses to be pastor to a divided congregation. Their spiritual formation requires that they live in open communion with one another.

In Romans 1–8, Paul deals with Jews, the insiders to the historic revelation of God in Israel and Jesus, who are using their ethnic distinction as a mark of privilege, setting themselves off as superior to the Gentiles. Paul argues vigorously and relentlessly that there is no difference, "no distinction" (3:22). All of Paul's biggest theological guns are brought out to demolish Jewish assumptions of advantage over the Gentile, Jewish attitudes of condescension to the Gentile. Eight chapters of this may seem like overkill, but they need it. The theological arguments are so brilliantly worked out, have become so fundamental to the entire Christian world of thought, and have such far-reaching implications that it is easy to overlook the obvious: the theology is being put to use in the Roman letter entirely in the immediate service of establishing and nurturing a Christian community, a congregation free from class distinctions.

In chapters 9–11, the tables are turned: "Now I am speaking to you Gentiles . . ." (11:13). Paul addresses the Gentiles, warning them against looking down on or excluding Israel. Gentiles, finding themselves included as insiders in God's ways of grace and salvation, could easily assume a place of privilege that has just been taken away from the Jews and now, in their turn, look down on or exclude Jews, reversing the process of discrimination.

In chapters 1–8, Paul prevents Jews from excluding Gentiles by insisting that they, the Jews, are sinners to the same degree as the Gentiles; in chapters 9–11, Paul prevents Gentiles from excluding Jews by arguing that they are only "in" by virtue of a miracle, God's miracle of "grafting" them into the salvation tree. Paul's image of the wild olive branch being grafted into the cultivated olive tree, the Gentiles finding themselves "in" only by God's action and grace, is set alongside the parallel image of the natural branch (the Jews), which has been broken off but can be put back in again ("for God has the power to graft them in again" [11:23]). Gentiles do not hold a position of privilege because of their miraculous status; Jews will also get in by means of miracle.

Paul argues differently to the two factions in his congregation, but the effect is the same in both. The sin argument ("all have sinned" [3:23]) directed to the Jews in chapters 1–8 is matched by the miracle argument ("life from the dead" [11:15]) directed to the Gentiles in chapters 9–11. There can be no categories in the Christian community that sort the members into first class and second class, insiders and outsiders: we are all first-class sinners; we are all miraculously "grafted" into God's olive tree. In effect, "You both get in by miracle. You're both sinners, but you're both miracles as well."

There can be no community where there is no mutuality. Privilege is a breeding ground for pride. And once pride is given class sanction it corrupts every person. Class designation of any sort (Jew/Gentile, rich/poor, young/old, capitalist/worker, male/female, white/colored, clergy/laity, literate/illiterate) is death of community. The frightening thing is that the moment we get our identity from a classification, we lose awareness of the other as person, and the gospel of Jesus is sabotaged at an unconscious level.

The first eleven chapters are Paul's intense struggle to make community. When he gets to chapter 12, he's got it. It's hard to make community. You can't just start out with it. Romans 1–11 is needed to get it in place. But then, at chapter 12, having gotten everyone thinking truly about one another, their minds scrubbed clean of distorting class assumptions, Paul addresses a community, a congregation of Jews and Gentiles of all sorts, and instructs them in life together. They are now standing on level ground, Jews and Gentiles alongside one another as

peers, brothers and sisters in the same family, their self-identities re-
structured by Paul's powerful arguments and images. There is neither
motive nor excuse now for Jew to push Gentile into the background or
for Gentile to elbow Jew to the sidelines. In these final chapters of his
letter (12–16), Paul addresses them in common, instructing them in the
ways of community ("I appeal to you therefore, brethren . . ." [12:1]),
and brings the letter to a conclusion in a flourish of personal names,
thirty-five of them, Jews and Gentiles mixed together with no racial or
religious distinction.

Paul addresses them not as discrete individuals nor as a generic
class — they are a community, a community that can only be achieved
and understood theologically, that is, in terms of what God has done
in Christ through the Spirit, and only dealt with pastorally, that is, as
persons-in-relationship. Pastoral theology is not interested in abstract
truths on the one hand nor private individual instances in the other,
but in the formation of community by the Holy Spirit in Christ.

Necessary pastors manage people, putting them in boxes and
groups by age, gender, ethnicity, and so on. Unnecessary pastors engender communities in which they themselves participate.

I grew up in a farming community and have farmer friends who have
told me of their experience with herbicides and pesticides during their
younger years. Agents of government agricultural laboratories and
salesmen from chemical companies came to them with impressive
studies and statistics, urging them to make their fields more productive
and efficient by using powerful chemicals to get rid of devouring in-
sects and destructive disease.

Impressed by the combination of expertise and enthusiasm, they
did it. The results were wonderful: production increased remarkably.
For a while. It took a few years to realize that the chemicals were killing a lot more than the bad bugs and malign diseases. Soon the fields
were sterile and could be kept productive only by the lavish applica-
tion of fertilizers. The soil was no longer a living organism. Along the
way, awareness gradually grew among the people who were buying
the grains and vegetables and fruits from these fields and making
meals of them, an awareness that the nourishing vitamins they were

putting on their plates were laced with lethal poisons. That is when the movement back toward "organic" began — finding ways to grow food without killing the soil in which it is grown and the people who eat it.

Every time I hear these stories — and I've heard and read a lot of them by now — I think of my own field of pastoral theology. The "herbicides and pesticides" that promised to revolutionize the work of spiritual leadership are rationalism and functionalism — the scholars in their attempt to clean up Scripture and the church management gurus in their attempts to clean up the church — which promised to banish ignorance and error in our biblical and theological thinking and to get rid of the inefficiency and waste in the way we conduct our community and institutional lives. We bought it, and they did, in fact, deliver on what they promised — made us far more knowledgeable about God and the Scriptures, made us efficient in the management of religion. But at a terrible cost: theology that is less and less interested in God-with-us; pastoral work that deals less and less with persons-in-relationship.

When pastor and theology get separated from their biblical sources and then through specialization separated from each other, everybody loses. Paul in Romans offers a substantial impetus to the recovery of an organic-biblical-pastoral theology: he offers himself, Paul — submissive to Holy Scripture, open to divine mystery, alive to metaphoric language, and insistent on the conditions of community.

Chapter 5

The Call to Triumph over the Principalities and Powers

MARVA J. DAWN

Let us remember that we are a community of learning together. The Lord be with you. [And also with you.]

Let us pray: Triune God, as we think about the powers of evil at work in this world, help us to take them seriously and always remember that you triumphed over them in the victory of Christ at the cross and the empty tomb. Through Christ's victory give us courage to look realistically at our world. Give us faith strong enough to hold at arm's length the struggles we must encounter so that we see more clearly their origins and the possibility of conquest over them. Help us not to resort to the principalities and powers as a scapegoat in order to get out of facing our own sinfulness, but instead enable us to recognize the legions of diverse forces in our broken world that pull us away from what we are called to be as servants of your Church. May those powers be exposed in our study today. May our uncloaking of them disarm them, and thereby may we join in Christ's triumph over the powers. We ask all these things confidently because we know it is your will for us to stand fast against all the workings of the evil one. In the name of Jesus the Christ. Amen.

I am grateful that in previous chapters Eugene cleared the deck of most of our false necessarinesses. In the process, however, he unintentionally rebuked me when he took to task those who explain away all of the mystery of God. Woe is me, for, indeed, I am an inveterate explainer — and will be so especially in this chapter because the subject of the principalities and powers is one that is grossly misunderstood. Eugene's gentle reminder helps to call me away from some of my less desirable habits, so I pray that my explanations will still be filled with awe at the mystery of God and at the same time clarify a challenging and controversial biblical motif.

Some of the misunderstandings of the topic of "the powers" arise because of the rash of books concerning it in the evangelical market — most particularly the novels of Frank Peretti.[1] Do not jump to the conclusion that I discount Peretti's work entirely. His novels have given us several important gifts, most significant of which is the forceful awareness his books generate concerning the central role of prayer in our battles against evil. The problem, however, is that his work reduces the principalities simply to a caricature of little demons flying around and spitting sulfur. The result is that we miss the many ways the powers are at work in the world — which we shall see below.

Another misunderstanding is to use the principalities and powers as a cop-out, to blame them for all our troubles and thereby avoid facing the deep fact that we ourselves are serious sinners. To know ourselves more honestly we need to wrestle with a crucial dialectic.

In live presentations I always illustrate "dialectic" with our elbows, so I would encourage you to try this posture as you read. Fold your hands as if to pray, and then raise your elbows until they are parallel to the floor and pointing outward in opposite directions. Now change the position of your fingers so that they are interlocking and tugging on the opposite hand as you pull both your elbows outward toward opposite walls. Think now that each elbow represents a truth, but that the two truths are seemingly contradictory. The only way to keep both truths in dialectical balance is to pull equally with both hands in the center. The hands must continue to grip each other so that you don't fall over on one side or the other. Keep pulling hard — then your hands represent the dialectic tension held in balance.

---

1. An example is Frank E. Peretti, *This Present Darkness* (Westchester, IL: Crossway Books, 1986).

For example, on your left elbow is the truth that Jesus is true God; on your right, that he is true man. Most of the major heresies in the history of the Church have arisen because of an overemphasis on one side or the other. Ebionism denied the incarnation and insisted that Jesus was solely a human being. Docetism taught that Christ was only divine and that his human nature was a phantasm. Both of these heresies exist in various "Jesus Quest" and Gnostic misconceptions still today. Throughout history there have been all kinds of versions of this dialectic concerning Jesus' divine and human natures — a good dictionary of religion will explain for you the Alogi and Artemonites, those who advocated Patripassianism, Sabellianism, Arianism, Apollinarianism, Nestorianism, Eutychianism, Monophysitism, Monothelitism, and so forth. The development of doctrine in the Church is not an empty exercise in theological obfuscation. Rather, it is essential for all of us to have good, strong doctrinal bones, so that the bodies of our churches are well formed, so that we are faithful to what the Scriptures tell us about who Jesus the Christ was and is and will be.

One of the most helpful dialectics ever named is Martin Luther's insight into *simul justus et peccata* — that we are totally saints and totally sinners at the same time. Put those two truths on your two elbows and see how tugging them in the center aids us in our Christian life.

If we don't keep those two truths in balance, we can fall into deep despair over our sinning. Look carefully at yourself: you might get rid of some of your most blatant sins, but then that sneaky sin of pride creeps in as you celebrate how good you are becoming. Many Christians become devastated over their backsliding, so devastated that they doubt whether they have faith. The plain fact is that we are sinners, *peccata;* it is our human nature, the "flesh" principle. I don't emphasize this to give us an excuse for sinning, but to help us face up to this terrible truth so that we can understand ourselves. Yet it is only one side of the dialectic, one elbow in the process of knowing the truth.

On the other side is the fact that we are saints, declared so by God through the merits of Jesus Christ and transformed by the Spirit at work within us to live out of our sainthood, to participate actually in God's work through us. *Knowing* that we are saints and *living* in union with God will give us both the motivation and the means to change. We are already set free, already named holy, already knit with Christ in his death and resurrection so that it is no longer we who live, but Christ who lives in and through us. Remember here all that we contemplated in Chapter 3 concerning the deep symbol of blood and all of Christ's work on our behalf that this metaphor represents. When we hold that sacrifice before us and envision our sainthood through the blood, we find the courage and desire to change. Moreover, we truly do no longer live from ourselves, but, as the Orthodox have taught us in their doctrine of *theosis,* we participate in God's work through Christ living by the power of the Spirit through us.[2]

As God keeps changing us, we know that we will never be perfect (until the end of time when our evil propensities are done away with forever); that old sin elbow will keep tugging. But if we turn our attention immediately to the saint side, we remember the true source for being refashioned. The metaphor of our baptism helps us know the whole truth; in its waters we have drowned the old nature and have been raised again with Christ living new life in us. Focus on that new life, that "Christ in us," and then we act like the saints that we are. Because it is totally "Christ in us," we can really learn how truly unnecessary we are!

It is like driving a car at night on a two-lane road. We will avoid a crash not by looking at the oncoming lights, for then our tendency will be to veer toward them. Instead, we learn in driver's education to focus our eyes on our side of the road. Similarly, to avoid crashes into sin, we look to the saint side and trust the "called-alongside" Spirit and the indwelling Christ to guide our path straightly and to live new life through us.

All of the foregoing perceptions concerning our sinfulness are

2. See the new insights into Martin Luther's understandings of this doctrine in Carl E. Braaten and Robert W. Jenson, eds., *Union with Christ: The New Finnish Interpretation of Luther* (Grand Rapids: Wm. B. Eerdmans Publishing Co., 1998). For an Eastern Orthodox perspective on *theosis,* summarized in the patristic formula, "God became human (without ceasing to be God) that humanity might become God (without ceasing to be human)," see Kenneth Paul Wesche, "Eastern Orthodox Spirituality," *Theology Today* 56, no. 1 (April 1999): 29-43.

necessary here lest we study the principalities and powers to excuse ourselves. In fact, the forces of evil are enabled to work because of our complicity with them. At the same time, however, it is not enough to know our individual sinfulness; we must also get to know more precisely the brokenness of the conglomerate world and the ways in which the powers function in it.

The Biblical Picture of "Principalities and Powers"

We begin by considering the semantic domain of "evil," which includes words such as these: *principalities, rulers, authorities, powers, death, demons, bad angels, Satan, the Devil,* and so forth.[3] It is an exegetical mistake to equate principalities and powers with angels and demons,[4] for the biblical terminology functions differently, although sometimes the terms are used together in various combinations on lists that emphasize the diversity of the numerous agents of evil. The letter to the Ephesians is not concerned with angels, but chapter 6 gives us very commanding clues about the powers for our comprehension and combat with them.

Next, let us ponder our human propensity to develop idolatries. We appropriately value some important matter, something that we need to take seriously, but then that something seems to overstep its bounds and become overly prominent in our life. It starts to usurp the place of God. For example, instead of God being the only true God in our lives, we might start to let money become a god. Of course it is right to be good stewards of our money. That is a basic principle for our faith. However, have we ever let that principle get out of hand so that we become such "good stewards" that we are no longer generous as the Bible invites us to be?

3. The entire semantic domain is carefully assessed by Walter Wink in the first volume of his three-part series on the powers, *Naming the Powers: The Language of Power in the New Testament* (Philadelphia: Fortress Press, 1984).

4. For a thorough explication of this topic, see Marva J. Dawn, "The Concept of 'The Principalities and Powers' in the Works of Jacques Ellul" (Ph.D. dissertation, University of Notre Dame, 1992).

Paul makes this development more clear in 1 Corinthians 8:4, which insists specifically, "we know that there is no such thing as an idol in the world, and that there is no God but one" — and yet in verse 5 he adds, "For even if there are so-called gods and whether in heaven or on earth, as indeed there *are* many gods and many lords . . ." (NASV, emphasis mine). How can we put together those seemingly contradictory comments? We must ask how the not-gods become gods.

A god that does not exist in tangible reality becomes a god if we worship it, even if (perhaps especially if?) we do not know we are worshiping it. In our unintentional, unknowing worship, we make gods. Idolatry is our construction — which takes us back to the problem of our human sinfulness.

Powers are somewhat similar, but not entirely, for they already exist. We don't create them. They already exist as a tendency, a force, an existing possibility, an institution. We will see how that affects us and how we affect them when we look more closely at Ephesians 6. At this point, however, we must note that the Bible never describes for us the essence of "the powers." We don't know what kind of "being" they have. We only really see how they function, what went wrong.[5]

Let us make a quick survey of the main details the Scriptures give us regarding the powers. There is not space in this book to do a full exegetical study of these passages (even my dissertation could not encompass the subject entirely), but we can gather enough main points to guide our reading of Ephesians.

> 1. For in [Christ] all things in heaven and on earth were created, things visible and invisible, whether thrones or dominions or rulers or powers — all things have been created through him and for him.
>
> Colossians 1:16

In this text Paul acknowledges that the powers were originally part of God's good creation and were created for good. It is essential

---

5. This is made more clear in Jacques Ellul's *The Subversion of Christianity*, trans. Geoffrey W. Bromiley (Grand Rapids: Wm. B. Eerdmans Publishing Co., 1986). I don't agree with the way Ellul reduces the powers to *only* their function, but he was brilliant to recognize that we search for the wrong thing when we try to discover their essence.

that we underscore this, for when I name some of the powers operative in our present world, I do not want you to think that I want simply to revert to an earlier epoch. For example, technology is one of the powers. I am not saying that technology is bad; it serves many good purposes (among which is how much easier it makes the writing of this book). I will only insist that technology often becomes a force for alienation, a power that distorts human relationships. Technology is certainly created for good in most instances, but inherent in it is a tendency that must be held in check.

Just as you and I were created for good, yet are fallen, so the principalities and powers share in the fallenness of the world and contribute to its patterns of evil. The powers do not become gods if we keep them in their rightful place, doing the functions for which they were created — functions that give God glory and contribute to his praise. However, we live in such a broken world that nothing stays within its functional limits. Everything tends to overstep its bounds. We do, too. We make ourselves gods all the time.

> 2. The creation waits in eager expectation for the sons of God to be revealed. For the creation was subjected to frustration, not by its own choice, but by the will of the one who subjected it, in hope that the creation itself will be liberated from its bondage to decay and brought into the glorious freedom of the children of God.
>
> Romans 8:19-22, NIV[6]

The powers, as part of the fallen creation, share in its brokenness. All of creation groans in bondage to the sinfulness we have brought into the world and participates in the destructions of our fallenness. In the overstepping of a power's bounds, the world's brokenness is manifested. Yet in that very brokenness, the power and the world are part of the creation that God came to save. Later we will consider the possibility of transforming the powers, but at this point let us focus more on what Paul calls the "bondage to decay."

Why is it that money, as one example, exerts such power over

---

6. I use the NIV here because it retains the word *sons*, the biblical importance of which was explained in Chapter 3.

people? It is just paper. What is in money that makes it so essential to us? Of course, the simple answer is that we need it to buy what is necessary for our life, but we immediately recognize the many confusions over what truly is necessary. By asking questions of money, we begin to wonder at its mystery. We grieve over all the problems it causes in the world. What is the spiritual "thing" about money that causes it to have such power?[7]

Jesus named it Mammon, the god that we let be our master instead of God. Money frequently transgresses its proper sphere and becomes Mammon. When instead we return it to God, use it sparingly, give it away generously, and in other ways desacralize it, we triumph over it. Let's scan a few passages about that triumph.

> 3. For I am convinced that neither death, nor life, nor angels, nor rulers, nor things present, nor things to come, nor powers, nor height, nor depth, nor anything else in all creation, will be able to separate us from the love of God in Christ Jesus our Lord.
>
> Romans 8:38-39

This is a great text with which to commence our contemplation of victory over the powers, for Paul's exuberant declaration of assurance gives us a bold confidence that nothing can shake. He expresses his conviction with a verb in the perfect tense *(pepeiomai)* to insist, "I have been persuaded and remain persuaded" that no force of evil can disconnect us from God's love. He lists ten that might threaten. For the Jews ten was a number of completeness, so this list represents every single kind of force that seems to detach us from God, even as Paul's tenth item, "nor anything else in all creation," makes us chuckle with its suggestion, "in case I forgot a few crucial things."

Nothing can separate us; absolutely nothing has enough clout. No matter how much we might feel we are slipping from God's grasp, we are assured by Jesus who told us, "no one will snatch [my sheep]

---

7. One of the best books on the subject is Jacques Ellul's *Money and Power*, trans. LaVonne Neff (Downers Grove, IL: InterVarsity Press, 1984). See also Rodney Clapp, ed., *The Consuming Passion: Christianity and the Consumer Culture* (Downers Grove, IL: InterVarsity Press, 1998).

out of my hand . . . no one can snatch [what the Father has given me] out of the Father's hand" (John 10:28-29).

I wonder what kind of list you and I would make to remember that not one single power can separate us from God's love. Neither health crises nor handicaps, neither manuscript deadlines nor malfunctioning computers, neither airline delays nor messed-up schedules, neither busyness nor waiting, neither death nor anything else in life can sever me from my Savior's grace. (But frequently I let these things pull me away, and then they become a power for evil.)

> 4. For [Christ] must reign until he has put all his enemies under his feet. The last enemy to be destroyed is death.
>
> 1 Corinthians 15:25-26

Death was the last enemy Christ defeated (more on that later), but it is one of the first enemies to afflict our daily lives. Reflect for a while on all the ways in which the inescapableness of your death influences your behavior. Why do we have such a need to make a name for ourselves, to be important, to be remembered? Why do parents often want their children to accomplish their own unfulfilled dreams? Why are we so frightened by disruptions in our health and so unable to "weep with those who weep" over their own health crises? The most obvious evidence of how much an enemy death can be is the extraordinary lengths to which people go in order to control it (as in the euthanasia movement) or to postpone it.

In contrast, I think fondly of my friend Toni, diagnosed with terminal breast cancer. At each stage of its progression as it metastasized into her spine and brain, Toni carefully listened to the doctors' proposals for treatment, and then she asked her questions: "How much time will this gain for me?" (she was concerned for raising her young children) and "How much ability truly to live will I lose in the process?" When the latter outweighed the former, she refused the treatment and prepared herself and her family for her death. She spent her last days without added encumbrances to the communication with her family that was most important to her, for she was ready to "go home" to her Father, Savior, and Comforter.

Toni could die like that because she knew with courageous conviction that Christ had defeated that last enemy, so no barriers separated her from God. We celebrate the empty tomb every Sunday[8] as we laugh in death's face and shout for Joy, "Where is your sting?!"

I confess: I still think I have too much to do before I die, so death still becomes a power in my life frequently. Why am I so slow in learning that I'm unnecessary?

> 5. God made you alive together with [Christ], when he forgave us all our trespasses, erasing the record that stood against us with its legal demands. He set this aside, nailing it to the cross. He disarmed the rulers and authorities and made a public example of them, triumphing over them in it.
>
> Colossians 2:13b-15

The work that Christ did against the powers, as described in Colossians 2, gives us a guide for our own battles. First Christ disarmed the principalities by submitting to them. He took away their power by not responding with power and thus "made a public example" of (or "exposed" them for) what they really were.

Paul's imagery is carefully chosen; victorious battle commanders would parade before the people a line of prisoners to make a public example of their defeat. Similarly Christ exposed Mammon by being available to the traitor in the garden, and the blood money stared Judas in the face until he had to throw it away. Jesus exposed sham religion, misguided politics, Roman oppression, empty bravado, and egregious violence. Because he made a public display of these, we are now able to see their falseness and triumph over them too.

One of the purposes of this chapter is to name some of the powers that seek to destroy true ministry, that make us feel necessary. By naming them, we have a clearer perspective from which to resist them, to stand against them, to make use of the weapons that we have been given in Ephesians 6 for confronting them.

---

8. After becoming totally separated from the Jews (precipitated in the fall of Jerusalem in 70 C.E. and finalized in the Bar Kochba revolution of 135), Christians made Sunday, "the Lord's Day," their Sabbath for worship because of the Resurrection.

6. [Christ] has gone into heaven and is at the right hand of God, with angels, authorities, and powers made subject to him.

1 Peter 3:22

Peter gives a victorious vision in this text to sustain his original readers in their times of persecution. Someday, he rejoices, these authorities, such as the Roman emperors, will be — and will be seen — in submission to the exalted Christ.

Still principalities and authorities of evil persecute Christians. In the Sudan, in China, in the Holy Land where Palestinian Christians' and Muslims' homes are bulldozed for Jewish settlements — even in the United States where the persecution is much more subtle — various human and supra-human agents oppress us temporarily. Even if the "temporary" lasts a long time, Peter assures us, ultimately the triumph over all the forces of evil begun at the cross will be completed and Christ's cosmic reign will be brought to its fruition.

I have emphasized that the principalities and powers are biblically distinct from angels and demons. At the same time, they are often grouped together to help us remember that they are all greater forces than merely human. The letter to the Ephesians sometimes adds the word *heavenlies* to its descriptions, not necessarily to name a geographical location, but to heighten our sense of spiritual realities greater than earthly materiality.

We have to recognize that we cannot resist the powers unless we take seriously those larger spiritual realms. Why is it that the United States is not able to solve the drug problem? The government's fallacy is that its efforts have remained on the human level. We have not understood the spiritual influence of the power of Mammon, which drives the production and distribution by capturing corrupt police officers or border guards, kids in ghettos who have no other work besides selling drugs, and farmers who make much less if they use their agricultural talents for growing regular food crops. At the same time we have not understood the spiritual vacuum that drives consumption and addictions. We won't solve these roots of the drug problem merely by pouring more money into drug czars and more police if at the same time our culture continues to reject human cries for spiritual meaning and for genuine compassion. We must address the spiritual roots and understand the principalities and powers that are the driving forces. On the other hand, Paul, in our next passage, underscores the human connections.

> 7. None of the rulers of this age understood [God's secret wisdom]; for if they had, they would not have crucified the Lord of glory.
>
> 1 Corinthians 2:8

This text invites us to remember the other side of the dialectic — not only the spiritual realities, but also the very human dimensions of the authorities and rulers. The officials of the Lord's age included Caiaphas and Pilate and Herod. Though they aren't mentioned by name, the reference to their act of crucifying Jesus underscores that the powers function in the human religious and political spheres. This alerts us to the disturbing fact that *churches* today can similarly be principalities acting for evil instead of good.

It is necessary to keep the spiritual and material dimensions of the principalities and powers in firm dialectical balance. Under the influence of books such as those by Peretti, many evangelical Christians these days fall off on the supernatural side, as was well illustrated by a "Eutychus and His Kin" column in *Christianity Today* many years ago. I failed to record the bibliographic information or the exact quotation when someone told me about the column, but the ironic jester wrote something like this: "I'm so glad we have learned what the principalities and powers are, because now we no longer have to have food banks and homeless shelters, or legal aid services and medical clinics for the poor. Instead we can simply walk around the city and cast out the spirit of poverty."

Both sides of the dialectic must be kept in mind. Though there is plenty of work for us to do on the physical/earthly/human level, we must never lose sight of the spiritual forces working through human agencies and controlling human affairs, so that we do not limit our understanding to the mortal agencies on only their material level.

It is essential that we remember these spiritual powers, for otherwise we will fail to rely on spiritual weapons and consequently will not be able to triumph thoroughly over those powers. We do, however, always recognize that the principalities and powers operate through human institutions, created things, rulers and authorities, other cultural elements — any of these that become separated from their God-given role to serve God's purposes and that function instead for harm. The person who most clearly articulated this dialectic of the human and spiritual was Jacques Ellul (as we shall see below), but first let's begin looking at Ephesians 6 — remembering that we are discussing what is beyond our ability thoroughly to define or grasp.

Totally by God's Power We Overcome the Powers

Finally, continually become empowered in the Lord and in the strength of his might. Clothe yourselves with the panoply of God for you to continue being able to stand firm against the methods of the devil, for our struggle is not against flesh and blood, but against the principalities, against the authorities, against the world rulers of this darkness, against the spirituals [i.e., the spiritual forces] of evil in the heavenlies. On account of this take up the panoply of God, in order that you might be able to stand firm against [them] in the evil day and, having accomplished everything, to stand firm. Stand firm, therefore, having belted your waist with truth, and having clothed yourself with the breastplate of righteousness, and having shod your feet in the readiness of the good news of peace; in all circumstances taking up the shield of faith, by which you might be able to extinguish all the flaming arrows of the evil one. And receive the helmet of salvation, and the sword of the Spirit, which is the Word of God.

Through all prayer and petition praying at all times in the Spirit, and with this in view being alert with all perseverance and petition concerning all the saints, and [pray] on behalf of me in order that a word may be given to me in the opening of my mouth in boldness to make known the mystery of the gospel, on behalf of which I am an ambassador in chains, in order that in that [task] I will declare it boldly as I ought to speak.

Ephesians 6:10-20

Right at the outset of this section from Ephesians 6 we are given the assurance that we can indeed triumph over the principalities and powers, for it is not by our own capabilities and strength that we win. Paul uses a triple underscoring of the source of our might — and threesomes usually symbolize the divine in Jewish literature. Perhaps I overstate the case of symbolic numbering because I am by nature a symbolic person, but it seems to me that Paul intentionally chose three terms to accentuate the divine genesis of our vitality.

Every culture uses numbers, colors, words, gestures, or whatever to accentuate things. For example, for hundreds of years churches have employed symbolic colors to represent certain aspects of Christian doctrine and particular seasons of the Church year. Because I find this symbolic undergirding helpful to my own mind-set, I often wear liturgical colors to remind myself of the present season in the Church year or to highlight the theology I am teaching. Thus, when I first presented the lecture on the principalities and powers at Regent's pastors' conference, I wore primarily purple because that is the color of repentance. I wanted to be conscious of my own need for confession of how much I let various powers control my life. I also wore white because that is the liturgical color for the victory of Christ in the Easter empty tomb — a color to remind me that my failures are always forgivable in the context of his triumph.

My clothes often reflect liturgical colors because that helps me get my bearings according to what the Church year is teaching me or to focus on the primary mood of my lecture. I always don black on Good Friday, frequently purple during Lent and Advent, perhaps red on Pentecost. Often I wear pink because that is the liturgical color for Joy.

I think Paul does something of the same with the Jewish symbolic numbers. Verse 10 of Ephesians 6 not only tells us that our capability for dealing with the powers is "in the Lord" but also triples the words of strength and potential and might to make it clear to us that we overcome only if our power is divine.

I find it fascinating that the Jews chose three to represent the sacred. All sorts of things are grouped together in threes in the First Testament, such as the *kadosh, kadosh, kadosh* ("holy, holy, holy") of the seraphim's antiphonal song in Isaiah 6 and Isaiah's frequent use of three names for God — *YHWH,* the Holy One of Israel, your Redeemer. It is wondrous to me that after centuries of such threes to highlight deity, the followers of Jesus would discover that their God in Christ was three, yet one![9]

The verb used in Ephesians 6:10 is the source of our English words *dynamite, dynamic,* and *dynamo.* The plural present imperative middle form of the verb *(endunamousthe)* emphasizes that "y'all" (together) *continue* to summon up vigor, utilize your potential, or put forth energy in God's might. We must never forget that only "in union with the Lord" do we "become capable by means of his great strength" (*SD* 74.7).

This stack of terms keeps us mindful that the only way it is possible to have victory over the powers and authorities is if the Lord triumphs in, with, and through us. Technology will turn us into addicts if we let it; sexual behavior out of the context of God's designs will enslave us. We can't conquer the drug problem without seeing its spiritual roots; we can't get rid of our propensity to turn money into a god.

We are simply silly if we think we can win against evils by ourselves. Instead we need a "dynamic" working of God, the Lord's strength. Alcoholics Anonymous is one of the most successful of all treatments for substance abuse, and it seems to me that the secret of that accomplishment is the confession of all who participate in the meetings that they cannot conquer alcohol by themselves, but instead that they entrust themselves to a higher power and the support of the community.

We keep trying to make it on our own though, don't we? We say things like, "I've just got to try harder." It kills you, doesn't it? "If I just try harder I'll be able to fix my life." Has that ever worked?

We are not very good at recognizing what grace is, which is why I spent Chapter 3 focusing on it. This is *all* the working of God — but

---

9. For more study of Jewish symbolic numbers, especially as understanding them makes the book of Revelation less frightening, without a "countdown to the end of time" approach, see my *Joy in Our Weakness: A Gift of Hope from the Book of Revelation* (St. Louis: Concordia Publishing House, 1994).

I'm not stressing this so that we can cop out. Rather, when we know where our strength comes from, then God's empowering truly sets us free to deal faithfully with the powers.

Now, remembering that it is solely by God's working through us, we prepare to be actively engaged in that work by following this command: "Clothe yourselves with the panoply of God." Let me underscore the use of the word *panoply,* for the original Greek term *(panoplia)* invites us to keep the Roman army and its particular array of equipment in mind as we think about the weapons with which we stand against the principalities and rulers. Why might Paul have chosen this word out of the semantic domain of terms for weapons and armor? The noun designates a complete set of instruments, and its emphasis is usually upon defensive armament (*SD* 6.30). We need every piece of the protection God gives us — all the necessary Christian virtues — so that we can resist evil by being and doing good.

Since the Roman army was the force that the original readers of the Ephesians letter would envision, let us ask what made that army invincible. Why did Rome conquer the known world? When we look at the weapons of the Spirit and imagine the Romans' pieces, their victory will make enormous sense. Furthermore, taking note of a few aspects of that panoply below will expand the metaphor in this text for the workings of the Spirit and give us deeper insight into how our standing against the powers will work.

The Methods of the Diabolical One

Verse 11 reads literally, "Clothe yourselves with the panoply of God for you to continue being able to stand firm against the methods of the diabolical one." As we begin to think about our combat against the functioning of the powers, we must seriously acknowledge their immense destructiveness and not take the battle lightly or prepare too shoddily. The conflict with them requires an entire panoply of weapons. What we do with those weapons, however, is not so much an act of aggression as an act of resistance. We are called simply to stand — stand our ground, stand firm, stand faithfully, take a stand against.

The first infinitive is a present one, so the text invites us to keep on being able to stand. And what is it that we stand against? Methods!

The original Greek word is actually *methodia*, which is used only twice in the New Testament — both times in Ephesians and both times pejoratively. What does Paul mean here by "methods," and why is the term *methods* a negative one? His rare use of the word causes me to contemplate how often our methods in our ministries and churches pull us away from our true call. How easily our methods degenerate into practices not of God, but of the diabolical one!

As one such method, consider a Vacation Bible School that advertised itself as the "fastest growing Vacation Bible School in the country." Every summer, its leaders offered an eighteen-speed bicycle to the child who brought the most friends to VBS. What is wrong with such a building-filling promotional tool? First of all, it fosters greed, consumerism, dependence on things for one's happiness, and competition. Second, if the young people are urged to bring other children because of the goal of a hi-tech bicycle, then consumerism becomes their motivation instead of the love of Jesus. Third, what kind of follow-up will there be with the children who were brought along?

How dangerous such a method is! This one pulls children away from the genuine love of their neighbor as a response to knowing the good news of the Triune God's love for them. It denies them the opportunity to practice honest evangelism, witness, and hospitality. However, lest we turn our critique too much into maligning this hapless congregation, let us all admit that we, too, resort to *methods* of the diabolical one. Jacques Ellul designated such measures "Technique."[10]

Take some time to think about the methods we use in our parishes. For example, what kind of gimmicks do we use for raising money? Do they function ultimately for evil rather than good? The pastors at the Regent College conference laughed when I told about churches that have used a stewardship program based on "pony express riders," who go to homes in the congregation carrying saddle bags to collect the members' pledges — but it is true. Such programs

---

10. See Ellul's definition in *The Technological Society*, trans. John Wilkinson (New York: Vintage Books, 1964).

exist. Why do we not instead simply talk about God's immense love for us, about his invitation to us to give generously and wholeheartedly, and about the mission of the community for which funds are needed? Perhaps your parish has not resorted to stewardship gimmicks, but if we are all brutally honest we have to admit that we have used some methods in other dimensions of church life that might have been questionable.

One of my principal areas of attention and anguish concerns the kinds of methods practiced in worship services, since many churches these days depend on marketing strategies to attract people. It is often easy to recognize pastors who rely overmuch on "Technique" by the way they read the Scriptures. If we don't believe that the Word carries itself in its own power, we begin to manipulate it by the way we read it. Worship degenerates if we become like talk show hosts — as if God is not convincing enough when we clearly make him visible.

The kind of patter that disturbs me is introductory comments like, "Now listen really closely to this text; it is really exciting" or "This song is so stirring; now really pay close attention to the words" or "I just love this song so much; it is SO moving to me — I hope it really moves you." Such comments keep pulling us away from God to focus our attention on the speaker. Let the text speak for itself. Let God speak in the text. Point out an image that might not be understood in a song or explain its biblical referent. But merely to tell its subjective influence on you is to pull the focus away from God to yourself.

This is not a criticism of certain kinds of music or worship styles, though such patter more frequently happens in churches that do not use liturgies of the whole Church. Nor is it an objection to using drama, art, dance, and other visual or poetic gifts. Rather, I'm trying to call attention to anything that is phony, superficial, subjective, personal but not corporate, lacking in integrity, performance rather than worship, or whatever we do that becomes a method of manipulation and thereby becomes a working of the powers.[11]

11. See chapter 11 of my *A Royal "Waste" of Time: The Splendor of Worshiping God and Being Church for the World* (Grand Rapids: Wm. B. Eerdmans Publishing Co., 1999), pp. 149-58.

Notice that it is the *methods* of the diabolical one which we primarily stand against and not the devil himself. That takes some of the fear out of the encounter. But we know that evil works in many subtle ways, so it is essential that in everything we do we ask ourselves, spouses, best friends, staff or presbytery or vestry or boards, and/or our whole worshiping congregation this very important question: Are we resorting to Technique or does what we do have integrity? Is it faithful as a method of God?

As Jacques Ellul noted, it is not technology that is a problem; it is the *Technique,* the technological mind-set that deceives us into thinking that if we get just the right technological fix we will solve our problems. If we choose just the right style of music, we'll attract great crowds to our churches. If we use the right methods, our youth group will grow. If we develop a good gimmick, our Vacation Bible School will be the fastest growing in the world!

What we don't realize is that each Technique carries disadvantages that ultimately matter more than the advantages. My favorite good example of a bad example is Scotch broom. I don't know what the plant is actually like in Scotland, but in the United States Scotch broom was planted along the interstate highways to stop soil erosion. What was not anticipated is that it spreads like crazy from along the freeways into the fields and chokes out crops. Furthermore, Scotch broom cannot be easily removed from the fields, but requires extreme endeavor. On top of that, a large proportion of the population is allergic to it, so many of us sneeze our heads off if we are exposed to its pollen. Perhaps it solves the erosion problem, but how much of the crops — not to mention the beauty of the fields — has been destroyed in the process?

Similarly, if we resort to techniques in our churches — or *once* we resort to them — it is very hard to get rid of them. Worship gimmicks create superficial Christians. Once we condition our congregation to Twinkies in worship, it is hard to help people appreciate good vegetables.[12] As spiritual leaders, we must be constantly on the alert

---

12. See Hebrews 5:11-14, which enunciates the problem even more forcefully than I've had the courage to state it.

against methods, gimmicks, marketing strategies, Technique. Don't think that I am picking on your pet projects since I don't know what yours might be. I only know that as a sinner I, too, find myself resorting to Technique, that I am indicted by the words of Ephesians 6:11, and thus I assume that they also indict you.

Continually we can keep going back to Eugene's wonderful image in Chapter 1 of using pitons for rock climbing, the requirement that we build in protection lest we fall into manipulation. Ask yourself Eugene's question again: What kinds of precautions can I establish for myself? One of the safeguards that is necessary for me is not to keep the royalties from the books I write. The royalties are channeled to ministries for the poor or for education, not because I am generous, but so that I don't fall into the trap of writing what sells. I need that sanctuary to protect myself from myself, so that I write only what God gives me to write, even if it doesn't sell.

My point is that we all need safeguards to prevent us from using manipulative methods. How can we in the community, in the family, and in our friendship circles talk together and find better questions and other means to help each other avoid such methods?

As an example, let me offer a mistake I made a few months ago at Washington Dulles airport. A delayed shuttle flight made it necessary for me to be pushed in a wheelchair at the airport because there wasn't enough time for me to hurry with my crippled leg down the stairs from the small plane, into the airport, down a long concourse, through a maze of shops and food stands, up an escalator, down another lengthy concourse, onto a bus, over to another terminal, and down a final concourse to catch my major flight across the country to Portland. My sin was that I didn't tip the wheelchair pusher enough.

He had worked very hard for me, but, as he was wheeling me, I let the power of Mammon rob me of generosity and him of the larger tip he deserved. By the time I got home I was overwhelmed with guilt about it and confessed my stupidity to my husband Myron, who is far more generous by nature than I am. So we made up this little signal: any time one of us catches the other not being generous, we will simply say, "wheelchair." That word will remind us of the story and will thereby help to expose and disarm the power of Mammon over us.

We can develop such aids in our churches or homes so that in public situations where a warning might be required, we need only say something like "wheelchair" to be shaken out of our inattentiveness, to be spared a falling into Technique. This is not in itself a Technique (as someone asked at the Regent conference), because it is a plea for honesty. It is perhaps a hidden plea, so that other people nearby won't know that we are getting rebuked at this moment by our spouse or church secretary or colleague. Indeed, it seems to me to be the deepest of non-techniques to be rebuked graciously by someone who loves us so that we can resist the methods of the powers.

Stand, Stand, Stand, Stand

> Clothe yourselves with the panoply of God for you to continue being able to stand firm against the methods of the devil. . . . On account of this take up the panoply of God, in order that you might be able to stand firm against [them] in the evil day and, having accomplished everything, to stand firm. Stand firm, therefore . . .
>
> Ephesians 6:11, 13, 14

To grasp the full impact of these verses we have to consider another symbolic integer, the number four. As we can note in the three verses above, the verb *stand* appears in the Greek text four times, which is for the Jews the universal number. In Revelation 5:9 the elders and living creatures burst out with a new song of praise and adoration for the Lamb's worthiness to receive the book and to open its seals. The song uses a symbolic four to declare that by virtue of the Lamb's sacrifice and death he has brought back to God persons from every "tribe and tongue and people and nation."

I frequently use gathering the laundry as an image for understanding the biblical use of symbolic fours to suggest the whole world. If I pile all the clothes and towels on top of the bedsheet, then it is easy to wrap them all in the sheet by grabbing its four corners, pulling them toward the center, and turning the sheet into a sack to flip over my shoulder and carry to the washing machine. Similarly, the Hebrew use of a symbolic four named the four corners in order to include everything else in between.

My professional last name actually comes out of one of my most favorite sets of four in the Scriptures. Since my maiden family name is for others often unpronounceable and unspellable, my publisher at the time many years ago suggested that I choose a pen name. However, my editor gave me so many rules for choosing one that I was not capable of doing so — until the Sunday morning that I taught Isaiah 58 and found my new name there.

In that text the prophet is rebuking Israel for their mistreatment and oppression of the poor, their hypocrisy at worship, their misunderstanding of God's desires, and their violation of the true Sabbath. In a comprehensive set of four, the LORD declares what he wants instead: not simply to have a soup kitchen, but "to divide your own bread with the hungry"; not merely to have a homeless shelter, but to "welcome the homeless poor into your own house"; to "cover the naked when you see him"; and "not to hide yourself from your kindred" or any other human being (v. 7, my paraphrase). The result of doing these things and everything else in between — in other words, universal care for all the needy we encounter — will be this set of four: "*Then your light will break out like the dawn,* and your recovery [restoration] will speedily spring forth; and your righteousness will go before you; the glory of the LORD will be your rear guard" (v. 8, NASV). The text continues with a double set of four in chiastic (a b b a) arrangement to give two more promises, two behaviors to avoid and two to practice, and then two more promises.

For me to use the pen name *Dawn* is to be constantly reminded of those four corners in verse 7 and everything else in between. My name is a constant question: How do I live to take care of the poor, since that is one of God's major instructions to his people? The LORD calls us to be doing and building justice all the time, to love the neighbor as ourselves, to respond to God whom we cannot see by serving those we can. My name helps to goad me, and it never lets me forget. Perhaps now that you know its source, if you ever think of my name and remember God's dawning grace in Isaiah 58, that can motivate you, too, to establish righteousness in the world.

The promises of Isaiah 58:8 are reminiscent of the Exodus, especially with the imagery of righteousness going before Israel and the LORD's glory (in the pillar of fire and cloud) serving as their rear guard. When we pour out our lives to secure justice for the oppressed, God's glory shines through us. (Recall what we discussed about glory in Chapter 3.)

Telling you about the fours related to my name is relevant to our study of Ephesians 6, for living justly is part of our standing against the powers of economics and politics. We need four occurrences of the verb *stand* to jolt us into the awareness that all of life is a standing against various powers of inequality, war-mongering, oppression, and division. We need a universal reminder to stand firm in every possible way against these forces.

The four "stands" are matched in verse 12 by four names for the forces of evil that we oppose: "for our struggle is not against flesh and blood, but *against the principalities* [in the first corner], *against the authorities* [in the second], *against the world rulers of this darkness* [in the third], *against the spiritual forces of evil [literally, 'the spirituals']* *in the heavenlies* [in the fourth]." And in between these four named adversaries lie many other powers of evil.

I called your attention to the four "stands" first so that when we hear the list of our enemies we remember that we have them surrounded. We have already — through the life and suffering and death and resurrection of Christ — won. Every authority or principality against which we contend can be withstood.

Another set of four, the uses of "all" (various forms of the Greek *pas, pasa, pan*) in verse 18, adds the reinforcement of universal prayer as the final weapon in our panoply. "Through all prayer and petition praying at all times in the Spirit, and with this in view being alert with all perseverance and petition concerning all the saints" — by this fourfold, comprehensive conversation with God, our stand against the powers will remain thoroughly immersed in prayer.

We can't help but acknowledge the universal presence of evil in our world, but equally we have the universal capability to stand against all its manifestations. Moreover, we have seven weapons of the Spirit with which to stand — and the number seven represents perfection in Jewish symbolism, so we are perfectly equipped for standing. (We will look more closely at some of these weapons later in this chapter.)

Remembering that we need the whole panoply, the seven weapons, and that with them we assiduously stand, let us look more closely at the names of the foes. At this point we find significant help from Jacques Ellul.[13]

Jacques Ellul on "the Powers"

Fifty years ago Ellul saw how the powers were at work in the modern, post-war world, and in some of his earliest articles published in 1946-47 he connected his faith with how he viewed these destructive forces in society.[14] I hope the following discussion will interest you in exploring further how his writings expose the workings of the powers in our culture.

I first began studying the works of Jacques Ellul in depth because

---

13. French sociologist and lay theologian Jacques Ellul was greatly misunderstood — to a great extent because he wrote on two separate tracks that he rarely connected. His European-style *sociologie* is not like U.S. sociology, which often specializes in statistics; Ellul instead painted with broad and sweeping brush strokes to sketch in strong terms the fundamental ills of our technicized, political culture. See, for example, *The Technological Society; The Technological System,* trans. Joachim Neugroschel (New York: Continuum Publishing Co., 1980); *The Technological Bluff,* trans. Joyce Main Hanks (Grand Rapids: Wm. B. Eerdmans Publishing Co., 1990); and *The New Demons,* trans. C. Edward Hopkin (New York: Seabury Press, 1975).

Because Ellul kept his theological, biblical, ethical books in a separate track, his *sociologie* is often critiqued as overly pessimistic. However, Ellul maintained that his faith gave him the courage to look realistically at society, while his Christian books (often written at the same time in an intentional parallel) provided the hope with which believers can be sentinels for the larger society. See especially *The Presence of the Kingdom,* trans. Olive Wyon (New York: Seabury Press, 1967).

As examples of works to read in pairs, see *The Political Illusion,* trans. Konrad Kellen (New York: Alfred A. Knopf, 1967), and *The Politics of God and the Politics of Man,* trans. Geoffrey W. Bromiley (Grand Rapids: Wm. B. Eerdmans Publishing Co., 1972).

14. See *Sources and Trajectories: Eight Early Articles by Jacques Ellul That Set the Stage,* trans. and ed. Marva J. Dawn (Grand Rapids: Wm. B. Eerdmans Publishing Co., 1997).

of a chance remark to my dissertation director, John Howard Yoder. The result redirected much of my life! I had planned to do my dissertation in Ethics and the Scriptures on economic redistribution — but Ellul's comments in *The Ethics of Freedom* about the principalities and powers piqued my interest, Professor Yoder said the subject needed much more study, and, as the saying goes, the rest was history. My new dissertation topic led to massive research in sociological methods and analysis, exegetical research on the biblical passages concerning the powers, and extensive reading in the corpus of Ellul, which includes more than sixty books and six hundred articles. Far more important for the work of pastors is that I discovered as my research progressed that my difficulties would be not academic ones, but spiritual ones.

Many contemporary persons, including some academicians, believe that the biblical notion of "the principalities and powers" is merely the vestige of an outdated cosmology that nobody believes anymore and that should therefore be discarded as were similar medieval conceptions and superstitions like that of the flat earth or the existence of a devil with horns and a pitchfork. Troubles with my dissertation made me look more closely at conflicts in academic settings more generally, and thereby I began to understand the workings of the powers in institutions.

Similarly, we all must learn to recognize how principalities function, how clever the powers are to attack us each in different ways, how we must put on the Spirit's armor in order to protect ourselves as we stand against them and resist their attacks. We need the protection of the Christian community, as we shall see below, when the flaming darts of the wicked one fly from complainers in our congregations, for example, who might judge us to be incompetent if we choose truly to be a pastor. Then we have to take seriously the nature of this evil so that we battle the accusations not on a human level but on a spiritual one. We will stop the complaints not merely by stopping mouths, but by dealing with the spiritual conflict that lies beneath the surface problems.

Jacques Ellul was an insightful and faithful prophet, and he is neglected only to our great detriment, for throughout his long career he gave insistent warnings about the subtle functioning of the principalities in such accusations. Consider, as another example, the forces of propaganda.[15] I grew up thinking that propaganda was only a problem in societies under the oppression of the communist U.S.S.R. Only under Ellul's tutelage did I learn how unremittingly deceptions and fabrications proliferate in our own North American culture. Furthermore, consider the ways in which the marketing gurus' propaganda is destroying churches by calling their leaders to false roles that we think are necessary and away from who we really are as the Church.[16] I would be in despair if I didn't know that Jesus is still Lord of his Church.

Propaganda in churches is, in many ways, similar to that of the communists, for it invites people to a perfidious dream that does not acknowledge suffering, sinful humanity, the dangers of false success, and the cost of discipleship. It is, then, the working of the powers of deception. You might think that I am overstating the case, but when we are pulled away from the proper ambitions, attitudes, and actions that Christ has modeled for his Church, then whose way are we following?

In doing research for my dissertation on Jacques Ellul and his understanding of the biblical notion of "the principalities and powers," I discovered that the subject of the powers is a valuable key for bridging the two tracks of his work — his biblical/theological/ethical works and his European-style *sociologie*. In the same way, the scriptural insight bridges our pastoral recognition of evil with our analyses of human problems and failures.

This critical connection first came to my attention because of Ellul's comments on "the powers" in *The Ethics of Freedom,* in which he lists the following possible interpretations for some of the biblical titles given to the powers in Ephesians 6:12:

15. See Ellul's *Propaganda: The Formation of Men's Attitudes,* trans. Konrad Kellen and Jean Lerner (New York: Alfred A. Knopf, 1965); *A Critique of the New Commonplaces,* trans. Helen Weaver (New York: Alfred A. Knopf, 1968); and *The Humiliation of the Word,* trans. Joyce Main Hanks (Grand Rapids: Wm. B. Eerdmans Publishing Co., 1985).

16. See Philip Kenneson and James Street, *Selling Out the Church: The Dangers of Church Marketing* (Nashville: Abingdon Press, 1997).

Are they demons in the most elemental and traditional sense? Are they less precise powers (thrones and dominions) which still have an existence, reality, and, as one might say, objectivity of their own? Or do we simply have a disposition of man which constitutes this or that human factor a power by exalting it as such . . . ? In this case the powers are not objective realities which influence man from without. They exist only as the determination of man which allows them to exist in their subjugating otherness and transcendence. Or finally, at the far end of the scale, are the powers simply a figure of speech common to the Jewish-Hellenistic world, so that they merely represent cultural beliefs and have no true validity?[17]

Ellul situates himself somewhere between the second and third interpretations, for these reasons:

On the one side, I am fully convinced with Barth and Cullmann that the New Testament *exousiai* and the power of money personified as Mammon correspond to authentic, if spiritual, realities which are independent of man's decision and inclination and whose force does not reside in the man who constitutes them. Nothing that I have read to the contrary has had any great cogency for me. Neither the appeal to Gnosticism nor reference to the cultural background seems to me to explain the force and emphasis of the New Testament writers in this area. In particular the opposite view has to follow the common practice of ignoring certain essential passages where Paul cannot be adequately demythologized.

On the other side, however, the powers do not act simply from outside after the manner of Gnostic destiny or a *deus ex machina*. They are characterized by their relation to the concrete world of man. According to the biblical references they find expression in human, social realities, in the enterprises of man. In this sense the occasion of their intervention is human decision and action. . . . [T]he

---

17. Jacques Ellul, *The Ethics of Freedom*, trans. and ed. Geoffrey W. Bromiley (Grand Rapids: Wm. B. Eerdmans Publishing Co., 1976), pp. 151-52. Page references to this book in the following discussion are given parenthetically in the text. I apologize to readers offended by Ellul's non-inclusive language, but texts would become too cumbersome if all Ellul's non-gendered uses of "man" were changed.

world of which the New Testament speaks is not just a spiritual and abstract reality but one which is identical with what man in general calls the world, i.e., society. (152)

Ellul's comments are significant, for they name the powers as entities external to human beings and yet inextricably contingent with human and social realities. Ellul avoids both extremes — excessively liberal rejection of the notion entirely as well as ultra-conservative positing of a medieval cosmology for the powers — by brilliantly placing a whole range of options between them, gravitating toward either of two focal points, the evil of human beings and the spiritual forces that go beyond human explanations. As Ellul continues his description of the cohesion of the powers with material realities, he makes the following very personal remarks:

> Political power has many dimensions, e.g., social, economic, psychological, ethical, psycho-analytical, and legal. But when we have scrutinized them all, we have still not apprehended its reality. *I am not speaking hastily or lightly here but as one who has passed most of his life in confrontation with their question and in their power.* We cannot say with Marx that the power is an ideological superstructure, for it is always there. *The disproportion noted above leads me to the unavoidable conclusion that another power intervenes and indwells and uses political power, thus giving it a range and force that it does not have in itself.*
>
> The same is true of money . . . [and] technology. (153-54, emphasis mine)

I believe that Ellul's insistence that he speaks out of a lifelong confrontation with the question of the powers justifies my conviction that the biblical notion should be kept in mind when reading Ellul's *sociologie* as the key for understanding why his assessments of society are so strongly negative. He declared that only on the basis of his faith did he have the courage to be "able to hold at arm's length these powers which condition and crush me . . . [and to] view them with an objective eye that freezes and externalizes and measures them" (228-33).

Ellul's incisive analyses give us, too, the courage to face seriously the workings of the powers that disrupt, interrupt, obstruct, or corrupt ministry. On the other hand, Ellul's theology brings hope and grace and freedom to the concrete situations of our struggles against the powers at work in the world.

As one example of the correlation of spiritual forces requiring human agencies to operate, let us consider money. Certainly the power that Mammon holds over us is not due to demons flying around and operating all by themselves; the spiritual authority of Mammon necessitates human cooperation. On the other hand, the material reality of money is not sufficient to explain its compulsion; as mentioned above, money certainly doesn't possess the kind of power it has merely by its own paper self.

Ellul explicates the nature of "the powers," and specifically that of money, as follows:

> This term ["power"] should be understood not in its vague meaning, "force," but in the specific sense in which it is used in the New Testament. Power is something that acts by itself, is capable of moving other things, is autonomous (or claims to be), is a law unto itself, and presents itself as an active agent. That is its first characteristic. Its second is that power has a spiritual value. It is not only of the material world, although this is where it acts. It has spiritual meaning and direction. Power is never neutral. It is oriented; it also orients people. Finally power is more or less personal. And just as death often appears in the Bible as a personal force so here with money. Money is not a power because man uses it, because it is the means of wealth or because accumulating money makes things possible. It is a power *before* all that, and those exterior signs are only the manifestations of this power which has, or claims to have, a reality of its own.

We absolutely must not minimize the parallel Jesus draws between God and Mammon. He is not using a rhetorical figure but pointing out a reality. God as a person and Mammon as a person find themselves in conflict. Jesus describes the relation between us and one or the other the same way: it is the relationship between servant and master. Mammon can be a master the same way God is: that is, Mammon can be a personal master.

> . . . Jesus is not describing a relationship between us and an object, but between us and an active agent. He is not suggesting that we use money wisely or earn it honestly. He is speaking of a power which tries to be like God, which makes itself our master and which has specific goals.[18]

It is especially important to note in this passage the idea that Mammon is not a power because of humanity's relation to it or use of it, but that "it is a power *before* all that." Furthermore, the final paragraphs quoted above indicate a separate existence in that the power functions as does God "as a person" and establishes its own purposes and mastery. Similarly, Revelation 13–14 makes it very clear that there are agencies of evil that try to be like God. In those chapters the dragon parodies God the Father, the first beast mimics the Son, and the second beast imitates the Holy Spirit.[19]

What is urgently important is Ellul's recognition that Mammon's existence as a power calls for vigilance and more critical engagement. Note this:

> Thus when we claim to use money, we make a gross error. We can, if we must, use money, but it is really money that uses us and makes us servants by bringing us under its law and subordinating us to its aims. We are not talking only about our inner life; we are observing our total situation. We are not free to direct the use of money one way or another, for we are in the hands of this controlling power. Money is only an outward manifestation of this power, a mode of being, a form to be used in relating to man — exactly as governments, kings and dictators are only forms and appearances of another power clearly described in the Bible, political power. (76-77)

Later in *Money and Power*, Ellul demonstrates how subtle the control of Mammon is. I had always thought that it was one of the

18. Ellul, *Money and Power*, pp. 75-76. Page references to this book in the following paragraphs are given parenthetically in the text. This book is an expansion of Ellul's earlier article, "L'Argent," *Etudes Théologiques et Religieuses* 27, no. 4 (1952).

19. See chapter 24, "Taking the Presence of Evil Seriously," in my *Joy in Our Weakness*, pp. 168-75.

powers that did not really bother me. I've never had too much of it to hoard it or not enough of it to crave it or scramble after it. However, having just enough of it and being a terribly good steward of it can lead to the idolatry of a careful management that is not generous. Whoops! I would guess that if we all scrutinize our lives thoroughly, every person who ever reads this book will have to admit that at some point in his or her life Mammon has been a corrupting power.

Notice, however, that it is not just you, not simply your own longing after money. Rather, money inherently carries within itself a spiritual force, the potential for idolatry — even though it's created for good. We will not win over money if we try to solve the problems it creates merely with human means, such as a good budget. Since we tend to divinize it, we can only conquer it by desacralizing it.

Who would have thought that the battle against the principalities and powers could be fun? Ellul's idea that we must desacralize them actually lets us be playful at times in doing so, especially because he stresses that the process of de-divinizing cannot be anonymous.

There I was, reading *Money and Power* as a graduate student on a limited budget and urged by Ellul not to let Mammon become a god in my life. I was extremely careful about my grocery dollars, kept them in a special envelope, tried to have some left over at month's end so that the next month could be a bit more celebrative. Suddenly I realized that this careful stewarding allowed Mammon to exert its control over me. It had to be desacralized!

The woman whose study carrel at the library was next to mine was married (I was single), had a child, her husband was unemployed, and her graduate stipend was the same as mine. Who needed money more — she or I? I knocked on her door one day and said, "You are going to think this is really silly, but I'm making a god out of these ten bucks that I have left in my grocery fund. I know it's not much — won't get you anything but hot dogs — but would you please take it so that it stops being a god in my life?" She started to laugh, said it was the funniest thing she'd ever heard. She wouldn't have taken it if I'd offered it to her as a gift — that would have been humiliating — but she was glad to help me desacralize my money.

We must understand clearly that it is because the natural is linked with spiritual power that it is not sufficient to deal with money simply by devising and following a good budget. We need to combat the spiritual hold that Mammon acquires over us. I thought I had to hoard that $10 to make sure that I would have enough money for the next month. I'm certainly not opposed to planning ahead, but why does Mammon affect so many of our decisions when Jesus has promised that if we first seek him and his kingdom everything else will be given to us?

Let us consider, then, the hold that Mammon has over our churches and the members of our congregations. Why is good budgeting not enough? How can we help parishioners learn to desacralize Mammon in their own lives? How can we stand against the power of money in our congregation's decisions?

The Powers and Their Functions

One of Ellul's most brilliant insights was that the biblical record never describes the essence or nature of the principalities and powers. We can know them only by their functions. Though in his later years Ellul became a bit more reductionistic about the powers and no longer held to some of his insights elaborated in *Money and Power* (as noted above), his naming of six of their functions in *The Subversion of Christianity* is helpful. This is Ellul's list:

> The Bible refers to six evil powers: Mammon, the prince of this world, the prince of lies, Satan, the devil, and death. This is enough. Concerning these six, one might remark that if we compare them we find that they are all characterized by their functions: money, power, deception, accusation, division, and destruction.[20]

Of course, Ellul is right to recognize that the Hebrew term *ha-satan* literally means "the accusing one," but he stretches things a bit to limit

---

20. See Ellul, *The Subversion of Christianity*, p. 176. This volume offers a very thorough explication of the powers' functions, though he digresses too much in limiting the biblical titles to *only* these functions.

the name *diabolos* to "division." However, he is accurate in noticing that it is the working of evil, of spiritual forces, when people are divided. Racial hatred is more than merely a human reaction. The deception of propaganda is a greater power than that of only words. Whenever money pulls churches away from their God-given purposes, then it is functioning as Mammon. Whenever technology divides you from people, then it is operating as a power. Ellul's list helps us to be more observant of how and when other gods are controlling social situations.

We could no doubt name more functions than his six, but his point is crucial that these functions cause human institutions, authorities, rulers, kingdoms, principalities, and other realities to overstretch their bounds. Look, for example, at medical technology. I have numerous handicaps and health limitations due to a measles virus killing my pancreas when I was a teenager. In recent years, specialists discovered a way to inject people with islet cells that produce insulin, with the result that some diabetic complications have actually been reversed. At first I thought, "How wonderful! Technology to the rescue — my life is prolonged!" However, then I discovered that the technologists obtained the cells from aborted fetuses. It is scary, isn't it? Ethics books already list cases of women purposely becoming pregnant in order to sell their fetuses for such processes. We have to be very careful lest medical technology overstep its moral bounds, and the resulting *Techniques* bring about unintended destructions.

I am encouraged that many doctors, nurses, and other medical practitioners are asking good ethical questions to put limits on technology. The language of "principalities and powers" helps us, for it teaches us to be more observant, to pose the tough objections, to challenge easy answers, to prevent Technique from transgressing its proper sphere. We, too, must ask better questions concerning technologies in our churches. At what point do these labor-saving tools overstep their proper roles and contribute to breakdowns in our community life? What technologies might be pulling us away from our pastoral call? What Techniques make us think we are necessary?

The First Weapon in the Panoply

Stand firm, therefore, having belted your waist with truth . . .

Ephesians 6:14a

Our opponents in the struggle against the *methodia* of the diabolical one are indeed enormously strong, but we are not defenseless. We do not have the space here to look closely at all the weapons in the panoply that God gives us to stand against the powers, but we must notice a few examples to see why the list is urgently important. The first piece of armor is the belt of truth. The Roman army used belts to "gird up their loins," to keep their togas off the ground so they wouldn't trip over them. Truth keeps us from tumbling into error.

Let us expand this with another Ellulian insight. In one of his best books, *The Humiliation of the Word,* Ellul distinguishes between reality and truth.[21] That is an extraordinarily helpful perception. Reality is what we see on the surface, the superficial perspectives we gain, for example, from the television's evening news. Truth is what is *really* going on in a certain situation. The reality is that our world is full of economic chaos and political mayhem; the truth is that Jesus Christ is still Lord of the cosmos. The reality is that my body is a wreck, with hardly any part of it performing properly. The truth is that God doesn't need me still to be an athlete in good shape to do the work to which he has called me. (I usually joke that he needs only my mouth, and that seems to work just fine.)

Being able to distinguish between reality and truth helps us immensely in our standing against the powers, for we expose them and thereby disarm them if we can name the truth of their functioning for evil. We also need constantly to remember the truth of Christ's triumph over the powers so that we have the courage to stand against them and resist them in his name.

As one example, let me point to the need to expose the truth about television in our society. I formerly talked reasonably nicely about television — urging parents to monitor it closely, to discern

21. Ellul, *The Humiliation of the Word,* p. xi.

carefully what might be suitable for their children. Then I read some of Jane Healy's research, which demonstrates that children who watch a lot of television actually have smaller brains.[22] This is the case, first, because simply watching the screen fails to bridge the brain's hemispheres for input and output. Also, in sitting passively rather than manipulating their environment children do not proliferate their dendrite connections as do those who actively play.

Whenever we *do* things, neurons have to jump over the synapses to make pathways. A healthy brain is a real mess, with pathways connected everywhere. (Recently I learned from David Walsh, founder of the National Institute on Media and the Family, that, having 100 billion neurons with approximately 1,000 dendrites for each, a baby has the potential of making 100 trillion synaptic connections.[23]) Children raised on television have fewer connections, not as many pathways, less bridging — and thus a smaller brain.

Once I started telling parents the truth about this hindrance to brain development, they became more serious about limiting their children's television viewing. Exposing the powers by telling the truth about them is half the battle; we thereby begin to disarm those forces.

By the time they graduate from high school, youth in the United States have spent more hours watching television than they have spent in school. A high school senior who watches the average amount of programming has seen 500,000 commercials.[24] It seems to me that this would produce a rather brain-dead person — and a rather greedy one, too, if all those advertisements were actually observed. Let's expose this truth; let's help parents to see the powers at work right in their own homes.

I wrote my book *Is It a Lost Cause?* out of passionate concern that parents ask serious questions about what is forming the character of their children. Is it the truths of Christian faith? Or is it television? Or

22. Jane M. Healy, *Endangered Minds: Why Our Children Don't Think* (New York: Simon and Schuster, 1990). See also her *Failure to Connect: How Computers Affect Our Children's Minds — For Better and Worse* (New York: Simon and Schuster, 1998).

23. See David Walsh, *Selling Out America's Children* (Minneapolis: Fairview Press, 1995).

24. William F. Fore, *Television and Religion: The Shaping of Faith, Values, and Culture* (Minneapolis: Augsburg, 1987), pp. 16-17.

the Internet? Which controls the most hours of young people's lives? If they get one hour per week of Christian education and perhaps a few minutes each day of family or personal devotions and then watch the average four and a half hours per day of television with all its violence, greed, sexual immorality, and passivity training, what has the greater chance of forming their values and attitudes and behaviors and goals?[25]

When I am asked to speak with youth about godly sexual character and tell them God's good designs as outlined in the Bible, they often respond, "I've never heard this before." Why not? If the media give them bad ideas about their sexuality ninety-five times a day, how often do we in the Christian community need to tell them good ideas? It is essential that we recognize the working of the powers in the media and take steps to resist them![26]

One of the worst problems of television is that it forms us to have the "Low Information-Action Ratio" mentioned in Chapter 2. Even now, as I write this, I want to reach out from the page and grab you by the collar and ask you if this book will change your life. I wonder if instead you might be sitting there happily reading it and saying, "Good point, Marva," but letting it stop there and not acting on what you learn.

Similarly, pastors, think what a television-produced "Low Information-Action Ratio" does to sermons! If people have been trained by the overglut of information in the media *not* to act on what they hear (because there is too much of it and they are immobilized, or because the information is out of their context so they are unable to act on it), how will we encourage listeners to become engaged in our sermons and in living out what we preach? How can we effectively teach the Christian faith and pass it on when various principalities and powers of technology and consumerism and media and politics are pulling us all away from that way of life?

---

25. This question is more thoroughly discussed, with positive alternatives, in *Is It a Lost Cause? Having the Heart of God for the Church's Children* (Grand Rapids: Wm. B. Eerdmans Publishing Co., 1997).

26. For ways to talk with youth about the goodness of God's design rather than the emptiness of the world's *methods*, see Marva J. Dawn, *Sexual Character: Beyond Technique to Intimacy* (Grand Rapids: Wm. B. Eerdmans Publishing Co., 1993).

Sociologists know that any group that seeks to be different from the dominant culture must have rites, rituals, customs, language, habits, memories, and manners that help its members know how they are different and why that matters. Most teenagers with whom I converse at youth convocations or in congregations where I am a guest do not really know clearly how they are different as Christians from the rest of society and why they should care about that difference. We are failing our children — and ourselves!

Let us help our young people have the resources of truth to resist the idiotic ideas the media feed them concerning their sexuality. It is essential that we enfold them in better ideas, that we encircle them with the belt of truth so that they don't trip and hurt themselves, not only physically, but also emotionally, socially, spiritually. Once I gave a college chapel sermon on sexual chasteness as consumer resistance. Our society has turned sexual intercourse into another shopper item, by deflecting it from its God-ordained design into merely something else for self-gratification.

The Scriptures instead show that genital union symbolizes the faithfulness of God, the mystery of grace, the covenant bond God makes with his people. Now that is a good reason to keep it special, to sanctify it as a gift to be shared only in a committed marriage relationship. Few of our young people understand that. I talk with them about their sexuality not to spoil their fun, but so that they can understand how beautiful God's design is. It is the truth about who they are in their sexuality, and the truth is SO good! The reality they are served in daily life, in contrast, is a pack of lies.

In this matter we constantly see the powers at work. When the media function as deception, we know it is a spiritual force that needs to be resisted. The television needs to be turned off; use of the computer needs to be limited; media consumption needs to be counterbalanced with human engagement; better questions need to be asked. Exploitative words in rock music should be made plain — we certainly don't want our kids to be constantly filling their minds with smut.

Even more important, we must teach our churches' children discernment. It is not sufficient merely to attempt to keep them away from the garbage, for it is too pervasive in our culture. Let us instead help them learn to distinguish what is not good for them and develop the will to resist it.

How can we in our pastoral call enable congregation members to discern these crucial differences between truth and reality? How can we equip them with skills to resist the dehumanizing and deceiving powers? How can we so immerse them in the splendor of God that they have the will to discard these false gods?

The Shield of Faith

One great gift for developing sufficient will is another weapon in the panoply, the "shield of faith, by which you might be able to extinguish all the flaming arrows of the evil one" (Ephesians 6:16). What was it about Roman shields that made Rome's armies so invincible?

For one thing, a soldier did not hold his shield entirely over himself, but rather two-thirds covered himself and one-third was held over the person next to him. Similarly, the soldier on his other side protected him with one-third of his shield. Because of this mutual dependency, the Roman lines would rarely break.

Furthermore, the shields were not just wee little ones, but long, oblong ones by which the Roman lines could create a complete shell of protection over their heads when they came up to an enemy wall. Even though the fortress defenders rained down "fiery darts" on them, they could be sufficiently safeguarded. That is how the faith of the Christian community supports us against the attacks of the Accuser.

Recently at a conference for which I was speaking, I was feeling somewhat inferior and was tempted to put on my glittering image. The other speaker impressed everyone with his splendid piano jazz that made all the pastors and spouses rise to their feet in enthusiastic applause, while the next day I was going to have to say some very unclappable things. In the midst of my feeling a bit daunted, a dear pastor came over to me and said, "Marva, don't forget: you are not competing with him. Remember only whose servant you are." How I cherished that sentence. (Furthermore, the next day, after I finished the presentation that included those unclappable things, he came to me and said, "Well done, good and faithful servant." What a pastoral heart he has!) Every time we are tempted as church leaders to compete with others, we need someone to be telling us, "Don't forget whose servant you are!"

We are lured by our own insecurities into trying to make ourselves better than others, instead of letting God use our gifts in faithfulness to and reliance on him. Faith is a shield against our misconceptions and competitions. Faith knows that our worth is derived from the One to whom we belong, that God's love embraces us and sets us free to be truly ourselves.

We don't have the space here to explicate thoroughly the topic of faith in relation to the powers or to look at the other weapons in the panoply.[27] It is essential for the work of pastors, however, that we remember that faith is a gift and that it is bestowed by God essentially through the community. The whole Church has passed on the testimonies and the Scriptures from which we hear the good news we believe. Furthermore, the whole community supports our faith as it stands against the powers of darkness, for we in our plurality are the light of the world, the city set on the hill.

For the Sake of the Gospel

The reason why all of this concerning the powers matters is given to us at the end of this section of Ephesians 6 in verses 19-20:

> and [pray] on behalf of me in order that a word may be given to me in the opening of my mouth in boldness to make known the mystery of the gospel, on behalf of which I am an ambassador in chains, in order that in that [task] I will declare it boldly as I ought to speak.

It is essential that we resist the powers so that we can proclaim the gospel, so that we are believable when we speak about the freedom

27. I will be developing further this study of the principalities and powers in my forthcoming *The Sense of the Call: Kingdom* Shalom *for Those Who Serve the Church,* to be published also by Eerdmans.

from idolatries and tyrannies that Christ creates for us, so that we might have boldness in sharing the good news of the rescue from sin we have in Jesus and his deliverance from all oppressions and enslavements. For that to happen now, we dare not have a Low Information-Action Ratio about the material in this chapter. Join me in my campaign for our churches to be exposing the powers, for our churches to be communitarian with our shields so that we — all the members of Christ's Body — can band together to help each other and our children know the faith. Let us cover ourselves with the helmet of salvation instead of arrogance, as Eugene cautioned us in Chapter 4.

Let me give a final example, this time to illustrate the kind of discernment we need concerning the powers for the sake of the gospel. Eugene has pointed out that part of our vow in serving our churches is love of the neighbor. Now let us ask about e-mail and whether it helps us love the neighbor or whether it might function as a power for evil in our lives.

People continually insist that I "just have to" get e-mail and get on the Internet. Now I certainly think that e-mail can be very good; it helps many people communicate with their loved ones far away. Similarly, the Internet is very useful for scholarship. However, these cyberspace tools can also become a reigning power these days. E-mail deprives us of true face-to-face intimacy and allows us to escape genuine vulnerability. The Internet is by nature addictive for many people, who feel compelled to waste enormous amounts of time jumping to every hyperlink and endlessly gathering tons more information than they could ever process (thus escalating their Low Information-Action Ratio!). Moreover, many young people have never been formed with an adequate frame of reference by which to know what data is worth knowing or how to shape the knowledge gained into wisdom. Where does one put all these bytes?

Please notice that I first acknowledged that e-mail can be quite good, and then I emphasized how dangerous it can be. The key is for each of us to discern the proportion of the advantages and disadvantages, to ask better questions before deciding whether to get connected. (Many people in our society simply grab on to whatever technology is "there.")

At this point I do not have e-mail. That might change later this year when my god-daughter goes to Africa as a missionary, and I will want to be able to communicate with her more easily. Right now, however, I had to choose not to have it because I don't yet take adequate care of my friend, a widow, who lives down the street. I cannot add another thing to my life when I'm doing such a poor job of what is on my plate now. It is a careful choice, continually reassessed.

I do not ask you to make the same choice, but I urge you to take the same care when making your own good choices about technology. Is a certain technological tool going to be a power in your life for good or for evil? Will it divide you from people? Is it a power that will deceive you with a pack of lies about all the great things you will be able to learn only if you can visit multiple sites on the Web? Or will it really be a tool for ministry? You must discern and weigh and test and reassess. But you don't have to do all that alone. You discern in the midst of a community of caring that helps you ask better questions, that enables you to keep the powers in their proper spheres, functioning according to God's creation for the purposes of good.

Let us pray: O God, teach us discernment and teach us to be a community, so that we, together as your Church, can resist the powers that seek to pull us away from our role as pastors and pastoral people. May we, in seeking to be your servants, always be conscious of the spiritual nature of the powers so that we never try to fight against them on our own and never cease receiving the strength of your might in order to stand in resistance. We ask this confidently, because we know it is your will for us to be energized in your victory over those powers. We are eager to see how you will use us to be agents to expose and disarm them for the sake of spreading the good news of your grace and triumph in Jesus Christ our Lord. Amen.

Chapter 6

Timothy: Taking Over in Ephesus

EUGENE H. PETERSON

Timothy enters into a congregational mess with the mandate to straighten it out. He inherits both the legacy (left by Paul) and the problems for which others were responsible (among whom were Hymenaeus and Alexander). Like the *tohu wabohu* of Genesis 1:2, pastoral vocation doesn't begin with a clean slate.

Congregational mess provides a particularly perilous condition for convincing us that we are necessary. Others have messed up, done it badly, behaved irresponsibly, and *we* are called in to make a difference. The very fact that *we* are called in must mean that we are competent in comparison to the incompetence of others, that we are capable.

We are flattered, of course. We've been noticed. "We need you," they say. "Get us out of this. We've read your résumé, called your references, heard you preach — rescue us."

And with those words, "we need you . . . rescue us . . . ," we become necessary pastors. Eventually, we become chained to the agenda set before us, a slave to the conditions we've entered into. The dimensions of our world shift from God's large and free salvation to the cramped conditions of what others need that through combinations of sin and incompetence have been left behind.

There's a neurotic aspect to this. It's like a person who gets caught up in a flood and, while being swept along by a torrent, grabs on to a branch and holds on for dear life. It takes days for the flood to

121

recede. Meanwhile, the person holds on to the branch — saved, rescued, alive. Eventually, the flood waters are gone and the poor soul is still holding on to the branch. People come by and say, "Come on down." But the person replies, "No way. I'm saved. This is where I found salvation; this is what saved me. I'm not going to leave this saved place." A successful attempt to save life has been held on beyond necessity. And pastors do this constantly. They enter messed up situations, fix them, and keep on with the same conditions year after year after year. "This is how I got saved and saved others. . . ."

This way of life accepts the conditions of sin as the conditions in which we'll work. Now, of course, we always work in sin conditions, but they don't define our world. They just provide the material for our world, for our gospel. The mess and need of congregations are not conditions that constrict us. They didn't constrict Timothy.

The Mess in Ephesus

Ephesus is the showcase church of the New Testament. It was a missionary church established by the eloquent and learned Jewish preacher Apollos (Acts 18:24). Paul stopped by to visit this fledgling Christian community in the course of his second missionary journey, met with the tiny congregation (there were only twelve of them), and guided them into receiving the Holy Spirit. He then stayed on for three months, using the synagogue as his center for preaching and teaching on "the kingdom of God" (19:8). That three-month visit, following the dramatic encounters with the seven sons of Sceva and the mob scene incited by Demetrius over the matter of the goddess Artemis, extended to three years. Three years Paul was in Ephesus, forming a Christian congregation.

Later, the name Ephesus was attached to a letter that reflects the healthiest, most mature of all of Paul's writing on the Christian life. All the other Pauline letters were provoked by something that went wrong, either wrong thinking or bad behavior, but the dominant mood of Ephesians isn't human problems, it's God's glory. After all the problems have been straightened out in the churches, Paul is free simply to write out the gospel the way it is. Ephesians is the result. It represents the best of which we are capable in the Christian life, calling us to a mature wholeness. "Ephesian," for many of us, marks the church at its best, most complete, healthy, and holy.

I have used Ephesians in the course that I teach on spiritual formation, which I called "Soulcraft." A year or so ago, when I taught this course, one person told me that he had been taking courses at Regent College for twenty years, and that this was the fourteenth time, all from different professors, that he had had a course on Ephesians. He remarked that Ephesians must somehow be the characteristic text of Regent College itself.

The Ephesian church didn't start out trouble free, but at some point it seems to have become what we might call the perfect church. There was plenty of groundwork that went before that: supplementing Apollos's Holy Spirit–deficient teaching; getting thrown out of the synagogue; dealing with the avaricious and entrepreneurial seven sons of Sceva; surviving the Demetrius-incited mob over the Artemis issue. But, eventually, there seems to have been a quiet and mature wholeness to that congregation, which we see in the prayers and affection and leave-taking in Paul's farewell visit with the Ephesian elders at Miletus.

At one point in St. Luke's story of the church at Ephesus, he wrote, "So the word of the Lord grew and prevailed mightily" (Acts 19:20). That sums it up.

This is the Ephesus to which Timothy is sent; but he is sent here not to enjoy a cushy post in ministry — Ephesus has become a mess. Good churches can go bad. Surprisingly, sinners show up. Wonderful beginnings can end up in terrible catastrophes. Not only can they, they do. Ephesus, the poster church, did.

Most of us, no matter how wonderful a place we enter into, are going to find ourselves in the middle of a mess sooner or later. For the Christian faith is always lived out in the conditions of the world; try as we may, we cannot isolate our Christian lives from the world in which we make our living. And this culture seeps into the church, just as it seeped into the Ephesian church. (The distressing thing is when we *invite* it in.)

We don't know the exact nature of what went wrong with the Ephesian church — nothing is spelled out exactly. What is clear is that the religion of the culture had invaded the gospel of Jesus Christ and was threatening to destroy it. Paul's two letters to Timothy give us glimpses of what was happening.

Paul tells Timothy to deal with "certain persons" who are obsessed with "religion" but apparently want nothing to do with God. Here is a sampling of phrases that describe the "religious" activities of these people:

> putting high value on myths and endless genealogies which promote speculations (1 Timothy 1:4);
> engaging in vain discussion (1:6);
> giving heed to deceitful spirits and doctrines of demons (4:1);
> being guided by the hypocrisy of liars (4:2);
> forbidding marriage and enjoining abstinence from foods (4:3);
> majoring in godless and silly myths (4:7);
> having a morbid craving for controversy and for disputes about words (6:4);
> imagining that godliness is a means of gain (6:5);
> participating in godless chatter (2 Timothy 2:16);
> holding that the resurrection is past already (2:18);
> starting stupid, senseless controversies (2:23);
> and wandering into myths (4:4).

We don't know with any precision what the "godless chatter" was in Ephesus. Scholars make learned guesses. It was no doubt a form of gnosticism, which essentially creates an elite body of insiders who cultivate a higher form of religion that despises common people, common things, and anything that has to do with a commitment to a moral life. Jesus, of course, would be far too common for people like this. The "godless chatter," whatever its actual content, would be shaped by the culture and not by the cross of Jesus.

What is most apparent about these phrases is that they refer to a lot of talk — speculations, controversies, and chatter. There is one reference to behavior (about marriage and diet) and one to an item of doctrine (resurrection), but mostly we are dealing with religious talk. These people loved to talk about religion. T. H. White's description of the older Guinevere, who had become a nun after the death of Arthur, could easily describe these Ephesian teachers: "She became a wonderful theologian, but cared nothing about God."

And this is what we are faced with continuously. This culture seeps into the church through the pores of our congregations: a religion without commitment, spirituality without content, aspiration and talk and longing, fulfillment and needs, but not much concern about God.

Diana of Ephesus and of Now

We have recently had a remarkable experience in our world of this old Ephesian stuff. At the end of August 1997 and for weeks following, the attention of the whole world, quite literally the whole world, was captured by the death of Princess Diana. I was in Ireland and Scotland at the time and got the entire drama served up to me blow by blow. I must confess that I knew next to nothing about Diana at the time, can't ever remember seeing a picture of her, and knew nothing of her trials with the royal family. But in three weeks, I got a crash course in Diana religion — for the thing that struck me most forcibly was that it was a course in *religion*. This was a totally religious event. There were political implications and family dynamics, but mostly, overwhelmingly, it was religious. Diana was treated with the veneration and adoration of a goddess. At her death, the world fell down and worshiped.

As I observed all of this, and reflected on it in conversation with friends, I realized that Diana was the perfect goddess for a world religion that didn't want anything to do with the God and Father of our Lord Jesus Christ, but was desperate to worship someone or something that would provide a sense of beauty and transcendence to their lives. It turned out that Princess Diana was absolutely perfect for the role. This supposedly godless world of ours is not godless at all — the capacity for worship is as strong as in any religious fundamentalist camp meeting. At her death, the world worshiped her.

At first, I noticed the parallels to the ancient Canaanite sex/fertility goddesses Astarte and Asherah. She was a perfect fit for the role: that fragile beauty, tinged with sadness; that poignant innocence, with suggestive hints and guesses of slightly corrupt sexuality in the shadows. Her popular identification with the poor and the oppressed, her photo with Mother Teresa of Calcutta, her compassion for people with AIDS, her campaign against the land mines that had destroyed the bodies of so many children, and her own victimization by the heartless royal family and rejection by her husband. She summed up the spiritual aspirations of a sexually indulgent culture that was at the same time filled with misunderstanding and loss and hurt and rejection.

Every day for a week in Edinburgh I watched long lines of men and women and children carrying bouquets of flowers, placing them on appointed shrines throughout the city — silent and weeping, unutterably moved by the death of their goddess. All week long, I read the meditations, *religious* meditations, on Diana in the daily newspapers. And then one day, I remembered that the Roman name for Artemis was Diana, Diana of the Ephesians. Now, Diana the sex goddess, who provided the mythology and set the moral tone to the city, was back — the fertility goddess of the ancient world taking over the imaginations of the modern world.

I'm not suggesting that the Diana cult of Ephesus and the Diana cult that we all witnessed since September 1997 have the same content, but the effect is the same. The Ephesian Diana cult was a pastiche of stories and superstitions and systems of thought endemic to the ancient east that served the religious needs of the city. (Much of it is accountable in general under what we in broad terms label gnosticism.) The recent Diana cult is also a pastiche of stories and longings and public relations that serve the religious needs of an astounding number of people who are nominally Christians and Jews, Buddhists and Muslims. Her death brought out into the open just how worldwide her influence extended, the untold millions who worshiped at the shrine of Diana.

Diana evoked the best of people — but it is the best of what they want for themselves, not of what God wants. She offered "good" without morality and transcendence without any God but herself. Diana epitomizes our world religion of today.

When Timothy was sent into Ephesus, it was to counter the effects of the Artemis/Diana religious substructure in the culture. We don't have to know exactly what it was he was dealing with — ultimately, he was dealing with religion that served the needs of people on their terms, their longings for completion, their hunger for meaning, their thirst for beauty and significance, and their impatience with a God who required anything of them.

But the gospel that Jesus brought and that Paul preached is not first of all about us; it is about God. It is about the God who created us and wills to save us; the Jesus who gave himself for us and wants us to deny ourselves and follow him wherever he leads us, including the cross; and the Holy Spirit who descends upon us in order to reproduce the resurrection in our ordinary lives. None of this involves fulfilling our needs as we define them. Our needs are sin-needs — the need to get our own way, to be self-important, to be in control of our own lives.

The wonderful Ephesian church that had begun so robustly, with such a sense of new life, discovering the revealed truth in the Scriptures and the presence of God in their lives by the Holy Spirit — this Christ-centered, Holy Spirit–created church was dissipating in a religious stew pot of hyped-up feelings and novel combinations of ideas, discussion groups, and interest gatherings.

Do you see how contemporary this is? Do you see how easily this can happen? Do you see how often it happens? Do you see how it is almost inevitable, that if it hasn't happened in your congregation yet, it will before too long? Do you see why, the moment he found out what was going on, Paul sent Timothy to do something about it? Do you see that you might have the same task set before you?

Diana/Artemis worship is in the air: it is on television, in the magazines, in church pulpits, and in school classrooms; it dominates business marketing, the entertainment industry, recreational addictions, and political arenas. Leaders acquire a following by evoking longings in us that are unfulfilled, and then either explicitly claiming or implicitly suggesting that their program or automobile or lifestyle or church can make us complete. Diana religion. Diana worship.

When the church finds itself overwhelmed by the culture, what is it to do? What was Timothy to do?

What Timothy Did

Conventional wisdom tells us that when the problem is large, the strategy must be large. We have to think globally; we need to acquire a "vision" that is adequate to the dimensions of the trouble. But that isn't what happens here. If we look for it, we're disappointed. Timothy isn't charged to refute or expose the Diana spirituality of Ephesus. Paul simply tells him to avoid it. He has bigger fish to fry: he is to teach and to pray.

The overriding concern in the Pastoral Epistles is in "healthy" or "sound" teaching. Eight times in all in these three letters we find concern for the "health" of teaching or words.

Sometimes "teaching" is translated as "doctrine" and so we get the impression that orthodoxy is at issue. But this isn't quite right. For Timothy is given a mandate to teach in a way that brings *health* to people. Words in Ephesus have gotten sick; the "godless chatter" in Ephesus is infecting the souls of people with disease. It is important not to see Timothy as a defender of orthodoxy, as someone who argues for the truth of the gospel. He is a teacher responsible for speaking in such a way that people get healthy again.

Let me digress here: if you have any desire or aptitude toward teaching, embrace the life of pastor. The vocation of pastor is the best of all contexts in which to teach. But it is a particular kind of teaching, the kind referred to here as "sound teaching." Frances Young translates the phrase as "healthy teaching" or "healthy words." Eight times the word is used to define the kind of teaching and speaking that is going to be at the center of the work of reforming the Ephesian church.

I give them to you here in the translation of the Revised Standard Version, followed by some brief comments and my translation in *The Message*.

1 Timothy 1:10

The first instance of the phrase "healthy teaching" or "sound doctrine" is in 1 Timothy 1:10. Timothy is instructed to "remain at Ephesus that you may charge certain persons not to teach any different doctrine" (1:3). Paul goes on to describe what results from the "different doctrine": fourteen instances of ways of life, acts, behaviors (1:9-10). Wrong thinking leads to wrong living. He contrasts this catalogue of bad, sick living with "*sound doctrine,* in accordance with the glorious gospel of the blessed God with which I have been entrusted" (1:10-11).

This sound doctrine is contrasted to those "who defy all authority, riding roughshod over God, life, sex, truth, whatever! They are contemptuous of this great Message I've been put in charge of by this great God."

1 Timothy 6:3

"If anyone teaches otherwise and does not agree with the *sound words* of our Lord Jesus Christ and the teaching which accords with godliness, he is puffed up with conceit, he knows nothing. . . ."

Words are important. Words and living are the heads and tails of the same coin. When words are wrong — diseased — they cause illness; they infect the soul. Sound, healthy words equal godly living.

"These are the things I want you to teach and preach. If you have leaders there who teach otherwise, who refuse the *solid words* of our Master Jesus and this godly instruction, tag them for what they are: ignorant windbags who infect the air with germs of envy, controversy, bad-mouthing, suspicious rumors."

2 Timothy 1:13

"Follow the pattern of the *sound words* which you have heard from me, in the faith and love which are in Christ Jesus."

Sound words are not information about God but a path to walk in by faith and love. Words and living are part of the same thing, not different realms of existence.

"So keep at your work, this faith and love rooted in Christ, exactly as I set it out for you. It's as *sound* as the day you first *heard* it from me. Guard this precious thing placed in your custody by the Holy Spirit who works in us."

2 Timothy 4:3

"For the time is coming when people will not endure *sound teaching,* but having itching ears they will accumulate for themselves teachers to suit their own likings. . . ."

Sound teaching obviously is not comforting and soothing; it is not background music to create a spiritual mood to keep your blood pressure in check. It's solid food. It's not what sounds nice but what's healthy.

"You're going to find that there will be times when people will have no stomach for *solid teaching,* but will fill up on spiritual junk food — catchy opinions that tickle their fancy. . . ."

(The next four citations are from Titus, substantiating what has already been given to Timothy and extending it into a new context.)

Titus 1:9

"He must hold firm to the *sure word* as taught, so that he may be able to give instruction in *sound doctrine* and also to confute those who contradict it."

This verse occurs in a passage that sets out what is required of an elder in the churches in Crete. Not only pastors are responsible for using words in a sound and healthy way; all leaders must have healthy doctrine so as not to lead in the wrong direction.

"It's important that a church leader . . . have a good grip on the

Message, knowing how to use the truth to either spur people on in knowledge or stop them in their tracks if they oppose it."

Titus 1:13

"This testimony is true. Therefore rebuke them sharply, that they may be *sound* in the faith."

"Stop that diseased talk of Jewish make-believe and made-up rules so they can recover a *robust* faith."

Titus 2:1

"But as for you, teach what befits *sound doctrine.*"

"Your job is to speak out on the things that make for *solid doctrine.*"

Titus 2:2

"Bid the older men be temperate, serious, sensible, *sound* in faith, in love, and in steadfastness."

This cluster of characteristics describes a person's life, not just his thoughts or beliefs. This is obvious, but it loses its obviousness in a Diana culture: teaching has to do with living, not with information gathering.

"Guide the older men into lives of temperance, dignity, and wisdom, into *healthy* faith, love, and endurance."

These eight uses of the word "sound" or "solid" or "healthy" or "sane" or "robust" begin to give us the hang of what Timothy is about as he enters this Ephesian disorder and confusion.

The phrase "sound words" or "sound doctrine," as J. N. D. Kelly puts it, "expresses [Paul's] conviction that a morally disordered life is, as it were, diseased and stands in need of treatment . . .

whereas a life based on the teaching of the Gospel is clean and healthy."[1]

The Greek word for "sound" is *hygiein,* from which we get hygiene. The main thing that Timothy is to do in Ephesus in order to clean up the mess is to teach sound words, sound truth, healthy thinking and believing. Verbal hygiene. Healthy gospel.

Scientia and *Sapientia*

Is this enough? Can words make a difference, especially in a society that is already saturated with words? They are not enough if we are obsessed with making a difference, convinced that we are necessary to the gospel enterprise. Words don't make anything happen. . . .

But words do matter. The way we speak and use words matters. Nothing a pastor does is more important than the way she or he uses words. However, words are devalued today in the church's ministry. We have made them marginal to images and programs and have reduced them to slogans and posters. Instead of using words carefully and accurately, we amplify them, thinking that we will convince by decibels.

Kathleen Norris in her book *The Cloister Walk* tells the story of the time she heard the poet Diane Glancy astound a group of pastors, mostly Protestant. Norris writes:

> She began her poetry reading by saying that she loved Christianity because it was a blood religion. People gasped in shock; I was overjoyed, thinking, *Hit 'em, Diane; hit 'em where they live.* One man later told me that Diane's language had led him to believe that she was some kind of fundamentalist, an impression that was rudely shattered when she read a marvelous poem about angels speaking to her through the carburetor of an old car as she drove down a rural highway at night. Diane told the clergy that she appreciated the relation of the Christian religion to words. "The creation came into be-

1. J. N. D. Kelly, *A Commentary on the Pastoral Epistles* (London: Adam and Charles Black, 1963), p. 50.

ing when God spoke," she said, reminding us of Paul's belief that "faith comes through hearing." Diane saw this regard for words as connected not only to writing but to living. "You build a world in what you say," she said. "Words — as I speak or write them — make a path on which I walk."[2]

But not all people use words that way. There is a great chasm in our Western world in the way words are used. It is an old split, but it has gotten worse century by century. It is the split between words that *describe* the world and reality from as much distance as possible through generalities and abstractions, and words that *express* the world and reality by entering it, participating in it by metaphor and command. Describing words can be set under the Latin term *scientia*, expressing words under the term *sapientia* — or in English, science and wisdom. Science is information stored in the head that can be used impersonally; wisdom is intelligence that comes from the heart, which can only be lived personally in relationships.

It is absolutely critical that we discern the distinction between these two ways of knowing, for if we don't we will treat matters of the gospel wrongly and therefore lead people wrongly. All knowledge, both science and wisdom, has content to it. But science characteristically depersonalizes knowledge in order to make it more exact, precise, objective, manageable. Wisdom, on the other hand, personalizes knowledge in order to live intensely, faithfully, healthily. For science, an item of knowledge is the same in any place or time for any kind of person. For wisdom, an item of knowledge is custom-made; timing, placing, fitting into the uniqueness of a person is essential. "Two plus two equals four" means exactly the same thing for a five-year-old kindergartner and a fifty-year-old Nobel Prize–winning economist. "I love you" means something different every time it is said, depending on who says it, the tone in which it is said, the circumstances surrounding the statement, and the person to whom the statement is addressed.

"Two plus two equals four" is science — generic fact.

2. Kathleen Norris, *The Cloister Walk* (New York: Riverhead Books, 1996), p. 154.

"I love you" is wisdom — lived truth.

The "sound words" that Paul writes about are all *sapientia*, wisdom-lived words. What the Ephesians were engaged in was *scientia*, "godless chatter." This is an important distinction to make because we are taught in school from childhood to speak in *scientia* but not in *sapientia*.

I belabor this a bit because we pastors, setting ourselves under the guidance of the pastoral letters, are told over and over again of the importance of teaching, and that we are the teachers. Frances Young points out this heavy emphasis here:

> *Didaskalia*, the Greek word for "teaching," occurs fifteen times in these three little letters, over against six in the whole of the rest of the NT. The urgency that church leaders (officials) be *didaktikoi*, "apt for teaching," appears twice and nowhere else in the NT. Uniquely, too, Paul is twice described as a *didaskalos*, or "teacher," alongside the usual *apostolos*. The noun *didache* and the verb *didasko*, in both simple and compound forms, punctuate the text, but their frequency elsewhere in the NT makes their use less dramatically striking. Other associated words for advising, exhorting, directing, commanding, etc. permeate the letters.[3]

Teaching is at the center of leadership work in the Christian community. Every piece of the gospel is to be lived, so we must keep on teaching. But what kind of teaching? Wisdom teaching, not science teaching; teaching people how to live, not teaching people how to pass exams.

We have two parallel institutions in which teaching takes place: schools and churches. Schools are primarily dedicated to the acquisition of information that we can use impersonally and objectively. Churches are primarily dedicated to first understanding and then internalizing the revelation of God so that we can live in obedience and love, in adoration and prayer. Unfortunately, we live in a time when

---

3. Frances Young, *The Theology of the Pastoral Epistles* (New York: Cambridge University Press, 1994), p. 75.

churches have taken on the ethos of the school in regards to teaching and learning. But when we do that, we abandon our proper work. If we think that by cramming theological or ethical or biblical information into people's heads we are helping them live better to the glory of God, we are badly mistaken. Getting the right information is the smallest part in the curriculum of wisdom. Living rightly and robustly in faith, hope, and love is what we are about. And that means, of course, that all our words must be lived words. What we say and the way we live are part of the same grammar. We teach as much when we are silent as when we are talking. We teach as effectively when we are praying as when we are lecturing.

And now I want to say something quite directly personal to you who are pastors. If you want to be a teacher, know that being a pastor in a church provides the best possible conditions for such work. And being a professor in a school is perhaps the worst place to be.

I put it this way because I fairly frequently have conversations with pastors who tell me that they feel they would like to, in their phrase, "go into teaching." What they mean by that is to get themselves a graduate degree and get a position as a professor in a school. I want to be careful about this, because being a professor in a school is honorable and can be Christ-honoring work. Professors are essential to the human community. The work of research, separating error from truth, getting things straight, training minds to think accurately — all this is terribly important. But it also takes place in conditions that treat knowledge as information, as something to be used. If you want to teach wisdom, you find yourself going against the stream constantly. Educational organizations and bureaucracies have no interest in how you live, or even if you do live. The primary ethical concerns of a school have to do with not stealing books from the library, not cheating on your exams, and not plagiarizing in your papers.

In saying this I am not putting down schools. I am, after all, a professor at Regent College and love what this school does. Schools, given the conditions of our times, are necessary. But I also must tell you that I was a much better teacher as a pastor in a congregation than I am as a professor in a school. Virtually everything I have taught at Regent, I taught first, and probably better, to my congregation.

In preparing for a recent summer school course, I was looking through a folder of accumulated notes and realized that I first taught it in 1968 to an adult class consisting of three women: Jennifer, a widow of about sixty years of age, with an eighth grade schooling, whose primary occupations were keeping a brood of chickens and a goat she was very fond of and watching the soaps on television; Penny, about fifty-five, an army wife who treated her retired military husband and her teenage son and daughter as items of furniture in her antiseptic house, dusting them off and placing them in positions that would show them off to her best advantage, and then getting upset when they didn't stay where she put them — she was, as you can imagine, in a perpetual state of upset; and Brenda, married, mother of two teenage sons, a timid, shy, introverted hypochondriac who read her frequently updated diagnoses and prescriptions from about a dozen doctors as horoscopes — the scriptures by which she lived. (Ironically, she lived the longest of the three.)

Looking back, I could not have picked a more ideal student body for my teaching. As I taught my fledgling course in spiritual formation, using Ephesians as my text, I soon learned the difference between information and wisdom, and that wisdom was all that mattered to these three women. It was slow work, but gospel words have power in them. These women learned with their lives. The three women are now dead. I sometimes wonder if they are amused as they see me teach this course in which they were the charter students, to bright and gifted students from all over the world who pay high fees to be in the class. They paid by putting a dollar or two in the Sunday offering.

In a sentence, all wisdom is acquired relationally, in the context of family and friends, work and neighborhood, under the conditions of sin and forgiveness, within the complex stories that the Holy Spirit has been writing and continues to write of our lives.

Paul tells Timothy: "continue in what you have learned and have firmly believed, knowing *from whom* you learned it . . ." (2 Timothy 3:14). *From whom* — that is the only way to get wisdom — from whom — a person. And so what better place to teach persons personally than in a congregation where you have access to everything that makes up their personhood — their families, their work, the weather, their neighborhood, their sins, their stories — and over a period of years, sometimes decades. In a school, you get them for a short period of time in a setting that excludes most of what makes them who they are, their uniqueness, their multifaceted lives. In a church, you get them in the setting where their main business is living, up to their armpits in life.

I can't think of a better or more important place to be a teacher, a wisdom teacher, which is the only kind of teaching I am interested in, than in a church. Timothy in Ephesus. You in your congregation.

As Paul put it: "If you put these instructions before the brethren, you will be a good minister of Christ Jesus, nourished on the words of the faith and of the good doctrine which you have followed" (1 Timothy 4:6).

Truth matters: simple, clear, lived.

Chapter 7

The Call to Be Formed and Transformed by the Spirit of the Ascended Christ

MARVA J. DAWN

Let us remember that we are a community. The Lord be with you. [And also with you.]

Let us pray: Blessed art Thou, O Lord the Christ, our risen and ascended Liberator. We celebrate that you sit at the right hand of the Father interceding for us. We celebrate that you returned to the Father so that you could send your Spirit to us. We celebrate that you are present with us now, wherever we are. We thank you especially that in your ascension you are able continually to form us, for you have reclaimed your authority and estate as God and thereby work in our lives through your risen presence and by the power of your Spirit. Guide us as we think about our formation. Knit the hearts of your people together so that we will be formed to be the kind of community you created and called us to be as your Body. Encourage us through each other. And let your Word change us as you have promised, for we believe that your Word will not come back empty, but will accomplish the purposes for which you send it. Amen.

Ascension Day and Pastoral Yearning

The lecture upon which this chapter is based was given on Ascension Day. When I was a child, the congregation to which I belonged always celebrated Ascension Day with a special worship service. Before continuing with our study of Ephesians (and actually as an introduction to the topic of this chapter), let me include comments made at Regent College to urge the conference participants to restore Ascension Day as a major church holy day. I do so because I have never seen in print a plea for recognizing the importance of this day.

Let's begin whimsically. Ascension Day is the perfect church holiday because the world can't steal it. The culture around us has quite ruined Christmas and Easter. Of course, the world owned Christmas as its festival for the restoration of the sun before the early Christians used it to disguise their celebration of Christ's birth. (And then the Church wisely made June 24th, when the amount of sunlight was diminishing, John the Baptizer's Day in keeping with his words in John 3:30, "He must increase, but I must decrease.") But the world has now stolen it back for its consumerist purposes and has seized Easter for the same idolatry. In my teen years I played clarinet in the high school band for the town Christmas parade at which Santa Claus was flown in by helicopter. Later, I heard, they flew the bunny in for Easter. But the world hasn't got the foggiest notion what to do with someone flying out!

Seriously, why should we celebrate Ascension Day? Most of the reasons are suggested by the prayer at the beginning of this chapter, but let's set out a full portrait of several of the gracious benefits and magnificent consequences of Christ's ascension. A most obvious gift is that otherwise, if Jesus had not ascended, we would all have to go over to Galilee to find him. Because he returned to the Father, he is ubiquitous. He can be found by all of us, everywhere.[1] He is present with you now as you read.

Philippians 2 introduces us to other dimensions as follows:

Let the same mind be in you that was in Christ Jesus,
who, though he was in the form of God,

---

1. Luke Timothy Johnson's new book, *Living Jesus,* accentuates the truth of Christ's resurrection that Jesus can be encountered in the world today, but his presence throughout the Christian community would not be possible without the ascension. Johnson's work is an excellent refutation of the claims of the Jesus Seminar and others who deny the Scriptures' revelation of Jesus. See *Living Jesus: Learning the Heart of the Gospel* (San Francisco: HarperSanFrancisco, 1999).

> did not regard equality with God
>> as something to be exploited,
> but emptied himself,
>> taking the form of a slave,
>> being born in human likeness.
> And being found in human form,
>> he humbled himself
>> and became obedient to the point of death —
>>> even death on a cross.
> Therefore, God also highly exalted him
>> and gave him the name that is above every name,
> so that at the name of Jesus every knee should bend
>> in heaven and on earth and under the earth,
> and every tongue should confess
>> that Jesus Christ is Lord,
>> to the glory of God the Father.
>
> Philippians 2:5-11

Paul uses (or creates?) in this text the early Christian hymn of the *kenosis* or "emptying" of Jesus. The Greek name of the doctrine comes from the past tense verb *ekenosen,* which means "to completely remove or eliminate elements of high status or rank by eliminating all privileges or prerogatives associated with such status or rank — 'to empty oneself, to divest oneself of position'" (*SD* 87.70). The hymn displays how thoroughly Jesus made himself nothing by giving up his God-powers in order to take the form *(morphē)* of a servant, though he was in the *morphē* of God. As a man Jesus did not assert his Godness, having laid that completely aside — for example, in not even knowing when the end of time would be. Only in the utter humility of his whole nature could he actually die for us.

The second glory of Christ's ascension, then, is that by it God affirmed Christ's total obedience and the completion of his earthly/ human work on our behalf. In the ascension Jesus took up again the fullness of his God-self, his deity; it was the end of the *kenosis,* the self-imposed self-limitation. Several texts in the letter to the Hebrews accentuate Christ's accomplishment of his work, as demonstrated by his taking his seat at God's right hand. For example, Hebrews 1:3 declares, "[The Son] is the reflection of God's glory and the exact imprint of God's very being, and he sustains all things by his powerful word. When he had made purification for sins, he sat down at the right hand of the Majesty on high." (See also Hebrews 10:12 and 12:2.)

The Philippians hymn also hints at another gift of the ascension in that Jesus was given the name — Jesus, Christ/Messiah, Lord — at which every knee shall bow. Other texts of the New Testament expand this notion to specify that all the powers have become subject to him. The clearest passage is 1 Peter 3:22 — that God saves us by the resurrection of Jesus Christ, "who has gone into heaven and is at the right hand of God, with angels, authorities, and powers made subject to him." The resurrection of Jesus signaled the final defeat of the last enemy, death (1 Corinthians 15), just as his exaltation to God's right hand indicates his rule over all other powers. (See also Luke 22:69, Stephen's vision in Acts 7:55-56, Colossians 3:1, and 1 Corinthians 15:25-27.) Our study subject, Ephesians, emphasizes this result of the ascension in 1:22: "And [God] has brought all things under control beneath his feet, and gave him to the church as head over all things." From that position of power Jesus will come again. Perhaps the greatest Joy of the ascension is its promise that someday soon Christ will come to reign eternally, to end all sorrow and pain, to take us to be with him. Jesus himself prophesied his return before the high priest in the parallel texts of Matthew 26:64 and Mark 14:62. Similarly, the angel promised his coming back to the disciples who watched him ascend in Acts 1:11.

Meanwhile, at that position of power and relationship with the Father, Christ stays to intercede for us. Romans 8:34 emphasizes, "Who is to condemn? It is Christ Jesus, who died, yes, who was raised, who is at the right hand of God, who indeed intercedes for us." Similarly, Hebrews 8:1-2 names Christ's present work since the ascension as that of the high priest: "Now the main point in what we are saying is this: we have such a high priest, one who is seated at the right hand of the throne of the Majesty in the heavens, a minister in the sanctuary and the true tent that the Lord, and not any mortal, has set up."

Jesus himself gave us yet another reason for the ascension when he told the disciples that unless he went away the Holy Spirit would not be sent to them (John 16:5-15). Peter proclaims this reason on Pentecost when he preaches in Acts 2:33, "Being therefore exalted at the right hand of God, and having received from the Father the promise of the Holy Spirit, he has poured out this that you both see and hear."

The result of that pouring out of the Spirit, furthermore, has been all God's gifts to the Church. This is specifically connected to the ascension in Ephesians 4 as follows:

> But to each one of us has been given grace according to the measure of the gift of Christ. Therefore it says,
>
> > Having ascended on high, "he took many captives with him" [*SD* 55.24],
> > he gave gifts to human beings.
>
> (But what does "he ascended" mean if not that he also descended into the lower parts of the earth? He who descended is also the one having ascended far above all the heavens, in order that he might fill all things.) And he appointed some [to be] apostles, some [as] prophets, some evangelists, and some pastors and teachers, in order to prepare the saints fully for [their] work of service, for building up the body of Christ, until we all attain to the unity of the faith and of the full knowledge of the Son of God, to mature manhood, to the measure of the stature of the completeness of Christ. . . .
>
> > Ephesians 4:7-13

This gifting of the Church with such leaders so that all the saints can do their work of ministry and build up Christ's Body, so that we may together be unified in faith and knowledge, so that we may all together achieve maturity and as one Body measure up to our Head — this gifting emerges in another astonishing consequence, that we the Church shall do greater works even than Christ. As Jesus foretold in John 14:12, "Very truly, I tell you, the one who believes in me will also do the works that I do and, in fact, will do greater works than these, because I am going to the Father." Can we even imagine such a stunning result of the ascension? Moreover, the works that are possible now in the name of Jesus are even greater because his Body has multiple manifestations. It is not limited to the single physical body of Jesus of Nazareth, but includes all the Christians throughout time and space. Now try to imagine the incredible possibilities!

All of these reasons for the importance of the ascension are underscored in Luke-Acts. In the Luke 9:51 announcement that Jesus "set his face to go to Jerusalem," we should notice something significant. Luke does not write that Jesus did this when it was time for him to die or when it was time for him to be raised from the dead. Rather, Luke explains, "When the days drew near for him to *be taken up,* he set his face. . . ." After this dramatic turning point for the whole Gospel account, Luke uses the verb *poreuomai,* "to go," as a constant drumbeat. Jesus set his face and goes . . . , goes . . . , goes . . . to his death, his resurrection, and then his ascension. The Gospel of Luke ends with the ascension (24:50-52).

Then the book of Acts begins with the ascension (1:1-11), demonstrating how important this event was for Luke's narrative. Following his account of the ascension and the pouring out of the Spirit at Pentecost, Luke takes up his drumbeat again and continues the *poreuomai* . . . , *poreuomai* . . . , *poreuomai* . . . with Peter and Paul going, going . . . to spread Christianity to Jerusalem, in all Judea and Samaria, and to the ends of the earth.

The going, going, going began with Jesus setting his face like flint for all the sacrificial work he was to do, which culminated in the ascension. Then, that very same ascension is the beginning of the commission to the apostles to go, go, go to the uttermost parts of the earth with the message of Jesus.[2] Thus, Christ's ascension is a pivotal point for Luke — the turn when Jesus regains his full authority as God and then passes on to his people the going that he had been doing, so that we, the Church, as his Body can do, by the power of the Holy Spirit, the greater works he promised.

Perhaps you might want to join me in campaigning for an Ascension Day celebration in your congregation next year. It offers several important aspects of our Christian language that have been lost. Ascension is a deep symbol that people don't understand anymore

---

2. I first learned this pivotal importance of the ascension in a graduate course with Luke/Acts scholar David L. Tiede, president of Luther Seminary, St. Paul, Minnesota. See his *Prophecy and History in Luke-Acts* (Philadelphia: Fortress Press, 1980).

because we so rarely discuss it. Ascension should be connected in our minds to Jesus' teaching the disciples about the kingdom of God during the forty days between Easter and his return to the Father. Thus, the festival day creates in us a longing for the completion of that kingdom.

Seasons of Longing, Fulfillment, and Proclamation

At an Interim Ministry Network conference a few years ago Chuck Olsen suggested that the Christian life has a rhythm of anticipation or yearning, celebration of a high point of fulfillment, and proclamation or practice.[3] After his keynote address in which he listed several examples, I found myself filling out the entire calendar of Christian seasons and was delighted to see how helpful his notion is for understanding the complete church year.

At the beginning of the church year, we observe a season of yearning in Advent as we imagine the longing of the Jews for their Messiah, as we hunger for Jesus to come more deeply into our own lives, and as we thirst for his coming again. The culminating celebration is Christmas, of course; and then the proclamation, the going out into life, is observed in the season of Epiphany, the observance of the coming of the Magi by God's light and the subsequent spread of God's grace to the Gentiles through all the ways in which Jesus is the Light of the world.

After the Epiphany season, we return to yearning with Lent. We need that time of longing, of meditating on all that Christ did for us, lest we take for granted the enormous gift of Easter. After the festival celebration of Easter, the proclamation or practice happens in the season of the forty days, during which time Jesus trained the disciples in

3. Olsen may have used other terms in his keynote presentation, but these are the words that have helped me remember his idea, for which I want to give him due credit. He specializes in enabling congregational leaders to serve more spiritually. For more information, see Charles M. Olsen, *Transforming Church Boards into Communities of Spiritual Leaders* (Bethesda, MD: Alban Institute, 1995). His organization can be reached at their web site, www.worshipful-work.org; e-mail address, worshpfulw@aol.com; or telephone number, (816) 880-0586.

the meaning of his resurrection and its promise of fulfillment in the final recapitulation of God's cosmic reign.

Ascension is again a time of yearning, for it initiates the disciples — and us — into the ten days of waiting for the pouring out of the Holy Spirit and for Christ's coming again. We celebrate the high festival of Pentecost, after which the entire season of "ordinary time" (formerly called the Trinity season, but now usually named "the Sundays after Pentecost") is a practicing of Christ's presence through the power of the Spirit.

The three high festivals are actually trinitarian, though most would think there are two celebrations of Christ. It seems to me that we would be able to avoid the overly romantic sentimentalizing of Christmas if we remembered that it is more fully a festival of the Father, the One who gave us the unfathomable gift of his Son. Christmas is not a cute baby in a cozy stable, but the harsh reality that God, the Creator of the whole universe, so condescended as to give us his Son as a creature in the flesh. Imagine if a shoemaker would become a shoe! The other two festivals are obviously those of the Son at Easter and the Holy Spirit at Pentecost.[4]

Moreover, to think in this way of Christmas as the Father's gift not only helps us to avoid the sticky sentimentality of the season but also enables us to link the Father more thoroughly into the sacrifice of the Son and thereby evade the "patriarchal oppression" ideas about the atonement to which nontrinitarian theologians often reduce Christ's death on the cross. Knowing the immensity of the Father's sacrifice in his Christmas gift of his Son enables us to envision more thoroughly how all of God suffers at the cross.

Why does it matter to think about this? one might wonder. It is simply my goal to help our churches be more trinitarian. To compre-

---

4. Another way to think about the seasons as trinitarian could be to celebrate Christmas as the Christ-festival, Jesus' initiation into his entire life of suffering, and then celebrate Easter as the Father's festival since many texts in the Scriptures emphasize that he raised Jesus from the dead and that during the following forty days Jesus taught about the kingdom of God. This schema has some advantages, but it would be difficult to teach since most of the church's hymns focus on Christ rising rather than the Father raising. I mention this only because we need continually to stretch our minds and question our categories in order to think more fully about God being Trinity.

hend Christmas as the Father's festival enables us also to think more thoroughly about the first person of the Trinity and to recognize his gift to the world of his Son as the fulfillment of his cosmic plan to restore his *whole* creation.

The three-step process of waiting/yearning, festival/celebration, and proclamation/sending gives structure to our Christian lives and congregational years. Moreover, it helps us keep societal powers from destroying our holy days, for these waiting times do not let us take for granted the great gifts of the festivals of Christmas and Easter and Pentecost.

Most people in our culture, for example, are disappointed in Christmas because they have been saluting it since September (or whenever the decorations and advertisements first hit the stores and airwaves). If we observe Advent, however, we are never disillusioned, for the Messiah for whom we long does indeed come to us!

When I was a child, it was not the presents we anticipated with great excitement, but the worship services at which we would exuberantly sing all the joyous carols and descants, all the new music my father had written during Advent. In those worship times we welcomed the Christ Child's coming with great Joy. At home our yearning was accentuated by our Advent wreath, which had a candle for every single day of the entire season. We kids could hardly wait for Christmas Eve when all the candles, especially the Christmas candle, would finally be lit all at once to celebrate that the Christ Child, the Light of the world, had come to our house.

As I look around me in our culture, I see many people — if not most! — disappointed in Christmas. Children don't get all the presents they wanted, or their toys break too soon or don't match what the advertisements promised. Adults are depressed because they are alone, because no matter how hard they try they cannot recapture the magic of childhood, because they have put themselves deeply in debt in the attempt to make the season "really special" and only know how to do that with stuff, because they wonder "Is this all there is?" You cannot help but be disillusioned if only Santa Claus comes to your house. But if the one you yearn for is the Christ Child, you will never be disappointed, for he always comes!

This is why I want to recapture also the yearning of Ascension

Day and its ten-day season. It provides a crucial lesson in waiting for the Spirit's empowerment and wisdom and gifts. For example, I yearn for God to give me the kind of pastoral wisdom that I see in Eugene. I yearn to be more faithful to the calling that God has given me. I yearn to teach with sound words. Advent, Lent, Ascension — they all whet my appetite for the presence of God.

Ascension is the primary season for whetting the pastoral appetite. In its culminating festival of Pentecost, the Spirit is poured out to anoint us with gifts, authorize us with the Word, and send us out for the sake of God's people and the world.

Formation

In the previous chapter Eugene has already superbly laid out the background of the Ephesian church and noted its maturity, so I need not cover that foundation again. However, I do want to add that I have always loved the letter to the Ephesians because its profound vision conveys so clearly Paul's heartfelt love for the Church's members at Ephesus and his urgent passion for what it means to be the community of Christ's Body. Thus it nurtures, with biblical formation, my own passion for the Church.

No doubt some of the readers of this book do not think Paul wrote the letter to the Ephesians. Remember that if we are considering these texts with a canonical approach, we can go beyond the liberal/conservative debate over authorship to consider instead what is gained by thinking about the text as it has been passed on by the Church. Especially for the topic of this chapter that will be helpful, for if we read the letter to the Ephesians as a love song from pastoral Paul, who spent three years in deep community life with the members of Christ's Body at Ephesus, then we hear important undertones of commitment and understanding, as well as overtones of knowledgeable critique and affirmation. Most significant, we hear an urgent melody as Paul leads his readers into the mystery, as he invites them to see what it would really be like when a church is truly Church.

One of the most surging streams through Ephesians which inspires our focus in this chapter is that of formation. However, two difficulties must be acknowledged before we turn to that theme. The first is that it is problematic to talk about the subject of formation since we cannot form ourselves. We must always be vigilant against thinking that we can grow ourselves in faith and faith-life or that we, pastoral servants, are "necessary" to the formation of congregation members.

The second is that all shaping of the spiritual life and a servant's character takes place in the midst of the entire Christian community throughout space and time. Properly, therefore, this chapter should follow Chapter 9, wherein we discuss building the community. However, because our culture is basically narcissistic, it will suit our habits to think first of ourselves and who we are becoming, and that will inevitably lead us to need the discussion of community, for this chapter will spur us to discern more deeply that we cannot manage without the Christian community that surrounds us.

If we skimmed through Ephesians to survey all the passages that deal with formation, we would be surprised at their extent. The second half of Ephesians 1, following the doxology that we studied in Chapter 3, is Paul's prayer for the saints at Ephesus, and it includes, after his thanksgiving for their faith and love, his petition that God's wisdom, God's revelation would form them. What is indispensably important for us here is to notice how so much of the prayer is about God.

It is urgent in our humanly centered (anthropocentric) times that we see how extensively Paul's prayer names God. If we pay attention to God, we will gain God's wisdom, receive God's revelation, and be formed to be more like God. The Trinity's grace (remember Chapter 3) is always quintessential.

One of the most severe failures in churches today is that so often preaching has become therapeutic instead of proclamatory. The point of sermons is not to tell listeners how to lift themselves up by their own bootstraps; we don't advise them on how to fix their lives and adjust their attitudes. Rather, we preach to paint so beautiful and compelling a vision of the kingdom of God that we enable the hearers to inhabit it.[5]

---

5. This image was first given to me by Walter Brueggemann, *Finally Comes the Poet: Daring Speech for Proclamation* (Minneapolis: Fortress Press, 1989).

I don't think it is possible to overstate this point. Probably those of you reading this book do not need this admonition to preach about God, but certainly many of your brothers and sisters in ministry do. Everywhere I go as a guest lecturer, across denominational lines, I hear sermons about us, rather than about God.

This has been especially frustrating to me in the past few seasons of Lent. For example, once a seminary intern gave a children's sermon about burying the "Alleluias" during Lent. He had written the word *Alleluia* on a piece of paper and took the children out the door to dig a little hole and bury it until Easter. However, he never told the children *why* we don't sing such a bright word during this time of the year. We were never invited into the sorrow of the season, the great grief that Jesus, whom we love so ardently, is bitterly betrayed, fearfully forsaken, spitefully scourged, mercilessly mocked, cruelly crucified — stricken, struck down by God, and afflicted, weighed down with grief and shame.

Frequently in the past few Lents I have heard sermons about *our* journey, *our* healing, *our* temptations — without a word about the way that Jesus walked, how he healed others but didn't save himself, and his victory over temptations on our behalf. In stark contrast, last weekend my husband and I went to Trinity Episcopal Cathedral in Portland for J. S. Bach's *Passion According to St. Matthew,* conducted by Eric Milnes. Bach faithfully set the text of the Gospel in its narrative parts and then assigned to soloists, choir, and the entire assembly arias, choruses, and congregational chorales in response to the Scriptures. Though our emotions are acknowledged and solemnized, the focus is predominantly on Jesus, the immensity of his sufferings for us, and the incredible wonder of it all.

For example, consider chorale number 46, which in Bach's day would have been sung by the congregation. These are the German words:

Wie wunderbarlich ist doch diese Strafe!
Der gute Hirte leidet für die Schafe,
Die Schuld bezahlt der Herre, der Gerechte,
Für seine Knechte.

This is my rough translation (not put into the music's rhythm or rhyme):

> How extraordinary indeed is this punishment!
> The good Shepherd suffers for the sheep;
> The Lord, the Just One, settles the debt
> For his servants.

It is Holy Week as I write this, and I have found myself repeatedly in tears as I listen again to Bach's *Passion* in my study — for his faithful music brings me a vision and the presence of the Suffering Servant. I can hear the immensity of Christ's love for me, the extent to which he loved his people "to the end." Thus I am wooed to respond in love to a Lover who would humble himself to such an extent, to such a death, for the sake of the unworthy beloved!

It is the revelation of God that forms us.

Moreover, many people in our culture don't know anything about God. We could never get done telling them all of what the Trinity did and does and will do, was and is and will be for us.

I am not advocating, of course, a proclamation that does not connect to the daily lives of people. We are not speaking about God in the abstract, but yet the focus remains on God and not on us.[6]

We are not going to change people by telling them that they ought to change. I know that from experience because of my physical handicaps, which frequently make me quite discouraged. People have actually said to me, "Marva, you shouldn't be depressed — you're a Bible teacher after all." Such a comment, of course, makes me more despondent. And then, when I'm more dejected, I feel so guilty about being depressed that I get more defeated and more desperate, which makes me experience even more guilt. It becomes a vicious cycle.

When people are in the depths of despair, Jesus does not say to them, "You ought to get out of that pit." Nor does he say, "Here are

---

6. This is the main theme of my book *Reaching Out without Dumbing Down: A Theology of Worship for the Turn-of-the-Century Culture* (Grand Rapids: Wm. B. Eerdmans Publishing Co., 1995): that true worship centers on God and, as a result of that concentration, will form us as individual believers and communities.

ten easy steps for getting out of pits." What he does instead is jump into the pit with us.

Our ministry to others is always to show them Jesus — that he went to the depths of the abyss on our behalf, that he is in the pit with us right now. Lent shows us how deep was the grave of sin in which we were buried so that we never presume that we could ever find life on our own. At the same time, Lent invites us to sit by the tomb of Jesus and know the truth of why he is there — from our side and from God's.

And, oh! then the exhilaration of Easter — this wild, ebullient, blazing Joy! This inconceivable victory, this unprecedented triumph, this monumental good news! Since every Sunday is a remembrance of Easter, how can we not preach sermons that proclaim this gospel, this truth of the resurrection that it is no longer we who live, but Christ lives in us? That is the theme of the first part of Ephesians 2.

How Desperate — and How Delivered — We Are!

And you, being dead in your wrongdoings and sins, in which you once walked according to the aeon of this world, according to the ruler of the authority of the air, [that is] the spirit now active in the sons of disobedience, among whom we also all lived at one time in the lusts of our flesh, doing the things willed by the flesh and by [our] thoughts, and we were children by nature of wrath as [were] also the rest . . .

Ephesians 2:1-3

I purposely left my translation awkward here to show how the beginning of Ephesians 2 stacks up, with image after image, a piercing portrait of how desperately we need resurrection and new formation. The first three verses show thoroughly that we are not merely bad because of sin. In our sin we are *dead!* One big problem in churches these days is that members don't know how dead they are.

We human beings have a great aversion to naming sin SIN. We want to euphemize it with terms like "brokenness" which make people feel cozy because it seems not to be their fault. Something else caused them to be "broken."

Now it is true that many outside forces do break us, but if we never take responsibility for our own self-centeredness, faults, missteps, and more blatant evils — in other words, if we never acknowledge that we are *sinners* — we can never get forgiven. This is indeed a real problem in North America: many persons carry around a pile of guilt which can never be removed and from which they can never be released because they have tried instead to turn it into a pillow by euphemizing it.

This is why we are so refreshed when we admit with the apostle Paul that we cannot do what we want to do and that we keep on doing what we wish we didn't do (Romans 7:15-20). Our churches teach us various ways to confess, our diverse denominations train us in different practices, but truly the announcement of forgiveness is the greatest gift the Church offers to the world. I hungrily eat up those words of forgiveness on Sunday mornings. I need the absolution that the pastor proclaims because I cannot forgive myself. Can you?

We can't forgive ourselves because we always hedge it. We turn back and wallow in our despairs, or we excuse ourselves too easily, or we put a penance on ourselves and try to earn forgiveness, or we assume that we are far too unworthy to be forgiven.

That is why it is such a Joy in worship to be able to confess our sins and sinfulness and to hear forgiveness and to taste it in the Lord's Supper. Forgiveness is a fact, a gift, that needs to be proclaimed, shouted from the rooftops, heralded, and declared gently to our burdened neighbors. When we know how dead we are, we comprehend, too, how desperate we are for forgiveness.

Notice how this deadness is tripled in Martin Luther's vast threesome of the Devil, the World, and our Flesh. As we saw in Chapter 5, talking about the principalities and powers does not let people cop out of their responsibility. Luther's triumvirate does not let us off the hook. Each one of the three contributes to the fault and mess. The devil and all his minions of demons and evil angels (however you understand them), the world with its temptations that are power-infested and principality-driven, and myself with my pride and panic and fears and foibles — all these help cause the muck in the world. It is certainly a bondage from which we cannot free ourselves, a thoroughly entombing deadness when we are under all three. We deserve nothing but the wrath of God, as does everyone else in the world.

This total bondage to death is the reason why Ephesians 2:4 offers one of the most beautiful contrasts in all of Scripture: "but God, being rich in mercy, because of his great love with which he loved us, and we being dead in wrongdoings, he made us alive together with Christ." Its introduction — *"but God!"* — then picks up steam, rolling on into the liberating passage of verses 4-9. As you read these verses, observe their comprehensive emphasis on gifts, riches, mercy, lavishing, God pouring out on us exactly the grace that we need.

Amazing Grace

But God, being rich in mercy, because of his great love with which he loved us, even when we were dead in wrongdoings, made us alive together with Christ — by grace you have come to be and remain saved — and raised us up with [him] and seated us with [him] in the heavenlies in Christ Jesus. For by grace you have come to be and remain saved through faith, and this not from yourselves, the gift [is] of God, not from works, so that no one might boast.

Ephesians 2:4-9

These verses engender complete freedom, liberated life. The Greek verbs in the phrases from verses 5 and 8 translated by the New Revised Standard Version as "by grace you have been saved" are both periphrastics, a combination of the second plural verb, *you are (este),* and the perfect participle, *becoming and remaining saved (sesōsmenoi).* My rendering above is an attempt to underscore the immensity of this truth: we didn't do anything to become saved, and we continue in God's salvation through no effort or merit or worthiness on our part. Coming to faith is a gift; remaining in it is also sheer grace. How could we ever stop being altogether amazed by this grace? Surely such lavish mercy on God's part forms us into thankfulness, wonder, freedom, commitment, eagerness, dedication to the praise of God's glory, and release from any necessariness.

Moreover, the following understanding of the nature of our lives underscores the grace once again:

> For of [the Triune God] we are the workmanship, having been created in Christ Jesus for good works which God appointed beforehand in order that we might walk in them.
>
> Ephesians 2:10

Once again we are astounded by the vision, this entirely new perception of our daily existence, of what we are and how we live as a result of God's incomprehensible, mysterious, overwhelming grace. What bliss it is to discover that since God has dealt with our deadness (totally because of his character!), we are, therefore, a work of art! It is such an unfathomable change: from casket to fresh creation, from colorlessness to craftsmanship, from deadness to great deeds, already planned by God for us to fulfill. God has choreographed the ballet and set us free to dance. Oh, the ecstasy of dancing when Someone has given us new feet and formed them in his steps!

Jesus proclaims to us the same freedom with a similar image to Ephesians 2:10 when, in Matthew 5:14-16, he calls us the light of the world. We are the lamp. No one, he says, lights a lamp and puts it under a bushel basket. Rather, a lamp is put on its stand from which it can give light to all in the house.

If we are the lamp in this parable, let's be consistent. We don't light ourselves, do we? Nor do we set ourselves on the lampstand. Nor do we invite the people into the house. God sets us on fire by grace, appoints us to our places of ministry by grace, brings the people into our lives by grace — and by grace liberates us simply to shine!

> Therefore, keep remembering that formerly you — Gentiles in the flesh, the ones called "uncircumcision" by those called "circumcision" (made in the flesh with human hands) — were at that time without Christ, estranged from the commonwealth of Israel and foreigners to the covenants of promise, not having hope and without

God in the world. But now in Christ Jesus you who once were far off have been brought near in the blood of Christ.

Ephesians 2:11-13

Exulting in the fact that we are works of art enables us to face even more deeply how dead we were. We Gentiles, the grafted ones, were not even a part of God's community. We had no part in the *polis*, the "people" of God. We were without hope for a Messiah, ignorant of God's covenant with his chosen ones, far away from all of God's promises and their fulfillments, without the covering of Christ's blood so that we could stand in the presence of God. If we keep remembering all this (the Greek verb is a continuing imperative), then we will certainly never take for granted the privilege of being part of the community of saints (see Chapter 9), and we will absolutely not want to continue in the way of life of those without God. That leads us to our next formative section in chapters 4 to 6 of the letter to the Ephesians.

Learning Christ

Therefore I say this and affirm it in the Lord, no longer [ought] you to be walking as the Gentiles walk in the futility of their minds, being and remaining darkened in their understanding, having become and remaining estranged from the life of God, on account of the ignorance which is in them, on account of the stubborn unwillingness of their hearts to learn; and they having thoroughly lost all feeling of shame gave themselves into behavior completely lacking any moral restraint in the greediness of practicing all kinds of impurity. But you did not so learn Christ!

Ephesians 4:17-20

Verse 17 seems to me to be an essential call for our times, the insistence that in the Lord we will not want any longer to continue living in our former patterns. I believe our churches need more of such urgency, the expectation that God's people will surely want to escape from the way of life we would follow if we were still without God.

Let me give you an example of one warning that I continually need for departing from the world's ways. What would happen here in North America if I would wear the same dress two out of four days at a conference? In some circles, people would think that to do so was appallingly fashionless. One has to wear something different every day, right?

A few years ago I gave a series of lectures at a seminary in Poland and visited a dormitory apartment where six of the women students lived together in a space not much larger than my study at home. Each person's entire wardrobe fit in a small pile on a short shelf. Most of the women owned only one change of clothing. These seminary students' simple life reproached me for the fullness of my closet. It is a frank invitation of the gospel that I leave my former way of life of having far too many clothes.

So easily we slip into the world's values — "Clothes make the person," "Be as glamorous as you dare," "You are what you wear." Do we really need all the stuff we own? Can we find a better balance between looking our best for the sake of the kingdom work we do and living simply for the sake of building justice in the world?

Paul beckons us away from whatever our practices might be that conform us to the world. This is the same message as that of these present continuing imperatives in my rendering of Romans 12:2: "Do not continue to be conformed to this world — don't be squashed into its boxes — but be continually being transformed from the inside out by the renewal of your mind." God gives us the language of faith in the Spirit's renewal of our minds, and then the Spirit transforms us into living it.

We must not confuse the explicit little instructions of Ephesians 4:17–6:9 with a legalistic religion. When we remember the grace poured out in the first chapters of the letter, we realize that Paul is not merely giving rules here. Rather, he is inviting us into the design God has for his people. He teaches us the language of what it means to follow the Christian community's way of life. His instructions are wonderfully helpful, as is demonstrated by this example:

> Every unwholesome word — let it not be proceeding out of your mouth, but if any [word is] good for building up what is needed, [speak it] in order that it might give grace to the ones hearing.
>
> Ephesians 4:29

I know that this rendering of verse 29 is awkward, but I wanted to accentuate as the Greek text does the importance of our staying alert so that every single unwholesome word is nipped in the bud in order not to let it come out of our mouths. Instead, as God's people we are invited to make sure that all our words are ones that will build others up, provide what they need, offer grace to every single person who hears us.

I have spent many years in graduate schools, which sometimes tend to be *macho* places, where the department ethos is to prove one's brilliance by demonstrating others' ignorance. Once I was told by a professor that others on the faculty did not think I was very smart. When I wondered how they had come to that conclusion (I readily admit to being not the brightest), he replied, "Because you never cut people down."

The ethos can be the same in graduate departments, business offices, marketing enterprises, church staffs. One worker says to another, "I don't think you understand what I am saying," to which the second person responds, "I understand what you are saying; I just don't understand why anybody intelligent would say it." Such situations offer us a choice. Are we going to accept that way of living or not? If we are formed by the Bible, by the narrative of the *Christian* community, will we instead not let any unwholesome talk come out of our mouths, but only that which is good for edifying? If we live that way, if we choose to upbuild others with our talk instead of tearing them down, it will cost us.

It will cost us to live this way because the world around us does not expect grace. People could think we're not too smart, might take advantage of our "naiveté," perhaps will dismiss us from the office or deny us advancement in our careers. But imagine what the world could be like if everyone lived according to God's design for language that uplifts, that imparts grace! This is not a rule to spoil our fun, but a great invitation to live together kindly and truly and well.

God's Spirit continually renews this invitation to let our character be formed by constructive texts. Remember what I wrote in Chapter 2 about immersing ourselves in a Shakespeare play so that we can improvise the missing parts. If we are improvising according to these instructions, we will also corporately pay a price. Our churches could grow, but they might not grow larger (or fatter) if we are truth tellers and grace speakers. However, they will certainly grow deeper if we will be what we are called to be. Meanwhile, people might suspect that we are being radical — but what better word could there be for the nonconformity of the gospel?

To be radical is to get to the root (Latin, *radix*) of things. We want to cut out the roots of sinfulness (which are tough to eliminate like dandelions and blow weedy seeds everywhere) and replace them with roots of grace that grow into transformation.

Our world needs us, the Church, to be formed by the Word of God, to be immersed in its instructions — if it is indeed a suffering immersion. It seems to me that Christian churches have such little impact in North America and most of the Western world because we are not willing to suffer. We are not willing to bear the pain and cost of really living true to God's instructions.

Can we let Paul woo us with the goodness of these instructions? He summons us to alternative attitudes, alternative words, alternative behaviors, alternatives of our whole being personally and corporately. What he wants is for our character to be formed into a certain kind of person, the image of God.

My husband is a superb example. Myron is kind in the best sense of that word, and kindness has never been one of my strong points. He willingly waits at the end of a line; I'm always in a hurry. One instance remains painted across my mind from early in our marriage. On our way to the doctor, we were stopped by a red light on a four-lane road. When the light turned green, the car in front of us didn't move. I kept saying, "Myron, you can go around now. It's clear, Myron. It's open; why don't you go?" Nagging is what I was doing. Finally, Myron in his gracious, good, generous self leaned over to me and said, "I am looking to make sure the woman in that car in front of us is all right."

Who has been formed by the gospel? That incident still stands out in my memory because it pricks me with my selfishness, competitiveness, bossiness, and inattention, and in contrast displays how Myron was formed to be merciful, supportive of others, and compassionate. He believes that part of his call in life is to help me with all my physical handicaps so that I can continue to teach and write. It is quite amazing, don't you think?

My side of that illustration demonstrates our deadness in sin; Myron's side manifests the possibilities of resurrection. I pray that God will use my being married to Myron to change me. (If I hang around with him enough, will his goodness rub off on me?) If we immerse ourselves in God's instructions and in the way of life of his people, God's invitations will transform us. His poured-out grace will give us the courage to face how dead we are, and, admitting that lifelessness, we can rise with Christ to life anew.

What does it mean to rise with Christ? Especially the notion emphasizes that the risen Christ dwells in us so that we learn his way of being in the world. One aid in all the instructions of the Scriptures is Paul's gentle rebuke, introduced with the strongest of Greek adversatives,

But you did not so learn Christ!

Ephesians 4:20

That verse ought to be underlined, circled, or starred in our Bibles and put up in our churches on broad, brilliant banners to help us keep remembering that the Christian community is an alternative society. We practice a way of life radically different from the ways of the world with its futility of mind, darkened understanding, estrangement from the life of God, ignorance, stubborn unwillingness to learn, loss of shame, behavior that lacks moral restraint, greediness, and diverse kinds of impurity (Ephesians 4:17-19). In immense contrast, we have learned Christ — and continue to be formed in his ways!

It is interesting to me that religious liberals and conservatives are often unwitting allies in their attempts to translate the gospel into the world's terms. But the biblical narratives teach us that this approach is backward. The early Christians did not try to translate their faith into something that was accessible to the world's darkened understanding. What they did instead was to engage in a way of life that was so different from the world that their neighbors wanted to be part of it. People nearby said, "Look at those Christians — how they love each other!" Thus, instead of translation, the early churches offered *catechesis*, deep and mentored instruction in the faith for those whom the Lord was adding to the Church.[7] They didn't simply translate the gospel, like French into English.

My own lack of skill makes this emphasis clear. Though large amounts of French reading for my dissertation on Jacques Ellul made me able to translate French words on paper into English explanations, I still can't *think French* very well. Recently I went to Quebec to visit my god-daughter, who is studying French before she and her husband go to Côte d'Ivoire as educational missionaries. Her schooling and life-immersion practice have taught her to speak French, to think it. Her increasing fluency makes me long to pursue further instruction and drill so that I can really *learn* the language. I don't want to have to translate French into English; I want to live French.

If faith is a language to be taught and practiced, then we spread it not by translating, but by immersing newcomers in it. The learners submit themselves to it and exercise its skills. Think about how children learn a language — by hearing it and imitating it, coming alive in the actions and grammatical usages of the people speaking around them. Similarly, the way to help our neighbors know Christ is to live his resurrection life in us so that they realize how Christ makes a difference and want to participate in his life too.

Churches find themselves powerless in the world and not able to invite our neighbors into the faith because we don't live in ways that give any warrant for belief. Observers don't seem to be saying, "Oh, you Christians have a superb attitude about time. I can see that in the way you observe the Sabbath." They don't say, "Oh, you Christians have a great perspective on money; you are so generous and don't seem to be scrambling after it like the rest of society," or "It amazes me that you Christians never try to pull power plays." The best evangelist I've ever known was a dear man who spoke English so poorly that he was pain-

---

7. For further information about catechesis in its early forms and present practices, see *Welcome to Christ: A Lutheran Introduction to the Catechumenate*, ed. Samuel Torvend and Lani Willis (Minneapolis: Augsburg-Fortress, 1997). This booklet is the first of a three-part series that also includes *Welcome to Christ: A Lutheran Catechetical Guide* and *Welcome to Christ: Lutheran Rites for the Catechumenate*, also published by Augsburg Fortress in 1997.

fully shy. He worked in an awfully boring factory job, but his grace and goodness were evident to all his peers. Anyone who ever needed any help went to Peter, for the people knew that he loved them.

God's love through us is the language we speak, the way of life in which we are engaged. The Trinity's grace undergirds our customs and practices and habits of faith, which show how we have learned Christ. The Holy Spirit uses Scripture and the community of faith and the risen Christ within us to train us in those traditions and disciplines and language. By these means God draws the world to himself.

The Christian Walk

One of the best passages in Ephesians concerning the formation of our character is this section from chapter 5:

> Therefore, be noticing accurately how you are walking, not as unwise, but as wise, redeeming the time, for the days are evil. On account of this, do not become foolish, but be perceiving clearly what the will of the Lord [is]. And do not be getting drunk with wine, which results in reckless deeds, but be continually filled with the Spirit, speaking to one another in psalms and hymns and spiritual songs, singing and making music in your heart to the Lord, giving thanks always and about everything in the name of our Lord Jesus Christ to God the Father, submitting yourselves to one another in reverence toward Christ.
>
> Ephesians 5:15-21

I love the old King James phrasing for verse 15, "Walk circumspectly." Recently I met with a bunch of teenagers in Iowa at their youth convocation, and we spent half an hour talking about walking "circumspectly." They were thrilled to learn that new word, for it captures well Paul's emphasis here that we are to look all around (Latin, *circum*) carefully as we walk/live.

The teenagers and I discussed why the image of walking is a favorite of the biblical writers for expressing what we call "lifestyle." They came up with these ideas among others:

walking is done at a more leisurely pace;
walking slows you down to God's pace, so you learn to go where
   God wants you to go;
you see more when you walk;
you meet other people and talk to them, which you don't do in
   your car;
you notice the scenery;
you have time to reflect;
you smile at people;
you experience the place where you live more thoroughly.

These images from the youth help us to practice the biblical exhortation to be more aware of the world we are serving. As discussed in Chapter 2, our faith is not simply intellectual agreement, nor is it an expression of universal religious emotions. These ways of understanding faith won't lead us to serving others and loving our neighbors. Rather, faith is a "walking," a language, a way of life.[8] We look all around us as we go through life to observe what is happening in the places where we walk, so that we remain culturally concerned though not culturally conformed — not necessarily relevant in the world's terms, but relational.

Karl Barth said that Christians should have the Bible in one hand and the newspaper in the other. I would like to make two modifications to Barth's comment. First, newspapers may show some reality, but they do not any longer give us enough of the truth. Newspapers increasingly give us only snatches of the whole story, and that is a flimsy way to know what is actually going on in the world. Some sort of deeper news journal is required to give us a more complete picture.

If we are going to walk circumspectly, brothers and sisters, we need a deeper perspective than that offered in the sound bytes and sensationalism and titillations of contemporary "news." It is valuable to read more thorough journals — and perspectives from opposite sides of the political, theological, and economic spectra — in order to get a truer picture of the whole situation.

8. See George Lindbeck, *The Nature of Doctrine: Religion and Theology in a Postliberal Age* (Philadelphia: Westminster Press, 1984).

I have a doctor friend who has frequently gone to troubled places in the world to serve in refugee camps or crises clinics. She has served in Sudan and Somalia, Rwanda and Sarajevo. She has survived gunfire as she raced to air transport and as the flight departed. Shortly after she left another site, the village was burned to the ground by enemies. She has often been extremely frustrated that we in North America have such erroneous notions of what is really happening in places of turmoil because we are given such lopsided perspectives in our news.

To walk circumspectly requires a more thorough look at the issues, not only with regard to wars and politics and economics, but also with regard to theological and ecclesiological controversies. Recently I spoke at a Christian college convocation on the subject of homosexuality and discovered that some of the students wanted to reduce that topic either to "this is my experience, so it must be right" or to an extremely rigid, almost homophobic hostility. We need instead to ask questions such as these:

- What gave rise in the late nineteenth century to the idea of a homosexual "identity"?[9]
- What factors in our society have led to the present power of genital idolatries both homosexual and heterosexual?
- How have our churches failed to deal with crises in families and communities that leave so many young people without positive models of male-female relationships and without biblical mentoring concerning their own sexual character?
- What does it mean truly to love our homosexual friends?

To walk circumspectly is to recognize the complexity of issues instead of reducing them to two polarized options.[10]

9. This is an extremely important question, hardly ever discussed. See David Greenberg's massive study, *The Construction of Homosexuality* (Chicago: University of Chicago Press, 1988).

10. The best ethical treatment of the subject I've seen and the best demonstration of biblical interpretation so that God's people can be formed by the Scriptures is Richard B. Hays, *The Moral Vision of the New Testament: A Contemporary Introduction to New Testament Ethics* (San Francisco: HarperSanFrancisco, 1996), pp. 379-406. See also Thomas E. Schmidt's *Straight and Narrow? Compassion and Clarity in the Homosexuality*

The second way we must modify Barth's comment is to ask why we need so much "news," most of which immobilizes us since we can't do anything about it, and especially since so many "news" stories focus inordinately on the catastrophic, particularly in television programs. Think, for example, of the incongruities when television shows us the "news." Imagine — as I saw recently on a bedtime news program in a small Midwestern city — an elegantly coifed and fashionably dressed woman who graphically but briefly detailed a half-dozen homicides and rapes and then smiled beautifully and benignly and said, "See you tomorrow." I had just heard enough murder and mayhem to last me the rest of my life. Why should I come back to it tomorrow?

Truly to "be Church" helps us make both of the modifications suggested above. We get a wider perspective concerning the whole world, because the Church is found throughout the world. We can learn more deeply the affairs of nations by listening to our brothers and sisters who live in them. Moreover, being Church keeps us from drowning in despair over the world's catastrophes, because we remember that Christ is still Lord over the cosmos, that someday God will wipe away these sorrows and struggles forever, that the Holy Spirit empowers us to be agents of justice and healing and peacemaking in the world now.

Another way to know more deeply the culture in which we live and the people whom we are trying to serve is to read novels. For example, Douglas Coupland's *Generation X* shows the profound longings of all human beings, especially as experienced by many young adults in their twenties and thirties.[11] His *Life after God* demonstrates even more profoundly the narrator's desperation for forgiveness and a new creation,[12] the primary graces and mercies of God and gifts offered freely by the Church.

Stories written for children are enormously revealing of the ur-

---

Debate (Downers Grove, IL: InterVarsity Press, 1995), which calmly and lucidly deals with social, political, medical, and biblical dimensions of the issues.

11. See Douglas Coupland, *Generation X: Tales for an Accelerated Culture* (New York: St. Martin's Press, 1991), and also "The Needs of Our Being," chapter 3 of Marva J. Dawn, *A Royal "Waste" of Time: The Splendor of Worshiping God and Being Church for the World* (Grand Rapids: Wm. B. Eerdmans Publishing Co., 1999), pp. 21-36.

12. Douglas Coupland, *Life after God* (New York: Simon and Schuster, 1994).

gent issues of our society. Barbara Dafoe Whitehead, author of *The Divorce Culture*, documents that in 1977 a comprehensive bibliography listed more than 200 pages of children's books dealing with problems of loss and separation experienced by kids in their divorced families; in 1989 the bibliography itself was more than 500 pages.[13] These books call our churches to respond to these pains and sorrows with ministries of genuine compassion and care and cultivation of different moral choices and behaviors. What is your congregation doing for the children of divorce in your neighborhood?

Walking circumspectly both keeps us from being formed by the culture (as we keep in mind our alternativity) and enables us to minister to our neighbors (offering the gifts of that alternativity). We can all certainly observe that a huge problem in our culture is the surplus of information (what Eugene called *scientia*) that is not processed into genuine knowledge and even less into wisdom *(sapentia)*. To walk circumspectly is to live within the framework of interpretation established by the canonical narrative of our promising God. If we are seeking formation by that narrative, then we don't change the Scriptures to fit in with the world; rather, the Scriptures redescribe the world for us. By means of that biblical redescription we understand more truly our neighbors, our milieu, and the gifts we offer.

> . . . redeeming the time, for the days are evil.
>
> Ephesians 5:16

Let us consider carefully what the phrase "redeeming [or 'buying back'] the time" might signify, since the Greek text utilizes the word *kairos* ("opportunity" or "era") rather than *chronos*, which usually refers more simply to chronological time. Many English translations help us contemplate this by rendering the verse with phrases such as "making the most of the opportunity." Translation guides Johannes P. Louw and Eugene A. Nida suggest similarly that the idiom urges us "to take full advantage of any opportunity" (*SD* 65.42), but they also add that the expression exhorts us "to do something with intensity and urgency" (*SD* 68.73).

---

13. See Barbara Dafoe Whitehead, *The Divorce Culture: Rethinking Our Commitments to Marriage and Family* (New York: Alfred Knopf, 1997).

Many Christians read this verse as a call to be workaholics, but I'm convinced that one of the best ways to make the most of our time is to observe the Sabbath. To work all the time will not use time best (do we think we are that necessary?), for we will exhaust ourselves, labor without adequate reflection, violate God's design for the care of our bodies, and offer a poor model to the world in our mistaken attempt to be some sort of messiah. Sabbath keeping, on the other hand, reminds us that God is in charge of the cosmos, that he uses us for the fulfillment of his plans, but that he never gives us more than we are able to do in the time given us. Ceasing our work one day a week enables us to look at it from God's gracious perspective.[14] We need to pull away from our busy-ness to let God determine how we live.

Similarly, we make the most of our time if we live prayerfully. It is rumored that Martin Luther once said, "I've got so much to do that I'd never get it all done if I didn't pray at least three hours a day." Though no one has yet documented that comment in Luther's works, it does seem to fit the better side of his character. He knew that unless he submitted everything to God's direction, he would waste his time doing the wrong things. Later in his life, when he was very ill, increasingly bitter, and sometimes exceedingly reckless, he wrote some diatribes (for example, against the Jews) for which Lutherans today have apologized, since these writings do not reflect God's guidance at all. Those writings stand as a sharp reminder to us all to avoid thinking we are "necessary" and to rediscover our call continually by much prayer.

To buy back the time is to render it to God. We are not really able to redeem it ourselves. All of time was bought back by Christ when he defeated the principalities and powers at the cross and empty tomb. It is redeemed for us when we participate prayerfully and painstakingly and placidly in God's time-full and timeless opportunities.[15]

We are to make the most of our time because the days are evil,

14. For further reflection on the gift and practice of this holy day, see my *Keeping the Sabbath Wholly: Ceasing, Resting, Embracing, Feasting* (Grand Rapids: Wm. B. Eerdmans Publishing Co., 1989) and *The Sense of the Call: Kingdom Shalom for Those Who Serve the Church* (Grand Rapids: Wm. B. Eerdmans Publishing Co., forthcoming).

15. For further study of this subject, I heartily recommend Robert Banks's *The Tyranny of Time: When 24 Hours Is Not Enough* (Eugene, OR: Wipf and Stock Publishers, 1997) and *Redeeming the Routines* (Grand Rapids: Baker Books, 1993).

verse 16 insists. The evidence that the days are evil has been obvious to us ever since human beings fell into sin. Evil's manifestations change with the times, but always our violence, greed, lusts, and self-absorption have been amply displayed. Therefore, we do our ministries — whatever they might be — with intensity and urgency in order to counteract, resist, avoid, and refashion what is personally and corporately, locally and globally evil. The connection of the evil of our times to the next verse in Ephesians 5 is momentous.

Knowing the Will of God

> On account of this, do not become foolish, but be perceiving clearly what the will of the Lord [is].
>
> Ephesians 5:17

How do we know what the will of the Lord is? If we are to do whatever we do with passion, persistence, and profundity, then we need to do all we can to know God's will as clearly as possible.[16]

Often when I am leading retreats or training workshops with youth, we have a session on "Everything you ever wanted to ask a theologian . . . ," and it is a gift of hope to me that teenagers and young adults ask such insightful and compassionate and provocative questions. What especially cheers me is that the most frequently asked question is, "How do I know the will of God?" Isn't it wonderful that their earnest desire is to obey God?

Unfortunately, an answer that is sometimes given to their question is to look for God's signs — and Gideon's challenge to the LORD in Judges 6 concerning the fleece is held up as a positive example. Earlier in that chapter Gideon had shown his lack of courage by accomplishing what the LORD commanded by night rather than during the day (v. 27). The LORD had told Gideon clearly what he wanted done (vv. 11-16), he had already given Gideon a sign (vv. 19-23), and the

---

16. David Hansen offers wonderful insights into listening to the Spirit to know God's will in chapter 3, "The Holy Spirit," of *The Art of Pastoring: Ministry* Without *All the Answers* (Downers Grove, IL: InterVarsity Press, 1994), pp. 42-59.

Spirit of the LORD had come upon him (v. 34). Still, however, Gideon wanted more signs (vv. 36-40). It is almost as if he said, "God, I'm not sure yet. How about this: I'll put out a fleece and you can make it wet. Wouldn't that be great, God? Then I'll know for sure that you *really* told me to defeat Midian." God condescended to humor him. If Gideon really needed such a sign, God would do it for him. Despite this, though, Gideon was not yet convinced, so then he said, "That was too easy, God. Let's try it again, and I'll make it a little harder this time. See if you can keep the fleece dry while you soak the ground."

I remember playing such a sign-from-God game when I was a kid. I had a newspaper route in the fourth grade, and one day when I wasn't quite sure what God would have me do about something, I said, "God, if it is your will [for such and such] let me hit the next porch." Our papers were quite small, however, and the wind would often deflect them from our aim. Then, when the paper missed the porch, I said, "Well, God, how about two out of three?"

The point is that we can so easily manipulate signs to make them say what we want them to say. How do you know how to read them anyway? I don't think the "Gideon and the fleece" story is in the Bible as a good example; God had told him clearly how he wanted Gideon to serve as Israel's leader. Instead, it seems that the narrative is there to show how gracious God is to use fearful and unbelieving people to accomplish his purposes. That is a great message, but it doesn't help us answer the question about knowing God's will since rarely do we see visions of angels who specifically give us God's instructions.

There are several better ways to know God's will. The primary means, of course, is through God's Word, for God will never contradict himself. If someone said to us, "God told me to have this affair," we would know that such a message could not have been from God since God is consistent in his commands for sexual faithfulness within the covenant commitment of marriage. If our lives are immersed in the Word, we will be able by God's Spirit to improvise more authentically, and thereby we will often discover the will of God.

Furthermore, we often ask the wrong question when we want to know God's will just for our personal lives. In *The Mustard Seed Conspiracy*, Tom Sine emphasizes that we should instead see what God is doing in the world and become part of his program.[17] We know that God wants us to love our neighbors and care for their particular needs, to feed the hungry, clothe the naked, shelter the homeless, build peace, secure justice, and spread the good news of salvation in Christ. If these are God's instructions to his people, how will we more fully participate in those purposes?

Sometimes open doors can reveal God's will, but not always. We must continually ask who opened the doors and whether we should walk through them. Open doors are like signs — ambiguous and not always reliable.

It seems to me that often we know God's will only in hindsight, after the fact. I don't think we have to be afraid of that. It might seem, for example, that my college and graduate work in the field of English literature was a waste of time since I turned instead to theology for my life's vocation. However, God hasn't let those years of work go to waste, for my English background not only guides my writing but also gives me skills for reading the Bible as literature that aren't usually taught in theological programs.

Even my motives for going to the University of Idaho for my M.A. in English were laughably mixed. I really do love to swim, and northern Idaho has some of the most beautiful lakes in the world. God used even that silly whim, as well as my desire to teach my own classes while earning the degree, to lead me to a place where I wound up teaching "Literature of the Bible" in the English Department and thereby found my life turned into theological directions instead. I don't believe these decisions and their outcomes are mere coincidences (nor do I believe we are "fated" to make certain decisions), though I certainly did not move to Idaho determined to make a turn into theology instead of English (both of which had been my undergraduate majors).

God's wisdom is far greater than our puny human intellects. Purposes far more vast than our major decisions are hinted at by the mysterious gifts we can see only after they have been given.

For this reason, two other important elements in any search for God's will are humility and calmness — we need not be under frightening pressure to fulfill God's purposes. As Mordecai said to Esther, "If

17. Tom Sine, *The Mustard Seed Conspiracy* (Waco, TX: Word Books, 1981).

you keep silence at such a time as this, relief and deliverance will rise for the Jews from another quarter. . . . Who knows? Perhaps you have come to royal dignity for just such a time as this" (Esther 4:14). In other words, God's purposes will be fulfilled whether you participate or not, but perhaps this is exactly why you are in the position you are in. This takes off the burden, a burden that often generates panic and fear. I have heard some young people say, "Oh, if I miss God's will, nothing will happen right, and everything will be spoiled."

God is sovereign. That truth is in a dialectical balance with our fallible human free will. We might make wrong choices, but God is too great for that to mess up everything. He certainly promises to work things ultimately for the good of those seeking his purposes. I love the courage, the hope in Mordecai. His confidence that God will accomplish his deliverance with or without Esther takes the pressure off our trying to find just the one right thing — our having to be absolutely sure that this is precisely what God wants us to do — and sets us free to pursue with gusto what we think we have discovered God's will to be. (This is the main intent of Martin Luther's famous saying, "Sin boldly; but believe more boldly still.")

Another biblical narrative that takes the pressure off by setting us free from our panic to find God's will is this text from Habakkuk:

> Then the LORD answered me and said:
> Write the vision:
>   make it plain on tablets,
>   so that a runner may read it.
> For there is still a vision for the appointed time;
>   it speaks of the end, and does not lie.
> If it seems to tarry, wait for it;
>   it will surely come, it will not delay.
> Look at the proud!
> Their spirit is not right in them,
>   but the righteous live by their faith.
>
> Habakkuk 2:2-4

Habakkuk had been given a vision concerning Israel's injustice and the Babylonian captivity as God's means for putting a stop to it. The point of this text is that God's plans will be fulfilled, even though we often have to wait. The prophet could be confident that the purposes of God would be accomplished in their appointed times — never too late or too early. In fact, the second line of the Hebrew text literally says that the vision "pants after its own fulfillment." Just as a pet dog pants eagerly in expectation that the master's movements indicate an upcoming walk together, so the purposes of God are ardently awaited and will surely be accomplished.

In all events of life we can have the same confidence. We need not panic as we wait for God's timing, for his purposes to be accomplished, for his will to be revealed. We all know that if we panic while taking a test, our brain will forget everything we do know because we are concentrating instead on what we don't know. In the same way, if we panic over finding God's will, we will miss the signals, the insights, the biblical truths. If we could stop giving in to our anxiety, we would discover that God *wants* to reveal his will to us. In God's own perfect timing, we will know what we need to know — that is, if our minds are not closed to his renewing Spirit and if our lives are committed to God's action through us.[18]

My second year of graduate study and teaching at the University of Idaho taught me a very important lesson about knowing God's will without panic. Before my final semester, I was offered a choice of teaching one or two classes and couldn't decide what to do. On the one hand, accepting only one class meant that I would have 350 fewer papers to grade. Certainly that would be a wise choice. However, I was teaching "Literature of the Bible," and many who signed up for the class as self-described atheists wound up encountering God and receiving his love. Was I going to deny thirty-five more students the chance to study the Bible for credit and perhaps meanwhile find their lives transformed? What would you have decided?

I still had not been able to figure out what to do on the day I had to give my answer to the department chairman. As I entered his office,

---

18. An important way of hearing the Spirit's leading and seeing God's action through us is spiritual direction. Eugene Peterson's works on the topic are especially helpful. See particularly *Working the Angles: The Shape of Pastoral Integrity* (Grand Rapids: Wm. B. Eerdmans Publishing Co., 1987).

he asked, "Have you decided yet?" When I responded, "I really don't know," he replied that certainly I was one of the stupidest persons he'd ever seen. Why anybody would teach two classes when only one was necessary seemed to him ludicrous. He was stunned when I exclaimed, "Thank you, sir. You have made it very clear. I will teach two."

The moment he had said that it seemed stupid for me to select two, into my memory flashed the verse, "Those who are unspiritual do not receive the gifts of God's Spirit, for they are foolishness to them, and they are unable to understand them because they are spiritually discerned" (1 Corinthians 2:14). It was almost as if God wrote the answer for me on the blackboard. If teaching two classes seemed foolish to someone who was not asking at that point about the spiritual ramifications, then perhaps that was the Spirit's way to give me insight.

Can we learn to wait for God's visions to be revealed and/or fulfilled? If they tarry, can we learn to trust in the meanwhile?

Perhaps the most important instrument for discovering God's will besides the Scriptures is one that many Christians do not know. I learned this from the Mennonite congregation to which I belonged while I was working on my Ph.D.: God's will is revealed in the counsel of the community.

During a time of confusion over whether to stay in my doctoral program, I asked the Mennonite pastor to pray for me. To my astonishment he answered, "Better yet, let's call a meeting to discern the Spirit." "A what?" I wondered. I'd never heard of such a meeting before. I was even more astonished that ten or so of my friends in the congregation gathered for an evening and gave me the gift of their time, their questions, and their prayers. Sometimes there would be silence, and then someone would ask a different question or pray again as the group worked to help me find God's purposes.

At first I didn't think we were getting anywhere, but gradually I began to see that there was movement, something like a funneling. Each comment or inquiry seemed to get me closer to a resolution. I had never had any "lightbulb" experiences in knowing God's will before, except for that conversation with the department chair in Idaho, but on that evening with my Mennonite friends one woman's question and following comment produced a breakthrough. She asked, "How do you envision your life?" and I responded, "I have always been somewhat of a bridge — between conservatives and liberals, non-believers and believers, Lutherans and other denominations, especially between scholars and lay people." "Well," she said, "a bridge needs to be firmly planted on both sides of the river." Suddenly the lightbulb went on! It was clear that I needed to finish the Ph.D.

Because of that glorious evening I decided firmly that I would never again make a major decision alone. Never!

Thus, on January 15, 1989, when Myron Sandberg proposed, I said, "Let's call a meeting to discern the Spirit." That meeting lasted two weeks because we didn't have a community in our local situation to give us counsel. Instead we wrote to trusted Christian friends in various places and asked them to pray with and for us, to ask us questions, to tell us what the Spirit said to them. We wanted to make sure that marriage was God's best for both of us and for our respective ministries, and the responses of the Christian community helped confirm our understanding.

We had intentionally asked two persons who we thought would disagree. One was a religious leader who had suggested that I should stay single for my freelancing work. The other was a good friend who had once teased, "If Myron ever proposes, I want a chance to make a counter-proposal." The former called to say that as he and his wife prayed about our question they had realized how good Myron was in supporting my work and had changed their minds. The second person said that he thought Myron would be a good husband for me, but that he hoped we would invite him to the wedding (which we did) and that we would still be friends (which we are).

I include all these details because they have confirmed for me the immense value of the community's counsel. Since every single person of all the people we asked brought us new insights that verified our decision to marry, Myron and I experienced a deep undergirding otherwise not possible. It seems to me that many decisions can be made on better grounds if we submit them to the community for the sake of discovering the will of God and the purposes of his kingdom.

During the two weeks of that process, I spoke at two Christian colleges on the subject of sexual character, and I suggested to the students that they not make major decisions about marriage or their careers or whatever else was important without the aid of the Christian community. When I told them about the process of discernment Myron and I were conducting, I thought they would all tell me we were crazy. Instead they said, "We don't have a community to help us."

Shame on us! Shame on us that we are not developing the kind of communal life in our churches in which young people can find guidance and counsel in gatherings with others in the Body. I continue to ask members of the wider Christian community to help me discover the will of God in such matters as whether or not I should accept faculty appointments. However, I long for my local community to develop the skills to hold a meeting to discern the Spirit.[19]

Life Filled with the Spirit

The rest of Ephesians 5 and the first nine verses of chapter 6 all hinge on this verse:

> And do not be getting drunk with wine, which results in reckless deeds, but be continually filled with the Spirit . . .
>
> Ephesians 5:18

Verse 18 contains two main verbs, both of which are continuing (present) imperatives. The first verb is difficult to render because it is the passive form of the verb rendered "to drink freely." We are urged to keep on not letting ourselves get intoxicated, for that "results in reckless deeds" (*SD* 88.96). If we want to serve God well, we certainly don't want to live senselessly, without thinking.

This text is critical for us because we've all got our addictions that result in behavior lacking in concern for the consequences. Our addiction might be workaholism, a messiah complex because we think

---

19. For a consideration of discovering God's will within the context of building the Christian community, see "The Constant Adventure of Discovering God's Will," chapter 6 of my *Truly the Community: Romans 12 and How to Be the Church* (Grand Rapids: Wm. B. Eerdmans Publishing Co., 1992; reissued 1997), pp. 46-55.

we are necessary — and the consequence might be burnout. My addiction too often is books. I start to make a "necessary" idolatry out of owning them, reading them, knowing them, writing them — and the result can be inadequate care for others. Whatever our divinizing habit or god, Paul exhorts us to be constantly being filled instead with the Spirit.

Everything hangs on the Spirit. Only total reliance on the Holy Spirit can free us from all our "necessarinesses." What a contrast Spirit-possession is to any other sacralizing, for it grants not the false freedom of inebriation and its resultant regrets, but the genuine freedom of *theosis*, God working through us!

Verses 18-21 list some of the results of being filled with the Spirit —

> speaking to one another in psalms and hymns and spiritual songs,
> singing and making music in your heart to the Lord,
> giving thanks always and about everything in the name of our Lord Jesus Christ to God the Father,
> submitting yourselves to one another in reverence toward Christ.

Each of these is important for our formation.

Notice the instruction about psalms and hymns and spiritual songs, which Paul also gives in Colossians 3:16. The combination of these three nouns gives us a sense of praises from the whole people of God throughout time and space.[20] Furthermore, the emphasis that we sing and make music in our *heart* reminds us that to worship God doesn't really depend upon our emotions, for the Greek word *heart* here emphasizes more an act of our will. Thus, we praise God because the Lord is worthy of our praise, so we can do it by the power of the Spirit even when we don't feel like it.

Another result of the Spirit's indwelling is giving thanks. In verse

---

20. This seems to me to argue against splitting our churches into those who want only "contemporary" music and those who prefer only "traditional." For extended consideration of why and how we can and should bridge these divisions, see especially chapters 2, 13-17, and 26 of *A Royal "Waste" of Time.*

20 it is important to note that the Greek preposition is *huper* ("about" or "in view of"), rather than *dia* ("on account of," as the cause or reason). I write this because some Christian groups insist that we should thank God *for* everything. I've even been told that my physical handicaps have not been healed because I have not thanked God *for* them. However, I do not believe God commands us to give thanks for what is evil, for such things as war or tragedy, illness or suffering. Instead, we give thanks "in the face of" everything, "in view of" everything. We counteract illness and fight evil, and meanwhile we give thanks that God works his purposes out in the midst of such things or in spite of them.[21]

Finally, a result of being filled with the Spirit is mutual submission, which is the basis for Ephesians 5:22–6:9. There is not space in this book for a complete discussion of that entire text, but a few words are in order because the passage has often been abused by churches.[22] It seems important for me to note a few aspects of this passage for the sake of women and for the sake of churches that don't know what to do with women. Such church bodies might be profoundly biblical, but usually they read such passages as 1 Corinthians 14:34-35 and 1 Timothy 2:11-15 too literalistically, without concern for the historic contexts that gave rise to these correctional instructions. Consequently, women are prohibited from exercising their spiritual gifts of leadership. Similarly, Ephesians 5:21-33 is used to justify a certain notion of the wife's "submission" that does not seem to me to be faithful to a text that begins with *mutual* submission.

In the previous chapter Eugene's comments about Artemis/Diana and what was going on in Ephesus clarify the context behind the troublesome verses in 1 Timothy 2:11-15. The passage urges Timothy to keep women who were heretics from teaching. Their "expertise" concerned the religion of the goddess Artemis, and consequently they be-

---

21. This topic is pursued much more thoroughly in my *Joy in Our Weakness: A Gift of Hope from the Book of Revelation* (St. Louis: Concordia Publishing House, 1994).

22. For a more thorough exegesis of this difficult passage than is possible here, an audiotape of my teaching in a congregation — #330, "A New Look at Ephesians 5:21-33" — can be ordered or borrowed from Dottie Davis, Christians Equipped for Ministry Tape Ministry, 10918 NE 152nd Ave., Vancouver, WA 98682, telephone (360) 892-3618.

lieved that Eve birthed the whole world, including Adam (and even God), though the biblical narrative taught Christians that Adam was created first. This passage does not suggest that Adam being created first puts men in a hierarchy over women. Rather, the text simply urges the young pastor not to let women teach who did not understand biblical revelation. Paul, of course, doesn't mean that all women in all times are never to teach or speak. After all, he was the one who commended Phoebe, the only named deacon in the Bible. Moreover, in 1 Corinthians 11 he urges the women to be properly dressed when they "pray" and "prophesy" in public.[23]

We can universally recognize the problem in human behavior (we see it often in our children and when youth first go to college) that people newly released from previous restrictions are easily tempted or develop the tendency to abuse their freedom. Consequently, Paul had to caution women who, formerly segregated from the men and uneducated in Jewish and Roman/Greek society, got carried away by their new privileges in the Christian community. In 1 Corinthians 14 their chatter (the Greek verb *laleō*) was disrupting worship; in 1 Timothy 2 they seem to have been usurping authority; both 1 Timothy 2 and 1 Corinthians 11 suggest that they were adopting hairstyles and fashions not befitting their Christian commitments.

The recognition that freedoms can be misused or misconstrued serves as an introduction to the problems associated with Ephesians 5:21-33. Contrary to the common assumption, this text is not primarily about wives' submission to their husbands. If we read the text carefully and write down in columns each usage of the name of Christ, each reference to the Church, and all the instructions about husbands and wives, we will discover that the passage is primarily about Christ's care for the Church and, consequently, that genuine marriage imitates, as well as symbolizes, the mystery of that union.

23. For thorough discussion of the false teaching in Ephesus and its implications for interpreting 1 Timothy 2, see Richard Clark Kroeger and Catherine Clark Kroeger, *I Suffer Not a Woman: Rethinking I Timothy 2:11-15 in Light of Ancient Evidence* (Grand Rapids: Baker Book House, 1992). See also my "Hermeneutical Considerations for Biblical Texts" and "I Timothy 2:8-15," in *Different Voices/Shared Vision: Male and Female in the Trinitarian Community*, ed. Paul Hinlicky (Delhi, NY: American Lutheran Publicity Bureau, 1992).

In the Christian community at Ephesus at the time this letter was written, women were newly set free from the patterns of the culture around them — and perhaps the men needed to curb an unbiblical (false) freedom. Whereas many men in Greek and Roman society did not love their wives, but perhaps loved the high-class prostitutes with whom they consorted while their wives were kept at home to raise proper children to continue the patrimony, Christian men were invited by this letter to recognize their virtuous role as husbands in light of Christ's love for the Church. How unusual the Christian community was — that the men would *love* their wives as their own bodies and cherish them for far more than only their raising of the children.

Women, on the other hand, were liberated from that repressive role in the surrounding society, were welcomed into the worship services along with their husbands, and were encouraged by the early Church to use their gifts. Consequently, they might have been tempted to forget that submission to their husbands had not been eliminated; rather, it had been modified into a mutual submission.

We know this because the verb *(hupotassomenoi)*, the form of which emphasizes submitting *oneself* or thus perhaps *choosing* to render obedience, occurs in verse 21, which underscores the mutuality and introduces the topic, but it does not appear in verse 22. The latter verse, then, seems to be more of a reminder to women not to overdo their freedom, but to continue instead placing themselves at their husbands' service, even as their husbands were newly doing the same.

Just as the uneducated women in 1 Corinthians 14 disrupted worship by calling across the aisle to their husbands when something was said that they didn't understand, so the women in Ephesus caused trouble for the church if they took their new freedom out of the bounds of mutual submission. For the sake of orderliness in worship, Paul wrote that the women should ask their husbands their questions at home instead of chattering and disturbing others in the corporate gatherings. (Perhaps that verse is newly applicable in our times when so many children are not taught by their parents that loud outside noises and unruly behavior are not appropriate in the midst of worship.) Similarly, for the sake of orderliness in daily life, Paul urges women not to forget their half of the mutual submission, even as their husbands needed to learn truly to love their wives.

If this is the general tone and intent of the end of Ephesians 5, then the text is not to be summarily rejected as many fanatical feminists do, nor does it give men an invitation to put women under their thumb, as many excessive conservatives do. Such polarizations are a typical reaction in an "Awakening" period in history.

Some scholars believe that our times will issue in a fourth Great Awakening. These periods always develop when there is great turmoil in society, as in the epoch of Jonathan Edwards. William Fore describes the pattern that a Great Awakening follows in this way:

> The beginning is a period of individual stress, when people lose their bearings, become psychically or physically ill, break out in violence against family, friends, and authority, or become apathetic and incapable of functioning. People may destroy themselves by alcohol, drugs, or suicide. Families come apart, children are abused.
>
> At this point there always arise a number of *traditionalist movements,* attempts by those with rigid personalities or with much at stake in the old order to insist that the solution to the current disorder is to adhere more strictly to the old beliefs, values, and behavior patterns. . . . In the final stage of each awakening, the traditionalists have polarized the alternatives, the traditional alternatives themselves are rejected by most of the populace, new leaders emerge who articulate a new and generally accepted worldview, and the society begins to rebuild its institutions.[24]

The issues concerning women and men are myriad in our time, including the complex connections of feminism with life/rights/responsibilities/abortion controversies, the problem of glass ceilings faced by gifted women in many occupations dominated by men, the multiple social problems that have arisen because of the lack of fathers in homes, the great difficulty men and women have in forming genuine friendships with each other in a culture bombarded with genital allurement.

24. William F. Fore, *Television and Religion: The Shaping of Faith, Values, and Culture* (Minneapolis: Augsburg, 1987), pp. 74-75.

Fore's observations are helpful because we can recognize this massive turmoil in our society and notice that the ultra-traditionalistic reactions are polarizing society. The situation has become so disjointed that most of society is alienated, caught between these extreme poles of the raging feminists who will not "consort with their enemy, men" and the ultraconservatives, neither of whom have a very good idea about relationships between women and men. Our culture needs new directions, and the biblical witness can be very helpful if the Church offers its biblical redescription clearly and compassionately.

We who are formed by the Scriptures are called to be good stewards of our spiritual gifts, in order to present God's many-sided grace to the world (see 1 Peter 4:10). All the normative biblical texts about spiritual gifts are not gender specific, so no limitations are put on who can do what in the service of God and neighbor. Furthermore, the Bible contains many descriptive texts showing women leading in many kinds of ways — as prophets (Huldah), singers and worship leaders (Miriam), judges (Deborah), missionaries (the woman at the well in John 4), first witnesses to the resurrection (Mary Magdalene), "rabbinic" students (Mary, sister of Martha), deacons (Phoebe), and so forth.

Consequently, when the three corrective texts of 1 Timothy 2 and 1 Corinthians 14 and Ephesians 5 disagree in intent with all the descriptive and normative texts (particularly the behavior of Jesus toward women) in the Bible, our hermeneutical responsibility is to ask what was happening in that specific culture and history that would give rise to such instructions. Since the cult of Artemis is no longer the problem against which the Church must contend, since women are now educated as thoroughly as men, since marriages in our time are suffering from all kinds of new societal pressures, then we need to think thoroughly about how the formative texts of Scripture can provide supremely valuable guidance for men and women in relationship with each other both in our churches and in our culture.

All of us in the Church are urged by the Ephesians letter to be different from the world. Today part of the role of pastors (seemingly unnecessary to the world) is to equip congregation members to resist the ethos of a society that is presently hostile to genuine marriage, true love, and mutual submission. Remember that this section is integrally connected with previous invitations to walk circumspectly, to discern the times and redeem our time, to discover the will of God, and to be filled continually with the Spirit. These are strong instructions. The world around us desperately needs us to be formed by them, but the Spirit's filling sets us free to live in them. God is the One at work in us to transform us into this way of life.

Let us pray: Ascended Lord, may we truly be your Church, each of us as individuals and all of us together fulfilling the functions of our part in the Body in accordance with your will. Kill us and raise us to new life in you. Fill us with your Spirit that we may rejoice in the way of life you produce in us. Teach us the faith language of the Bible; use it to form us. Display your presence in and through us for the sake of our neighbors and to your honor and glory and praise for all eternity. Amen.

Chapter 8

Titus: Starting Out in Crete

EUGENE H. PETERSON

Pastors have an extremely difficult job to do, and it's no surprise that so many are discouraged and ready to quit. Though it may not seem like it at face value, pastors are persecuted in North America, and I don't believe I am exaggerating when I say that it is far worse than in seemingly more hostile countries. Our culture doesn't lock us up; it simply and nicely castrates us, neuters us, and replaces our vital parts with a nice and smiling face. And then we are imprisoned in a mesh of "necessities" that keep us from being pastors.

The Russian poet Irina Ratushnakaya *(Gray Is the Color of Hope* and *Pencil Poems)* was imprisoned in the Gulag for writing poems that were not so much anti-Communist as they were simply true. Sitting in her cell, she needed no one to tell her that words make a difference. Her prison proved that they do. And so she kept on writing, carving her poems into soap and memorizing them or stowing them away on any scrap of paper she could get her hands on. She knew that her situation was desperate, and she used words to fight for freedom, not for herself alone (she was very free in the Gulag) but for her fellow Russians as well.

While Ratushnakaya knew the desperateness of her condition, most North American pastors are fairly oblivious to their own. We've been treated nicely for so long that we've forgotten that we are in enemy territory. While poets and pastors in other countries may not need to be reminded of the desperation of their situation, we do. Again and again. We simply cannot submit unprotesting to the conditions of our imprisonment. We are the ones proclaiming the gospel of freedom. We are called to use our words and our vocations in the freedom of the gospel, not in the necessities of our imprisoning culture. Through determined, prayerful, and patient attention, we must cease our accommodating to the culture that is robbing the gospel of its power.

Contrary to popular opinion, pastors are not jacks and jills of all trades. We have been bullied long enough by well-meaning but ignorant demands telling us what we *must* do, telling us why we are necessary to this or that program, this or that life. Everybody and his dog has a job description for the pastor. Everybody knows what a pastor *must* do to be a real pastor.

That's a problem, but what complicates and compounds it is that it's nice to be so needed, nice to have culture and congregation alike interested in defining our work and giving us instructions on how to go about it. It's nice to be so much in demand . . . until we find that none of the job descriptions seem to agree. It's even worse when we discover that virtually none of the people who write our job descriptions seem to have ever read or even heard of the text, the Holy Scripture, that orients our work, or to have been present at the ordinations that define our work. Necessity is laid upon the glorious but beleaguered life of pastor.

That is why, in this book, Marva and I are trying to set you free, set you free from the necessities that burden your life. We aren't trying to set you free from Jesus or the authority of the Scriptures. But being a slave of Christ is far better than being a slave of culture.

Titus, in the newly evangelized island of Crete, is given responsibility for laying the foundations for a Christian community in a culture that doesn't know much about spiritual community or a life of discipleship.

We have looked at Paul in Rome, finishing up his life of leadership in Christ's church. Once upon a time, he had written to the Romans; it was his most famous letter, and now we see him coming to terms with the completion of his life there. A nice conjunction of writing and living: the encompassing letter written to Rome, the coming-to-completion life of a pastor in Rome, the early church's most prominent missionary pastor ready to step out of the action. (It is important to note that a word that must always be linked with the ministering of Paul is "suffering." He never had a "successful" ministry, *but* he was always free and zestful.)

We have looked at Timothy in Ephesus, entering the mess of a congregation that is confused and conflicted about what it means to be persons created and saved and blessed by God. The famous Ephesian church had fallen on hard times. No church, no matter how wonderful, is exempt from disintegration, and we saw Timothy at the pastoral work of mopping up other people's messes. The response: Timothy is simply to teach, but in a healthy, life-giving way.

And now Titus. We know less about Titus and Crete than about Paul and Rome and about Timothy and Ephesus. In fact, all we have is a hint — but the hint is enough to discern the different setting in which Titus works, a setting we can easily identify as still characteristic of pastoral work. The emphasis in Titus is on building community and on leadership, two ideas that we must keep together.

Like Timothy, who was left in Ephesus (1 Timothy 1:3), Titus has been *left* in Crete. (By and large, we don't choose our ministries, we are given them; they are handed to us. Like the place we were born and the street on which we grew up, like the bodies that we inhabit and the parents we are given, like the children who are born to us — we take what is given.) But, unlike Timothy, who was left to reform an established but messed-up church, Titus has been left behind to set in order what had not yet been accomplished, namely, the *appointing* of elders in the various churches over the whole island (1:5). Communities come into being when the gospel is preached, and Paul seeded these communities through his evangelistic activity. But that's not the end of their story; these communities need tending, cultivation by Titus. In a way, seeding is the easiest part — cultivation is the hard work of farming. Planting seed is fine, but the hard work of cultivation and harvest is what pastors are called to do (and this includes suffering). Therefore, providing for ongoing leadership is an important part of pastoral work. Gordon Fee concludes that "the churches of Crete were more recent. . . . Since the churches on Crete are newer, the concern in Titus focuses less upon false teachers per se and more upon the church as God's people in the world."[1]

I characterized Timothy's pastoral task as teaching, but teaching of a particular kind, the teaching of wisdom — a knowledge of God and his ways that is worked into the fabric of muscle and spirit, mind and emotion, home and work. Ephesus seems to have been a place seething with ideas and schemes, words disconnected from actual living — living is a lot harder than just getting things straight in our heads — a church where there was a lot of talk, interesting and "deep" and even intoxicating, but talk that left people free to live pretty much any way they wanted.

I want to characterize Titus's pastoral task as developing leadership that honors the gospel in community. After getting the gospel straight (with Timothy), getting the community straight (with Titus) is the next item on the pastoral/leadership agenda. And just as the gospel is, as the scholars say, *sui generis* (one of a kind, lacking real parallels, useless to comparative religion studies), so is the community of Jesus. A spiritual community that is not formed under the shaping influence of Jesus is vulnerable to anyone with a strong, charismatic, authoritarian personality, whether it has anything to do with Jesus or not. High on the agenda of pastoral work, therefore, is the development of a counter-leadership, a leadership of a Holy Spirit community. This is countercultural leadership, refusing to buy into the power-based management styles our culture presents.

There is only one recorded visit by Paul to Crete (Acts 27), but that was a mere stopover at the harbor Fair Havens on his way to Rome as a prisoner. Those of us who believe that Paul was the actual author of Titus conjecture that Paul was released from that first Roman imprisonment and had several years of unrecorded travel, travel that may have included his long-anticipated visit to Spain and would have included Crete, where he preached and es-

---

1. Gordon Fee, *1 and 2 Timothy, Titus,* A Good News Commentary (San Francisco: Harper & Row, 1984), pp. xxiii-xxiv.

tablished a number of churches. This evangelistic/missionary activity would be background to the Titus letter, but we have no stories about that, no facts.

Crete: A Wild West

It is tempting to caricature Crete as a kind of first-century Wild West, a semi-anarchist society without much social savvy — independent spirits, do-it-yourself lone rangers. I imagine them as a rough-edged mixture of Yukon gold rusher, Texas cowboy, Saskatchewan sodbuster, and Montana militia man. These people are the context in which Paul seeded these Holy Spirit communities.

Crete, to be sure, had an esteemed civilization behind it. Archaeologists have uncovered old ruins that show that, a thousand years before Paul arrived, there were impressive capabilities in art and language. One of the most impressive philology stories in this century is the decipherment of a puzzling language of early Crete, designated as Minoan Linear B. In 1953, a couple of English philologists, Ventris and Chadwick, figured out the script and opened up a huge new chapter in our understanding of early Greek language. Crete, therefore, figures into the most sophisticated of language studies. But that was the past, and the popular image of Crete in the first century is more along the lines of what I am proposing as a Wild West. The myth of Minos gives the flavor.

Minos, king of Crete, had a wild bull of which he was very fond — bull riding and bull jumping were big in Crete, as evidenced by the painting on shards of Minoan pottery. But one of the gods got angry at Minos for being so selfish with his bull and fixed it so that Minos's wife, Pasiphae, was overcome with passion for the bull. She had herself turned briefly into a cow, consummated her passion, and then gave birth to a monster that was half human and half bull, the legendary Minotaur.

The only food this wild, ferocious Minotaur would eat was live humans. To protect himself and his kingdom, Minos had Daedalus and his son Icarus design and build the Labyrinth as a corral for the monster. The Labyrinth was cunningly constructed so that anyone who entered it would never be able to find his or her way out and would eventually be devoured by the Minotaur. Meanwhile, Minos had subdued Athens on the Greek mainland and forced them to pay a tribute every year (some accounts say every nine years) of seven maidens and seven young men, which were fed to the Minotaur.

Enter the hero. Theseus, the son of the king of Athens, decided that enough was enough and set sail to Crete to kill the Minotaur. On landing, he met Minos's daughter, Ariadne, who fell madly in love with him. And just before he entered the Labyrinth to do battle with the Minotaur, Ariadne gave him a thread so that he could find his way out again, something no one had ever done.

Well, it worked. Theseus made it to the lair of the Minotaur, killed it, and then, by following Ariadne's thread, found his way out again. He took her away with him and they sailed off into the sunset. There's more to the story, but that's enough to give the flavor.

You can't get a more basic Wild West story than that: a story to glorify violence and romance, the ferocious beast and the solitary outsider who shows up to save all those innocent young men and women from a brutal death each year — and then carrying off the beautiful Ariadne from the clutches of her bestial father. I'm surprised they don't reenact it at the Calgary stampede every year.

In this way, Crete is not unlike the Canadian and American West, with a legendary and fabled past of first nation people and intrepid pioneers, but a past without a living connection with us. The past is all myth, which gives color to our lives but no connections. The present is rough hewn and macho, independent and idiosyncratic.

The one phrase in the letter to Titus that gives us some backup detail for what I am conjecturing — and it is a most unflattering one — is a proverb by a poet of Crete, Epimendes of Cnossus, a religious teacher of the sixth century B.C., and it confirms this Wild West reputation: "Cretans are always liars, pernicious beasts, idle bellies" (1:12).[2]

---

2. J. N. D. Kelly, *A Commentary on the Pastoral Epistles* (London: Adam and Charles Black, 1963), p. 235. Elsewhere Paul quotes from Menander (1 Corinthians 15:33) and Aratus (Acts 17:28), showing, again, his love for metaphor and poetry.

J. N. D. Kelly speaks of the "shocking reputation for mendacity which the Cretans had in the ancient world. So prevalent was this that the verb 'to Cretize' (Gk. *kretizein*) was a slang word for lying or cheating."[3] In addition to being liars, they are called "pernicious beasts and idle bellies," rounding out the caricature of an island of boorish malcontents. In this kind of soil, Titus was called on to cultivate the seeds of Holy Spirit community.

Crete and Cretans provide the conditions for a certain stream of pastoral work: we find ourselves with people who know nothing about the Bible or Jesus, but neither do they know anything about good manners or an ethical life. Unlike the Ephesians, who are sophisticated and learned in all manner of religion, Cretans are rustic, rough-mannered newcomers to all this business of patience and love and humility. The Cretans are not promising material for building community. They don't know much about living together on any terms, let alone God's terms.

In some ways this is refreshing — we start from the beginning.

A good pastor friend of mine, Perry Monroe, became a Christian through an odd set of circumstances during World War II. And though he had no history within the church, upon returning to New York at the end of the war he decided that he would become a pastor. His friends, who were all lapsed Catholics and had a good degree of respect for priests left in them, thought this was a great idea, and so they threw a huge party for him the night he was to leave for Princeton. Perry got so drunk they had to put a sign on him so that the conductor could help him off the train when it got to his stop. In the morning, he woke up in the Princeton train station, went to school, and became a pastor — a good one, too.

Perry was one of those who had to learn what it means to be a Christian from the ground up. He didn't know anything. He didn't know that you weren't supposed to get drunk. All he knew was that when you do something big, you have a party. And while Perry had to deculturalize himself from the world's side, he forced me to decultural-

3. Kelly, *A Commentary on the Pastoral Epistles*, p. 235.

ize from the church's side everything I thought about a pastor. Through him, I had my first sustained deculturalization process of what it means to be a pastor.

Newly saved and drunk like Perry Monroe, this is the congregation Titus was given.

Tempting as it is, in situations like this, the pastor can't do it all by himself or herself. We have to develop community, and to develop community there must be godly leadership. So, we turn to the Titus letter as a kind of paradigm for the development of community and its leadership.

The Jesus Way of Leading

There is a great deal of advice given today about cultivating leadership. There is a popular journal with that title, *Leadership*. Counsel in how to be leaders is unending, but it all has to be tested against our Scriptures. There are a lot of good ideas out there, but when they take over the core of what we're doing, we end up in the Gulag, enduring an unrecognized persecution.

Against all leadership counsel we have to set Jesus, and not so much figure out how to be leaders from what he said and did but enter into the world that he lived in, the relationships that he cultivated, and assimilate his style. This leadership is not techniques and strategies culled from a superficial reading of the Gospels that knows little of Jesus himself, but a Jesus-leadership spirit, mind, sensitivity. It is a leadership that is conspicuously lacking in the exercise of power and the attraction of followers.

Henri J. M. Nouwen captures this well:

I am deeply convinced that the Christian leader of the future is called to be completely irrelevant and to stand in this world with nothing to offer but his or her own vulnerable self. That is the way Jesus came to reveal God's love. The great message that we have to carry, as ministers of God's word and followers of Jesus, is that God loves us not because of what we do or accomplish, but because God has

190

created and redeemed us in love and has chosen us to proclaim that love as the true source of all human life.[4]

This is the gospel, and I take it seriously. Next to it, hear this statement that I copied from a student's term paper:

> I've had my own experiences of seeing pastors' attitudes change towards me when I did not do what they wanted. If you are not a cog in the machine that they are running they discard your importance. . . . Leadership seems to be taken up by people who have a wrong concept of it.

In order to develop community in Christ, we have to deal with people the way Jesus deals with them. The corollary to this is that we have to make sure we don't treat them the way the culture deals with them. The culture thinks organizationally, functionally; the gospel thinks relationally, personally. The gospel says, where two or three are gathered together, there am I in the midst of them. The culture says, where two or three are gathered together, one has to be the chairperson and another take the minutes.

To reinforce a Jesus leadership, Scripture gives us two terms by which to think of people: *baptism* and *image of God*. The place to begin our understandings of leadership is baptism. Baptism is not something we do, but something that is done to us, and done equally. We are the baptized, the reborn, those set apart to God, holy, saints.

Next to this is the image of God, a metaphor that reminds us of the God-imprint that is unerasably stamped into each of us. And, again, this has nothing to do with what we do and everything to do with how God has made us and how he views and cherishes us.

With baptism and image of God before us, woe to us if we functionalize these God-bathed, God-imaged persons placed in our care — as Cretan as they may be. But as we saturate ourselves with these two very countercultural ways of dealing with people, we will cultivate a Christ-mind toward them.

4. Henri J. M. Nouwen, *In the Name of Jesus: Reflections on Christian Leadership* (New York: Crossroad Publishing Company, 1989), p. 17.

Salvation: The Theological Substructure of Leadership in Community

It is essential to acquire a theology adequate for community, and the Pastoral Epistles concentrate on *salvation*. There is a consensus among scholars of the pastoral letters that salvation is the theological center-piece. Philip Towner names it the "centerpoint" of the message in the Pastorals.[5] Frances Young writes, "It is characteristic in the Pastorals that God is called Saviour. Designation of God as Saviour is found in these letters six out of the mere eight times it occurs in the entire NT. The verb 'save' is used six times. Jesus Christ appears as Saviour four times."[6]

Salvation, in other words, is the work of God/Jesus that provides the substructure for what the pastor and other leaders do. Therefore, in developing leadership we have to work out of this substructure or we will be developing a leadership that has nothing to do with who we are as a community of Jesus.

So let me sketch out our Savior/salvation orientation.

1 Timothy 1:1, the initial greeting, describes Paul as "apostle of Jesus Christ according to the command of *God our Savior.*"

1 Timothy 2:3 states that "this," namely to spend a gentle and quiet life in all godliness and holiness, "is good and acceptable before *our Savior God,* who wishes all to be saved and to come to knowledge of truth."

1 Timothy 4:10 speaks of hoping in the living God, who is *Savior* of all human beings, especially believers.

2 Timothy 1:9 describes God as "the one who *has saved us* and called us with a holy calling, not according to our works but accord-ing to the divine purpose and grace." The passage goes on to speak of this plan of God being "granted to us in Christ Jesus before an-cient times and revealed now through the appearance of *our Savior Christ Jesus.*"

2 Timothy 2:10 shows Paul enduring everything for the Christian

5. Philip Towner, *The Goal of Our Instruction* (Sheffield, Eng.: JSOT Press, 1989).

6. Frances M. Young, *The Theology of the Pastoral Epistles* (New York: Cambridge University Press, 1994), p. 50.

community, "in order that they might attain to the *salvation* which is in Christ Jesus with eternal glory."

2 Timothy 4:18 expresses confidence that "the Lord will rescue me from every wicked act [referring to attacks on Paul's person, given the context in the previous verses], and will bring me *safe* [Greek = save] into his heavenly kingdom."

Titus 1:2-4, in the course of an elaborate greeting, refers to the "*kerygma* with which I was entrusted according to the command of *our Savior God,*" and the greeting ends with "grace and peace from God the Father and Christ Jesus *our Savior.*"

Titus 2:10 directs that slaves should behave in such a way as to show they can be trusted, so that "they make the teaching of *our Savior God* attractive to all."

Titus 2:11-13 speaks of the "*saving* grace of God" appearing to all human beings. The activity of God's saving grace is said to be teaching. The teaching produces lives that refuse ungodliness and worldly desires and produce self-control, righteousness, and piety. Such lives are lived in anticipation of "the blessed hope and the glorious appearing of the great God and *our Savior Jesus Christ.*"

Titus 3:4 sings of the appearance of the "kindness and love [*philanthropia* = love toward human beings] of *our Savior God.*" God is described as having "*saved* us not through works of righteousness we had done [presumably good deeds], but, according to the divine mercy, through the bath of re-birth [presumably baptism] and the renewal of the Holy Spirit which was poured out rightly upon us through *Jesus Christ our Savior.*"

Young writes, "What is noticeable is that the community to which these texts belong lays claim to the universal God in a special way as 'our Saviour God', while retaining the universal perspective. This God wants to save all."[7]

Alongside these texts, I want to set the "faithful sayings," *logos pistos.* These three letters are punctuated by "faithful sayings" — five of them — each of which is centered on salvation. They are as follows:

7. Young, *The Theology of the Pastoral Epistles,* p. 52.

1 Timothy 1:15: "The saying is sure *(pistos)* and worthy of full acceptance, that Christ Jesus came into the world to save sinners. . . ."

1 Timothy 3:1: "The saying is sure *(pistos):* If any one aspires to the office of bishop, he desires a noble task." (But this phrase may refer to what was written just before, about women being "saved" through childbearing.)

1 Timothy 4:8-9: "for while bodily training is of some value, godliness is of value in every way, as it holds promise for the present life and also for the life to come. The saying is sure *(pistos)* and worthy of full acceptance."

2 Timothy 2:11-13: "The saying is sure *(pistos):*
If we have died with him, we shall also live with him;
if we endure, we shall also reign with him;
if we deny him, he also will deny us;
if we are faithless, he remains faithful —
for he cannot deny himself."

Titus 3:5-8: "he saved us, not because of deeds done by us in righteousness, but in virtue of his own mercy, by the washing of regeneration and renewal in the Holy Spirit, which he poured out upon us rightly through Jesus Christ our Savior, so that we might be justified by his grace and become heirs in hope of eternal life. The saying is sure *(pistos)*."

Young comments on these sayings, noting:

The 'faithful sayings' are words of salvation. Of salvation there is no definition as such in the Pastoral epistles, but we can glean what it is supposed to consist in by careful attention to these . . . passages. The nearest to a definitive statement is **Titus 2:11-14** which speaks of the saving grace of God appearing, and
". . . by it we are trained to refuse ungodliness and worldly desires, and to live a life of self-control, righteousness and piety in the present age, looking forward to the blessed hope and the glorious

appearing of the great God and our Saviour Jesus Christ. He it is who gave himself for us, to set us free from all wickedness and to purify for himself a chosen people, eager to do good."[8]

Young later adds, "the kerygmatic content (that is, salvation) is advanced to ground the author's call to the community to live out the new life."[9]

Salvation is not merely a matter of eternity, getting to heaven, "getting saved" from eternal separation from God; it is a way of life in community. The "saved" are those we deal with, give leadership to, these baptized, image-of-God men, women, and children. We are "a chosen people, eager to do good." Salvation is not just a matter between the soul and God; it is the soul and God and house and kids and work and play — the works. The saved life is a way of life in which God is both the present and the eternal substructure.

Now, one more set of texts to back up this encompassing salvation world. These texts are christological — that is, they focus on the Jesus who effects this salvation among us. These texts show signs of being used liturgically — that is, in worship as creeds and/or hymns — a sung theology. When you form a Christian community, the basic thing you do is worship, develop Christ-centered, salvation-based worship. These passages are evidence.

Using the translation of the Revised Standard Version, I have arranged the lines to give a sense of the oral and hymnic quality of these texts, emphasizing the God-originating save/Savior/salvation words in bold print:

1 Timothy 2:5-6
> For there is one God,
> and there is **one mediator**
> **between God and men,**
> the man Christ Jesus,
> who **gave himself as a ransom for all,**
> the testimony to which was borne at the proper time.

8. Young, *The Theology of the Pastoral Epistles*, p. 57.
9. Young, *The Theology of the Pastoral Epistles*, p. 118.

1 Timothy 3:16

> **He was manifested** in the flesh,
> vindicated in the Spirit,
> seen by angels,
> **preached** among the nations,
> **believed on** in the world,
> taken up in glory.

1 Timothy 6:13-16

> In the presence of God who **gives life to all things,**
> and of Christ Jesus who in his testimony
> before Pontius Pilate made the good confession,
> I charge you to keep the commandment
> unstained and free from reproach
> **until the appearing of our Lord Jesus Christ;**
> **and this will be made manifest at the proper time**
> by the blessed and only Sovereign,
> the King of kings and Lord of lords,
> who alone has immortality
> and dwells in unapproachable light,
> whom no man has ever seen or can see.
> To him be honor and eternal dominion.
> Amen.

2 Timothy 1:9-10

> [Jesus] **saved us** and called us with a holy calling,
> not in virtue of our works
> but in virtue of his own purpose
> and the grace he gave us in Christ Jesus ages ago,
> and now has **manifested through**
> **the appearing of our Savior Christ Jesus**
> who abolished death
> and brought life and immortality
> to light through the gospel.

2 Timothy 2:11-13

> The saying is sure:

If we have died with him, we shall also live with him;
if we endure, we shall also reign with him;
if we deny him, he also will deny us;
if we are faithless, he remains faithful —
for he cannot deny himself.

Titus 3:4-8a
. . . when the goodness and loving kindness
of **God our Savior appeared,**
he saved us,
not because of deeds done by us in righteousness,
but in virtue of his own mercy,
by the washing of regeneration and renewal in the Holy Spirit,
which he poured out upon us richly
through Jesus Christ **our Savior,**
so that we might be justified by his grace
and become heirs in hope of eternal life.
The saying is sure.

These six texts embedded in the Pastoral Epistles provide a "salvation-fashioned, Jesus-saves" backdrop against which to understand the kind of community-building, leadership-developing work that pastors are involved in. If we lose the awareness and continual ministry validation of this continuous work of God among us, we are prey to every self-willed, self-promoting style of leadership offered up to us. Without this detailed, salvation-saturated context, no authentic Christian community will develop. Salvation-generated worship is prerequisite.

Young explains that "These key passages are often doxological or hymn-like interjections, difficult to translate, allusive in quality, so that for many of them it is hard to provide a clear and definite exegesis. . . . [Such poetry has] the ring of liturgical tradition, and therefore defies analysis in terms of systematic doctrine."[10]

10. Young, *The Theology of the Pastoral Epistles*, p. 61.

Developing Community and Its Leadership

We can't get community right if we don't get theology right, but with a sense of this substructure of theology — that is, thinking that is informed by God's presence and saving action — we can pick up the theme of community and its leadership.

The Pastorals, and now Titus in particular, are concerned with how a congregation grows and maintains itself, how people go about the day-to-day business of being Christians in the world. More than in any of the other biblical writings, attention is given to the nitty-gritty stuff of proper behavior in being a community in the world.

But before we look at what is involved in this community stuff, let me summarize the conditions: We have a culture that knows nothing about community, and we have a salvation that requires community to be lived rightly. Brought up with Wild West ideas in their heads, they encounter the gospel and enter the church with the culture still ringing in their ears.

And the *culture* is a lying, self-indulgent, violent culture — both Crete and North America. The violence and the self-indulgence are fed by the lies. Most of the ruin of our present culture comes from our lying words. Language that is at the root of creation, salvation, and community is abused and debased continuously and sacrilegiously.

Psalm 12 (taken here from *The Message*) is contemporary:

Quick Yahweh, I need your helping hand!
The last decent person just went down,
All the friends I depended on gone.
Everyone talks in lie language,
Lies slide off their oily lips.
They doubletalk with forked tongues.

Slice their lips off their faces!
Pull the braggart tongues from their mouths!
I'm tired of hearing, "We can talk anyone into anything!
Our lips manage the world."

Into the hovels of the poor,
Into the dark streets where the homeless groan, God speaks:
"I've had enough, I'm on my way
To heal the ache in the heart of the wretched."

God's words are pure words,
Pure silver words refined seven times
In the fires of his word-kiln,
Pure on earth as well as in heaven.
Yahweh, keep us safe from their lies,
From the wicked who stalk us with lies,
From the wicked who collect honors
For their wonderful lies.

In contrast, *salvation* is rooted in the God-revealing Word — the true Word, Jesus — and creates community. The same salvation that takes care of our eternal destiny plunges us into community relationships. Language, the means by which we reveal ourselves to one another and develop responsibilities among one another, is essential to community.

So, with this context in place — culture that knows nothing of community and a salvation that requires community — we are ready to look at how the Pastorals as a whole (but focusing in on the Titus text) take care of this business of providing leadership for community.

Paul's metaphor for the church community is "household of God." He writes, "I am writing these intructions to you so that, if I am delayed, you may know how one ought to behave in the household of God, which is the church of the living God, the pillar and bulwark of the truth" (1 Timothy 3:15).

Paul uses a literary form for giving instruction in this "how one ought to behave" that has parallels in other writings in the first century. The form is called "house codes" (German: *Haustafel*). "In the house codes the predominant concern is about correct relationships, duties and obligations in a community which regards itself as a teaching environment with a pattern of virtuous behaviour and a set of authoritative writings."[11]

What I want to highlight is that the way people are referred to in the Pastorals is in terms of social relationships and social identities, not tasks and talents. More often than not, we identify the people in our congregations in terms of what they can do: tithers and non-tithers, leaders and followers. Many of us develop systems for identifying skills and experience, which are computerized these days so that when you want someone who can paint a Sunday school room you pull up a file; likewise for potential youth leaders, people who have vans, secretarial skills, financial experience, flower arranging, singing voices, etc. There are things to be done in a church, and we need to know what people can do so that we can put them to work. We all do this; I did it myself and would do it again.

What I want to point out is that this way of looking at and identifying Christians in community has a way of functionalizing them in our minds, thinking of them not for who they are in community, in relationship, but for what they can do. It is significant that as the Pastorals refer to the members of the community it is as men and women embedded in relationship — Paul was looking for character, not ability. In the Pastorals, five pairs of social relationships are mentioned: men and women, husbands and wives, parents and children, masters and slaves, citizens and state. And ten social identities are given: young men, young women, older men, older women, widows, bishops, elders, deacons, wealthy, poor. None of these identities is used to evaluate the people, to put them on some kind of scale of usefulness or competence or value. They are used to give some focus to guiding and encouraging the formation of character in community.

If we identify people functionally, they turn into functions. We need to know our people for who they are, not for what they can do. Building community is not an organizational task; it is relational — understanding who people are in relation to one another and to Jesus and working on the virtues and habits that release love and forgiveness and hope and grace.

11. Young, *The Theology of the Pastoral Epistles*, p. 83.

Pascal has a wonderful image in this regard: "We think playing upon a man is like playing upon an ordinary organ. He is indeed an organ, but strange, shifting and changeable, with keys that do not follow the scales. Those who only know to play an ordinary organ would never be in tune on this one. You have to know where the keys are."[12]

Now, what I want to do is single out just one of these house codes, the one in Titus having to do with elders: "This is why I left you in Crete, that you might amend what was defective, and appoint elders in every town as I directed you." Here, Titus's task is essentially "to organize the Christian communities in the island by setting up responsible ministers."[13]

Christians sometimes come to these texts in the Pastorals to find a biblical mandate on how to organize a church. Along with most commentators, I don't see this letter to Titus (or either of the letters to Timothy) giving us an authoritative scheme for church order. All we can conclude is that developing church order is essential — we just don't know the particular form that order is to take. There is no biblically authoritative church order. We're never given enough information to systematize one — and probably for good reason. Elders are named in Titus, deacons in Timothy. Bishops and elders don't seem to be clearly distinguished. We know, of course, what bishops and elders and deacons do in our churches now, but we can't read our job descriptions back into the New Testament; we just don't know enough.

Along with trying to figure out an operational flow chart from the Bible, we talk about finding people's gifts. But that is just a euphemism for "how can we use these untapped resources." People do have gifts; the Holy Spirit does give them. But we have made a cultural shift away from the way the Holy Spirit works and what he wants and toward our management styles and organizational goals, functionalizing people where the Spirit personalizes them in his gifting. So, if we quit looking for a job description or a gift identification, it is interesting to see what is, in fact, here.

12. From Pascal's *Pensées* 172; quoted in Hans Urs von Balthasar, *The Glory of God*, vol. 3 (San Francisco: Ignatius Press, 1986), p. 206.
13. Kelly, *A Commentary on the Pastoral Epistles*, p. 229.

Here's the code for elders (three items):

blameless,
husband of one wife,
and having children who are believers and not open to the charge
of being profligate or insubordinate.

And here's the code for a bishop (eight positive and five negative items):

blameless,
not arrogant,
not quick-tempered,
not a drunkard,
not violent,
not greedy for gain,
hospitable,
lover of goodness,
master of himself,
upright,
holy,
self-controlled,
and holding firm to the sure word as taught that he may be able
to give instruction in sound doctrine and also be able to confute those who contradict it.

It is essential to note that not a single item (except possibly for
the last one) in these lists refers to job description or to ability. The final item in the bishop list is a partial exception — "able to give instruction in sound doctrine." But if we see it as referring to a person
whose life is oriented and shaped by Scripture and whose speech flows
out of that orientation and shaping, it is more a matter of character
than of skill. This is the wisdom we pointed out in Chapter 6 — lived
truth, lived gospel — this is the kind of person to look for. The way
you live is what qualifies or disqualifies you from leadership.

We don't find a job description. What we do find is a concern for
character formation — the task is to develop men and women who

know how to treat a congregation right. We aren't told what these leaders are to do or how they are to do it. Leaders are not distinguished by their functions or, as we might say it today, their "gifts" but by their character.

If we let our imaginations be trained by the Pastorals when we go to work developing leadership in the community of faith, we are not going to be looking for talented people whom we can use. We will seek nurturing souls who are trustworthy and faithful.

This is miles away from what is current among us regarding leadership development, and it just might account for the difficulties we find ourselves in. As community diminishes, the frenzy for leadership accelerates, but it is more often than not a leadership that destroys community by functionalizing people. The more "effective" our leaders become, the less community we get.

Christian community is developed by the Holy Spirit using men and women who are mature in their relationships, who have acquired the habits of the heart that make it possible to live in faith and faithfulness. What we call the "ability to lead" has almost nothing to do with it. If we want to develop community in Christ, we have to scrap most of what we are told today about leadership. Forget about charisma, go for character.

As a general rule, in selecting leaders in our congregations go for the little people, the ordinary people, the unimpressive people. They aren't as apt to have been corrupted by the world's functionalism; they are less apt to be identified by their job descriptions. Their character formation is more likely to be mature — not necessarily, of course, but more likely.

Look for the "poor in spirit." Learn to recognize the sphere of leadership not among those who excite admiration, who energetically get great things done, who become advertisements for the vigor of our congregations. Those kinds of leadership are useful, to be sure, and we are grateful for them. But when it comes to developing community, we need a few souls in whom love is gently at work, covering a multitude of sins.

We would do well not to be enamored by the kind of leadership that is so prized by politicians and CEOs, the kind that is conspicuous and, as we say, "effective." In Crete, that kind of leadership was epitomized by Minos and Theseus. Paul doesn't instruct Titus to match those mythological leaders with some Christian equivalent. He is looking not for someone who can *do* something spectacular but for someone who *is* something regardless of whether anyone notices. In the church communities, we work with different standards and have different goals. It is almost always a mistake to recruit exceptional people for leadership; look for ordinary Christians — that is mostly what you have anyway. But prize them, value them, and appoint them as leaders.

When we are looking for the people who will help us become a community of Christ, we are looking for people distinguished not by achievements, but "by whatever they have kept that is intact, pure, by that which remains in them of their childhood, regardless of how deeply we have to look for it."[14]

---

14. Georges Bernanos, quoted in Hans Urs von Balthasar, *Bernanos* (San Francisco: Ignatius Press, 1996), p. 32.

Chapter 9

The Call to Build Community

MARVA J. DAWN

As with my previous chapters, we begin this one with prayer — this time with two petitions taken from *A Guide to Prayer* because these summarize well what we have been doing so far in studying Ephesians and what we seek to do in this final chapter. As we begin, let us remember that we are working together as a community.

The Lord be with you. [And also with you.] Let us pray:

Almighty God, you have called the Church into being and have gathered us into one family. By the powers of your Holy Spirit help us to live in unity and peace with all of your children. May our actions this day be fruit of our faith in your kingdom, in the name of Christ. Amen.

Almighty God, you have created us, called us, chosen us to be your people. We wait now to receive your word of guidance and blessing. Grant unto us ears to hear, eyes to see, and faith to respond to your love and leadership, in the name of Christ. Amen.[1]

1. Rueben P. Job and Norman Shawchuck, eds., *A Guide to Prayer: For Ministers and Other Servants* (Nashville: The Upper Room, 1983), pp. 178 and 173. These prayers were the ones for the church-year weeks before and during which the Regent College conference was held. I have modified the punctuation for grammatical correctness and capitalized *Church* to signify the one, holy, catholic, apostolic Church throughout time and space.

Human beings have a strong need for public ritual.[2] In the communal prayers of a worshiping body, participants will find it more engaging if the leader says something like, "Lord, in your mercy," so we can all join with the rest of the congregation in responding, "hear our prayer." When we say these words together, we find ourselves not just listening to a prayer, but engaging verbally with the whole community in the utterance of prayer.

I feel a profound yearning for *corporate* lament with an extra sharpness because the largest longing in my life is somehow to find community. As a freelance speaker/writer, I spend a large proportion of my time away from my local worshiping community.

When the conference that gave rise to this book was held at Regent College in Vancouver, B.C., I found myself immersed in a community that brought great healing and comfort to my wandering soul. Their communal gifts offer excellent models for the community life in our churches. For example, Eugene Peterson was the beloved teacher at Regent, and I was mostly unknown — and yet Eugene warmly welcomed me to be a partner with him, as did the participants at the conference. That was an important beginning of community for me, for I have been part of some conferences where participants didn't attend the sessions of lesser known speakers or where the other speaker seemed to be competing rather than serving together with me in collegiality.

Furthermore, some students from a course I had taught two summers before at Regent invited me into their home and into their conversation and concerns about the future. Another former student took me to dinner with his present colleagues so that I could hear how he was serving and what the congregation in which he taught was doing in ministry. These events gave me opportunities to go beyond the formalities of lectures and into sharing more deeply in the lives of col-

2. These comments in the original presentation at Regent College were called forth by our learning about the high school shootings in Springfield, Oregon. One of the participants of the conference was pastor of a nearby congregation, so he and his ministry to the grieving community were included in our prayers. When there are such tragedies and crises in our church bodies and larger local communities, we need public rituals that welcome everyone into actual verbal participation in the corporate prayers. At the same time, we need those rituals to be truly *public,* so that they allow us to grieve corporately and thus find release from our overwhelming private confusions and agonies.

leagues in ministry. (As a freelancer I have no local colleagues for spiritual partnership.) Moreover, the participants at the Regent College conference were very exuberant in responding "and also with you" at the beginning of each of my sessions.

All these particulars give us some hints for how we might build community in our own congregations. Together we can practice such gifts as hospitality, words invested with meaning, sharing our concerns and dreams for the future, praying together about all these concerns and dreams, and discussing together how we can be faithful to our call. How deeply do the members of your congregation converse about their ministries in the world?

Please reflect for a moment also on what it is that causes you — both inside and outside your pastoral role — to experience community. If you are not presently benefiting from such fellowship, why not?

While at Regent for this pastors' conference, some of the participants and I went to a classical concert at a theatre on the University of British Columbia campus. The staff at the concert hall were amazingly generous, for we had told them of my visual handicap, and they had saved a few seats close to the stage so I could see the classical guitarists who were playing with the symphony. That was delightful except for this: there were not enough seats up close for everyone who had come from Regent. Throughout the concert I felt a bit guilty that my privileged place potentially undermined community since others were left out of it. The situation reminds me of how important it is that all of us be aware of things that might contribute to building community or that might pull us apart.

The reaction of those sitting further back extends the lessons, for their graciousness about not having close-up seats prevented the distinction from actually fracturing our community life. We all shared in the delight of the concert because they didn't let jealousy invade. To build community requires a wide diversity of efforts, including vigilance against envy or resentment, as well as the more positive labors of offering hospitality, engaging in conversation, and persisting in prayer for one another.[3]

3. For intensive exegesis and discussion questions concerning the building of community, see my *Truly the Community: Romans 12 and How to Be the Church* (Grand Rapids: Wm. B. Eerdmans Publishing Co., 1992; reissued 1997).

Factors in Society That Militate against Community

Our very culture militates against community and yet talks about it all the time because it is starved for it. Jacques Ellul is the scholar who helped me most to understand some of the reasons why modern Western culture has become so devoid of true community.[4] Let us look at his insights concerning the progression of relationships in world culture, beginning with the creation of the world.

The liturgical convictions of Genesis 1 display how thoroughly God originally designed the world with harmony and orderliness, with everything in relationship to everything else and with him. This harmony, of course, was broken in the Fall, which is the fundamental reason for our present lack of community.

Over the course of the history of the world, by and large, society was organized into small groups — clans, tribes, families, ethnic conclaves. I am not idealizing these groups — the communities were often very violent — but the basic social fabric was conducive to community life (often for the sake of surviving against the antagonistic forces of nature).

These more intimate groupings in home life and local milieu remained the pattern through most of history until the onset of the Industrial Revolution. Before that time, families worked mostly together, sharing the same cares and concerns. For example, consider the family farm (before the huge collectivized or bureaucratized farms of the twentieth century). Each member of the family had his or her own chores that contributed to the well-being of the whole. All of the members together had the same anxieties about the weather and the soybean prices. Young children imitated their parents at work and were mentored into full responsibilities and mature skills for carrying on the family heritage.

Many kinds of occupations could provide such a communal mi-

---

4. See especially Jacques Ellul, *The Technological Society,* trans. John Wilkinson (New York: Vintage Books, 1964); *The Technological System,* trans. Joachim Neugroschel (New York: Continuum, 1980); *The Technological Bluff,* trans. Joyce Main Hanks (Grand Rapids: Wm. B. Eerdmans Publishing Co., 1990); and *The New Demons,* trans. C. Edward Hopkin (New York: Seabury Press, 1975).

lieu. In the case of my own childhood, our whole family was concerned about the Christian school my parents served. My father was the principal, and Mom was the school secretary. Dad taught eighth grade, and my mother taught third. We all spent most of our time at the school (or on its playground) and worked hard for it to flourish. My brothers and I thought other children were deprived because they didn't get to stamp textbooks and push desks around in the summers.

Such a social fabric that more easily nourished community began to break down in the society of the Industrial Revolution. Instead of working in the family cobbler shop, the husband/father found employment at the shoe factory, which put him in a separate community from the rest of the household. Consequently, he had different psychological strains, different economic concerns, a different set of people with whom he spent his time. When he returned home from this separate world, there was less intimacy than in the former milieu because his identity partly resided in another community.

The breakdown took another dramatic leap with World War II, when women went to work for pay. Before that, their work centered in the home or family enterprise, but now they went to the office, while their husbands (returned from the war) worked at another site. With Mom in her office and Dad at his factory (and eventually with their child working at a fast food joint), they all had different workgroups, emotional and mental strains, financial concerns, sets of friends and colleagues, and work environments. Now when they came home, there was even less social fabric for intimacy. The milieu was now a diffusion of communities, instead of one that included home and work together. This dispersion of life was aggravated by the development of such things as the automobile (which allowed family members to go further from each other in their separate work lives) or youth sports teams (which organized play into formal structures not linked to the neighborhood).

The most extreme leap in the breakdown of the social fabric came with the onset of the technological milieu. Jacques Ellul states that technicization brought as drastic a breach as the Fall, but that is a typical Ellulian overstatement. Though nothing could be as decisive as human entry into sin, Ellul is right to recognize how terribly (and subtly) disruptive of the communal fabric our present milieu is, to a great extent because the very tools we work with and the toys with which we play pull us away from each other.

For example, consider dishwashers. We might think they are great labor-saving devices, but we do not as easily notice how they have stolen part of our household fabric for intimacy. When I was a child, my brothers and I did the dishes together and sang in three-part harmony while we cleaned them. I won't falsely romanticize that intimacy — we also whacked each other with towels — but the potential for enjoyable singing and good conversation was there. We also sang together with our parents in the car on our way to Wisconsin to visit our grandparents; when we were in college (a time when lots of siblings lose touch with each other), my closest brother and I used to make up fugues on the train home for holidays. The point is that we had established the practices of fellowship and nurtured them while we did dishes. If a family uses a dishwasher, taking care of the dishes is usually a solitary job. In addition, think of all the technological toys, like Walkmans and solo computer games, that keep us from singing with each other in our society.

Other aspects of the technological society are similarly disruptive of community. Children can rarely imitate their parents' work. With Mom at the office and food coming out of a bag, families no longer make cookies together, and little girls no longer imitate their mothers with their little toy rolling pins. With Dad gone to the factory, little boys don't take their miniature milking stools to the barn to emulate their fathers. (In order not to affirm gender stereotypes, let me add that my father mentored me in playing football and baseball, and my mother trained my brothers in cooking and housecleaning.)

Consider television sets. We never owned one when I was small. Instead we played games and various sports together. These days, if my husband and I go for a walk in the evening, we notice that in some houses as many as three different television sets are on at the same time in different rooms. What kind of camaraderie is possible in a family that spends its time so separated?

I am grateful for technological tools. (I am not a Luddite!) The problem is that we become too enthralled with their advantages and don't ask good questions about how much they take away from us.

For example, computers are much faster than typewriters for writing books; I'm glad simply to punch "Print" after making corrections instead of retyping everything. However, computers can also contribute to our alienation far more than we realize.

A friend who is a librarian complains that she never sees people anymore. Now she sits in her little cubicle and sends everything over the modem. Similarly, a news journal recently featured an article on how large corporations that formerly utilized lots of telecommuting are discovering that their workforces lack the comfortable interactions that spurred creativity. Consequently, they are building new headquarters buildings that look like a small village, with shops and park benches and "street corners" to foster the kinds of conversations that lead to new ideas and greater contentment in working.

Our culture is starved for community. It is hungry for genuine intimacy since we no longer have the basic social texture, the skills, or the time to learn how to develop it. One of the major reasons for the frantic genital idolatry of our environment is that people are so ravenous for social intimacy, but do not know how to create it.[5] Meanwhile, the media bombard them 95 times a day with the message that the only way to have intimacy is to jump into bed with somebody. Many young people especially resort to genital union out of their desperation to find some sort of love. Because our English language has only one word for "love," too many think that "sex" is the only kind of love to be found, but when sexual intercourse is ripped out of the context of God's design for it within a permanent marriage commitment, it can hardly be ultimately satisfying.

The Greeks have plenty of words for "love" besides *eros* (from which we get the word *erotic*) in order to help us develop many kinds of intimacy. Other terms for love include these:

> *storgē* — the love of parent for child or "blood love," which is becoming more and more absent in our culture as families break down;

5. This is the fundamental thesis of my book *Sexual Character: Beyond Technique to Intimacy* (Grand Rapids: Wm. B. Eerdmans Publishing Co., 1993). The book offers positive ways to discuss intimacy with young people and a thorough explication of God's lovely design for true love in friendship and marriage.

philia — friendship love, which our culture has largely lost because of our lack of time for sharing common interests and because such forces as competition and the idol of climbing the corporate ladder have kept work colleagues from becoming friends;[6]

philastorgē — tender affection (as in Romans 12:10), which deepens friendship love into a kinship as firmly fixed as a blood tie;

philadelphia — brotherly/sisterly friendship love, which is best exemplified in the Christian community when we can *truly* call each other "sister" and "brother";

agapē — love that needs no love in return, that is intelligent and purposeful, always directed to the need of the other.

This last love, of course, is the richest of all. Though many of the ancient Greek philosophers thought that *agapē* was least important since it is disinterested, the Christian community wisely recognized that it is the best term to describe God's love for us. Furthermore, all the biblical commands for us to love each other use the verb *agapaō;* truly the best intimacy we could offer members of the community and our neighbors is the extravagant, opulent, profuse love of God.

Because our culture scarcely knows these other kinds of love, extensive training is required for our congregations truly to be communities. Genuine, non-genital intimacy requires deliberate and diligent practice. Simply to have the name *church* does not mean we are a real community.

Rarely in my travels do I find congregations that are seriously committed to being genuine community. Recently at a women's luncheon I asked what it meant to be a Christian community, and the church members responded with such answers as "we care for each other" and "we share things." I kept responding, "Yes, and what else?" After a while I

---

6. On the work of the pastor as "friendship," see chapter 8 of David Hansen, *The Art of Pastoring: Ministry Without All the Answers* (Downers Grove, IL: InterVarsity Press, 1994), pp. 117-33. He reminds us that "It's better to recognize that our friendship is essentially unnecessary to people" (123).

could tell they were getting a bit exasperated with me, so I finally confessed, "I find it odd that no one has said, 'We would die for each other.'" They were noticeably unsettled, so I pressed this point further: How thoroughly bound to each other are we?

And how thoroughly hospitable to our neighbors are we? "Welcoming the stranger" needs to be taught in our parishes, for out of our fears of violence we instruct our children *not* to talk with strangers. If someone unknown to any one in your congregation showed up on a Sunday morning, would it be likely that a member would ask, "Would you like to sit with me for worship?" If the guest sits alone, would the person sitting next to him or her lean over and say, "Welcome to worship. Let me show you how our order of service goes so that you can follow along"?

As a freelancer for more than twenty years, I have been a guest in churches more than half the Sundays of all those years, and after so many experiences I must honestly say that most churches are quite atrocious at truly welcoming strangers. (I put on my perfume and am basically a friendly sort of person, so I don't think I'm the major problem.) My point is simply that the skills of community life are no longer instilled by our society. If our churches will truly be Church and nurture the profound intimacy and generous hospitality for which our culture is desperate, it will require schooling and sanctification, sacrifice and suffering.

There are so many ways in which we can be very practical about being and building a community. One necessary key is committed intentionality. So easily we have a "Low Information-Action Ratio" on the subject; we hear too much about the failure of community in our churches and become immobilized. Why not start now? Put down this book and consider what you might do to nurture in your congregation's members a deeper desire to care more truly for the needs of fellow saints. Where might you start? What could be your first step for building more genuine commonality within your parish?

Reading the Bible in the Plural

One important step is to teach Christians to recognize that the Bible is most often written in the plural — and then to equip them for acting on that plurality. I first became aware of how much we overlook this critical truth more than twenty years ago in leading a college Bible study. The student sitting right next to me when we discussed Philippians 4:4 complained, "I can't do that." "What can't you do?" I asked, and she replied, "I can't rejoice in the Lord always."

When I answered, "The text doesn't say you have to," she insisted, "Yes, it does. It tells me twice: 'Rejoice in the Lord always; again I will say, Rejoice.'"

Actually, the text does not command that. It says, "Rejoice, y'all." (Even more accurately, it says, "Keep on rejoicing, y'all," since the imperative is a present continuing one.) We all need to become Southerners to read the Bible correctly, because to inhabit its world is to speak about our lives as *y'all* (plural), instead of *you* (singular).[7]

About the only individual instructions in the Bible are those given to Timothy, Titus, and Philemon, since these three received personal letters, rather than congregational ones. Most of the rest of the descriptions and commissions in the Bible are plural: "Be blessing those persecuting you, y'all" (Romans 12:14); "Y'all consider it all joy, brothers and sisters, when y'all fall into diversified testings" (James 1:2); "Do not be thwarting the Spirit, y'all" (1 Thessalonians 5:19).

It requires compelling training for church members to learn to read the Scriptures this way. I participated in a small-group Bible study

7. It seems to me a setback that the English language has erased its pronoun distinctions between "thee" and "ye." Some European languages are beginning to follow suit by no longer requiring the formal, respectful form of the singular, which in those languages often is the same as the plural. In losing our vocabulary for respect in the United States, we have also renounced titles (like "Sir" or "Mrs." or "Professor") that reminded us that we still need mentoring from those older and (usually) wiser than we. Our language changes are both symptomatic of and contributive to the decline of community in our culture. To distinguish between "you" as an intimate acquaintance, "you" as someone I do not address in intimate terms because of respect or a less-developed relationship, and "you" as a larger group in which I am but a part helps me to have a more truthful sense of my place in the whole.

for several years before one woman eventually said, "You are always talking about 'we.' I finally get it." It takes a long process to change the Western individualized vocabulary that is ruining *our* church.

I certainly am not denying that it is essential for each of us to have a personal relationship with Jesus Christ or that we will stand before God's judgment individually. However, that "personal" emphasis regarding faith has been so overdone as to cause us to forget that both we and our faith are *formed* in the Christian *community*.

If we could stop thinking about ourselves in individualistic terms and recognize that everything in faith is communal, contingent, and corporate, we would find life and affliction and labor more bearable. When I had cancer and was so sick that I couldn't sing, I needed someone beside me to sing for me.[8]

The Christian Community Is an Alternative Society

This is one of the most important sentences I ever say or write, so if you are reading this book silently, read this out loud: *The Christian community is an alternative society.*

Another important step in building the community life of our congregations is to recognize that true corporate vitality in the Church will involve many values far different from the culture's. If you have been reading between the lines of this book, you have probably noticed this idea on almost every page. Our mutual concern for this alternativity is a major source of rejoicing and gratitude for me in the gift of Eugene's friendship. Our conversations keep revealing our common presupposition that to "be Church" is to follow Jesus in all the oddness of that calling. (That is my way of phrasing it; Eugene would say it better.[9])

To emphasize only our alternativity, however, is inadequate, so

---

8. For further discussion of the importance of community for those who suffer, see my *Joy in Our Weakness: A Gift of Hope from the Book of Revelation* (St. Louis: Concordia Publishing House, 1994).

9. See, for example, Eugene H. Peterson, *Subversive Spirituality*, ed. Jim Lyster, John Sharon, and Peter Santucci (Grand Rapids: Wm. B. Eerdmans Publishing Co., 1997).

let us add the word *parallel* and say this again out loud: *The Christian community is an alternative, parallel society.*

We need this dialectical balancing. The words *alternative* and *parallel* pull us in differing directions that more appropriately display the dynamic tension we live in if we are biblically formed. We are to be alternative in order to resist the modes of the world and to recognize the gifts we offer that the world needs. On the other hand, we understand ourselves also as parallel so that we remain close enough to the world still to speak in witness to it. Furthermore, we must recognize with the word *parallel* that we can't ever get the world out of us. We are still tempted by its treats, warped by its ways.

It is a tough balance to hold — resisting, gifting, witnessing, acknowledging. Jesus described it in terms of being *in* the world, but not *of* it. We can easily dwell so thoroughly in the surrounding culture (merging rather than parallel) that we blend in with the world and do not have any alternative gifts to offer. Then the world can't comprehend why Christianity matters. On the other hand, we can become so extremely alternative that we pull away into a provincialism that does not connect with our neighbors in order to offer our gifts.[10]

Think what tremendous alternatives God's people formed by the gospel exhibit to our society. The world doesn't need any more models of powerful success — it has plenty of those. Imagine how important it is for us to display instead our suffering servanthood. Our culture has no need for more big money enterprises; envision how valuable it is, rather, to demonstrate "poverty" and "simplicity" chosen willingly for the sake of building justice in the world. Societies don't need any more violence; visualize alternatively the impact of a people dedicated to reconciliation and peacemaking. Our neighbors do not crave more lies. Everyone is searching for truth.

---

10. See other terms for this dialectical balance in *Confident Witness — Changing World,* ed. Craig Van Gelder (Grand Rapids: Wm. B. Eerdmans Publishing Co., 1999). Compare especially William Burrows's notion of churches as "zones" connecting us with "home truth" in "Witness to the Gospel and Refounding the Church," pp. 189-202; Douglas John Hall's image of a "diaspora existence" in "Metamorphosis: From Christendom to Diaspora," pp. 67-79; and Mary Jo Leddy's reference to Václav Havel's description of the Czech "parallel cultures" in "The People of God as a Hermeneutic of the Gospel," pp. 303-13.

Mary Jo Leddy, in her closing plenary address at a conference sponsored by the Gospel and Our Culture Network entitled "Confident Witness — Changing World," described the "parallel cultures" developed by Václav Havel and other dissidents in Czechoslovakia and other iron-curtain countries when they began to ask, "How can we live the truth in a culture based on a fundamental lie . . . ?" This is her sketch:

> They had underground study groups. They studied Plato. They had drama. They had music groups. They wrote novels and poetry, and published them underground. . . . Over time, the truth became stronger and stronger, and at a certain point people began to walk in the streets and to say to the system, "We don't believe you anymore." And the system fell. It fell, not because of the power of Western nuclear equipment, but because the people said within the system, "We don't believe you anymore." It was a vision that had been nourished within those parallel cultures.[11]

Is that not one of the finest pictures of the Church? As a parallel society, we gather together on Sunday mornings for the most important thing we do, for the only thing the culture cannot do — worship! And when we worship

we pray our prayers;

we sing our songs that speak a different language from the world's;

we read our story, the grand master narrative of the promising God.

We learn from that meta-narrative how God was (and remains) faithful throughout (and in spite of) the history of Israel, how he most dra-

---

11. Leddy, "The People of God," p. 311. Leddy quotes Miroslav Václav Havel, *Living in Truth,* ed. Jon Vladislav (London and Boston: Faber and Faber, 1989). The essay from which she quotes, "The Power of the Powerless," written in 1978, also appears in Václav Havel, *Open Letters: Selected Writings 1965-1990,* ed. Paul Wilson (New York: Alfred A. Knopf, 1991), pp. 125-214. This book contains several additional references to, and descriptions of, "parallel cultures" and "parallel structures" in other essays.

matically fulfilled his promises in the resurrection and ascension of Jesus Christ and in the sending of the Holy Spirit, and how these covenant fulfillments give us confidence that God will continue to keep his promises all the way into eternity.

As we keep telling each other this story, and praying our petitions, and singing our hymns, we learn the truth so well that we can go out to the world and say, "We don't believe your lies anymore." Then we offer our truthful gifts, for which the world is starved.

Everybody in the world is searching for identity, asking "Who am I?" We trinitarians tell them the truth of the gospel and particularly of our baptism, that each person is the beloved of God, made in his image, and adopted into his family by grace.

Everybody is digging for roots, a larger story, a master account, an extended history that helps make sense of one's life and answers the question, "How does it all fit together?" Our Christian meta-narrative began with the creation of the world and became focused with God's creation of a special people for himself (through Abraham and Sarah and all their children in faith) for the sake of the world.

Everybody is looking for love, for loyalty, for sure solutions to the lonely yearning expressed in the questions "To whom do I belong?" and "Whom can I trust?" Our churches offer the gift of a genuine community that is trustworthy (and when it is not we offer confession and absolution) and the greatest gift of the truth about the totally reliable God to whom we all belong.

Everybody is investigating values and wondering "By what shall I live?" God's people possess a way of life that gives direction for our use of time and money, for our friendships and marriages, for our sense of occupation and vocation, for our priorities.

Everybody is pursuing enough power to survive, a remedy for the problems "How am I going to cope with the chaos of the world?" and "How can I make my way over against others?" We who follow Jesus know that all power rests in God and that we can submit to the world's derived power when appropriate, counteract it if necessary, resist it without violence, and exert it graciously.

Everybody is probing for meaning and trying to answer the question, "What is the purpose of my life?" We in the Church have discovered the mission of our existence in loving God and glorifying him forever.

Everybody is hunting for hope, harboring an aching desire to know, "How can I find the courage to go on?" Christians nestle in the loving arms of God and trust his promises for the future. Because we await the day when God will do away with evil forever, we anticipate that final culmination of his reign by practicing and passing on his reign in the present.[12]

These are some of the alternative gifts that we offer the world if we stay close enough to it and in it to be able to witness and share, welcome and care. We must continually return to our "beloved community"[13] in order to be reminded of our master story, to sing our truth again, and to pray for empowerment so that we can improvise our Good News in daily life for the sake of our neighbors.

Rediscovering Reconciliation

One major function of the pastor that seems unnecessary to the world is to equip the congregation for its reconciling work in society and to make sure that congregants remain reconciled with each other. The pastor keeps demonstrating that Christ is the bridge between any distinct groups or disparate causes that threaten to divide the community or separate it from the neighbors.

One very weighty passage in Ephesians concerning reconciliation is 2:14-22. Remember from Chapter 7 of this book these words of verses 11-13 which introduce the distinctions:

> Therefore, keep remembering that once you — Gentiles in the flesh, the ones called "uncircumcision" by those called "circumcision"

---

12. These seven needs of all human beings are elaborated and exemplified, with excerpts from Douglas Coupland's *Generation X: Tales for an Accelerated Culture* (New York: St. Martin's Press, 1991), in "The Needs of Our Being," chapter 3 of my book *A Royal "Waste" of Time: The Splendor of Worshiping God and Being Church for the World* (Grand Rapids: Wm. B. Eerdmans Publishing Co., 1999), pp. 21-36.

13. Mary Jo Leddy uses this phrase, adapted from poet and farmer Wendell Berry's expression "beloved country," in "The People of God," p. 312.

(made in the flesh with human hands) — were at that time without Christ, estranged from the commonwealth of Israel and foreigners to the covenants of promise, not having hope and without God in the world. But now in Christ Jesus you who once were far off have been brought near in the blood of Christ.

Ephesians 2:11-13

Now we look to the continuation of the text to gain further insight into the basis by which all barriers between people are eliminated. Paul proceeds as follows:

For [Christ] himself is our peace, he who made both [groups] one and he who "with his own body broke down the wall that separated them and kept them enemies" (*SD* 20.53), having rendered ineffective the law of the commands in decrees, in order that he might in himself create the two into one new person [thereby] making peace, and that he might reconcile both in one body to God through the cross, [thereby] putting to death in himself the enmity. And having come, he proclaimed the good news of peace to you [who were] far off and peace to the ones near; for because of him we both have boldness in the Spirit to address the Father with confidence (*SD* 33.72). So therefore you are no longer strangers and temporary residents (*SD* 11.77), but you are fellow citizens of the saints and members of the family of God, having been built upon the foundation of the apostles and prophets, Christ Jesus himself being the cornerstone, in whom the whole structure is joined together and grows into a holy temple in the Lord, in whom you also are being built together into a place where God dwells through his Spirit.

Ephesians 2:14-22

Notice how unnecessary we are to this entire process of reconciling and building. Christ Jesus did it all in his own body, by his cross, through his proclamation and effecting of the Trinity's *shalom*. This is a difficult paradox for us constantly to rediscover: that we are totally unnecessary for the accomplishment of this construction and yet that it is important for us to recognize what God has done and thereby to live in the peace that Christ has created (though we do that by means of

God dwelling in us through the gift of the Spirit). It is indeed essential that we actively receive God's gracious establishing and shaping, for our world's many divisions and discords amply demonstrate its inability to live in peace.

Our active participation is released from any sense of our necessariness if we recount God's work to build the temple of which we are a part. Christ broke down the barriers between Jew and Gentile, abolished the walls between us, released us from laws and commandments and decrees, made us all one people, destroyed all the enmity between us, laid the foundation of the apostles and prophets, gave us in himself the perfect corner so that the walls could be lined up straightly, joined us together in himself in spite of our diversity, nourishes us so that we grow, reconciled us to the Father, and poured out the Spirit to dwell within us.

However, even though the Triune God has fully implemented all the aspects of this construction, still churches constantly disrupt it and divide their community. We split over silly issues or erupt into "irreconcilable" (in our view) polarities. For example, I keep saying that these days we have to rewrite "neither Jew nor Greek" to say "neither Boomer nor X-er, neither lover of hymns nor lover of jazz, neither guitarist nor organist." It seems obvious that Christ could unite us all in praising him despite our differences in musical tastes, and yet increasingly congregations are split over "styles" of worship. Could we not instead engage earnestly in the community process of discernment that is required to see Christ's breaking down of walls and experience his creation of one people?[14]

What *could* the Church look like? Long ago I worked in a small but lively congregation serving its small city and two university campuses. In the summers when many of the professors were away for re-

---

14. If your congregation is divided over worship matters, let me once again urge you to make use of the questions and reflections in A Royal "Waste" of Time for the purpose of engaging in congregational processes that build unity. The royalties of that book provide scholarships for young musicians of faith so that they, too, can learn to build unity with music. This training in church music is provided by the Lutheran Music Program at its summer institutes for high school vocal and instrumental musicians. For more information, contact the executive director, Dr. Victor E. Gebauer, at 122 West Franklin Avenue, Suite 522, Minneapolis, MN 55404; phone (612) 879-9555 and fax (612) 879-9547.

search and the students were gone, our numbers were limited enough for the entire parish to have Sunday school together. One Sunday we built a church.

I explained to the children that in biblical times the cornerstone was chosen because it had the truest right angles, so that the walls could be positioned accordingly and be made straight. They then picked a well-aligned Bible to be Christ, and we discussed how he is the cornerstone by which we judge everything in our church.

Then we laid the foundation of the apostles and prophets. Each child could set down a Bible as one of the structural stones by naming a scriptural writer whose letter or prophecy helped to form us.

On this foundation we built our church out of shoeboxes, one for each person present. In pairs of young and old, they all helped each other color on their personal boxes a picture of themselves and the gifts they offered to the whole community. When they brought them back to the entire group, they told everyone else who they were as they fit their stone into the whole temple.

I will never forget five-year-old Michael. Every Friday he went with me to sing at the convalescent center, where he demonstrated his uncanny gift of knowing exactly who needed to hold his hand. When we built our temple, he drew on his shoe box a great big smile. As he placed it in the center of our construction he said to the whole congregation, "My gift is to make people happy." That child knew how important he and his gifts were for the community.

What would it be like if every single person in our pews knew that if he or she were absent the church could not be complete? Do you think anyone would be missing? What will we do, then, in our congregational language to pluralize it so that everyone knows that he or she needs the others, and then to emphasize that each one of us is indispensably important for the essential well-being of this community in this place?

At one time I worked in a congregation that included a fellow who loved to sing, but was quite a monotone. One week when he was away, the congregational singing was terrible, and I was stumped, wondering what made it so much worse than usual. The next week, when I was paying attention, he was there, singing full blast all on the same note. However, his exuberance caused everyone else to sing full-voiced, too. Perhaps they all knew that they weren't so bad in comparison; possibly they thought they could drown him out. Whatever the reason, if he was there, his great delight in singing inspired everyone else to sing more eagerly. The whole community benefited from his presence.

It is an odd gift, isn't it? However, it fits quite well with Eugene's comments in Chapter 8 that the supposed "little people," rather than the ones who are more dramatically great, are usually the best at creating community — and they often do it in surprising ways. There are many who lead congregational life and worship with great talent, and I do not intend to diminish their contributions. Nevertheless, it is critical that we recognize that such skills are not "necessary." They don't happen to be the main means by which God's Spirit shapes community out of a bunch of saved sinners.

I am quite distrustful of the little tests often given out in churches to determine which of seventeen or eighteen biblical spiritual gifts a person might have. The test makers who organize these lessons fail to understand that Paul's and Peter's lists are symbolic. For example, in Romans 12 Paul mentions seven (the Jewish symbolic number representing perfection) to illustrate all the rest.

All spiritual gifts are means of grace — the Greek term is *charismata* in plural form, deriving from the root *charis* or "grace." Thus, the Spirit uses the spiritual gift to convey grace to and in the one exercising the gift and, through that person, to impart more grace to those people who receive its fruits. Consequently, we can imagine that there are myriads upon myriads of spiritual gifts. Here is one of my favorites: the gift-of-the-person-who-does-dishes-after-a-potluck-congregational-dinner-with-so-much-Joy-that-everybody-wants-to-be-in-the-kitchen-helping.

Have you ever seen that gift listed in those inventories? Yet I know a person who has it. She diffuses more grace over soap suds than anyone I have ever met. Every church construction needs such a person.

Leadership for Building the Church

After the wonderful picture in Ephesians 2 of barriers broken down, a right-angled foundation, and diverse groups of stones fitted together into one temple, Ephesians 3:1-13 identifies the kind of leadership required for genuine community. Since Eugene has already covered most of this thoroughly, we need only sketch the main components of our pastoral character here, as Ephesians delineates them. With Paul and other leaders in the Church we want to be

> willing to be a prisoner for the sake of others (v. 1);
>
> aware of God's economy (*oikonomia;* see Chapter 3) in conferring grace upon us for the sake of others (v. 2);
>
> receptive to God's mystery (*mustērion,* see Chapter 3) made known by revelation (v. 3);
>
> eager to tell others of God's mystery to help them understand (vv. 3-4);
>
> having a sense of the meta-narrative concerning God's revelation of the mystery and of one's place in that master plan (v. 5);
>
> thoroughly convinced that Gentiles are fellow receivers *(sug-klēronomos),* co-members *(sussōmos),* and partners *(summe-tochos)* of the promise in Christ Jesus through the gospel (v. 6);
>
> attentive to God's power working to make us God's ministers as gifts of grace (v. 7);
>
> humbly acknowledging our unsuitability to have the privilege of proclaiming the unfathomable riches of Christ and thereby of enlightening others spiritually (vv. 8-9);
>
> perceiving that the God who created all things is also the one who now uses us to enlighten others concerning the economy of his mystery hidden from eternity (v. 9);
>
> conscious of the Church's calling to make known to the rulers and authorities in the heavenlies the multifaceted wisdom of God (v. 10; see Chapter 5);
>
> responsive to God's accomplishment of his eternal purpose in Christ Jesus and thereby obedient to him as our Lord (v. 11);

bold and completely confident to approach God through faith in
Christ (v. 12);
able to trust that sufferings, too, are a gift for the sake of those to
whom we minister (v. 13).

Simply by compiling this list from the Greek text, I am overwhelmed at the immensity of the privilege that is ours to serve God by
learning ever more of the wonders of the mystery of God's economy,
by nurturing the Christian community, and by proclaiming God's
Good News to those already participating in it and to those still to be
grafted on to the promise! We become aware of how essential it is that
God's economy involves a community, for none of us can know well
enough by ourselves the multifaceted wisdom of God. God's mystery is
too great for us to grasp, so we always serve as only one part of the entire fellowship of co-participants, co-sharers in God's immense bounty.

Family Relationships as Icons of Community

We have already looked (all too) briefly at Ephesians 5:21-33 to consider how it displays a vision for the character of men and women in
our churches. Now let us glance at it again to reflect on the larger intent of that passage — namely, to form marriages that let us see more
clearly Christ's relationship with his Body, the Church.

This text is particularly poignant for me as the broken-bodied
wife of a husband who does indeed love me as his own body, in imita-
tion of Christ's care for his Church. In our marriage Myron without
doubt is for me an icon through which I see much more clearly the
faithfulness of God in Christ.

We married later in life — and since that time Myron has stood
faithfully by me through my shattered foot; broken, then crippled leg;
numerous times on crutches or in wheelchairs; loss of hearing in one ear;
loss of vision in one eye and then for a while also in the other; cancer and
failing kidneys; failure of nerves in legs and intestinal tract; jaw deterio-
ration and demineralization of upper torso bones; and so forth. Isn't it a
wonder that he has patiently borne all that with me? Consequently, we

celebrate our month-versaries (having had an especially big fling on our 50th and 100th!). Today as I write this, I'm celebrating that it is our 119th-month-and-5-day-versary. During all this time, our marriage has been the most important icon for me of God's patience with my brokennesses, of God's tender care for me, of God's nourishing love.

Ephesians 5:21-33 teaches us that marriage is an icon for the relationship of the Christian community with Christ. Consequently, it urges us to celebrate marriage richly in our life together. How might our consciousness of that importance influence the way we conduct marriage preparation in our churches? or the way we solemnize wedding rites and commemorate marriage anniversaries? How might the image of Christ as the Bridegroom of the Church teach us better to honor and nurture the sexual chastity of single persons in our communities? Both heroic roles[15] — of faithful marriage and chaste singleness — are desperately needed by our sin-sick, lonely, uncommitted, confused society. By demonstrating relationships characterized by mutual submission, true love in its many kinds, and genuinely cleansing forgiveness, the Christian community presents to our neighbors icons that reveal to them the gracious faithfulness of God.

Our culture has made sexual gratification the be-all and end-all of human existence. In contrast to that, the Christian community as an alternative society offers not merely "the nuclear family," nor a prudish rejection of sexual union. We simply know that considering "sex" the source of our fulfillment is an idolatrous illusion.

In contrast, we know that sexual union is the icon of something far greater — the mystery of Christ and the Church. Thus the alternativity of our churches includes not only marriages but also single people and extended families all belonging together as part of a greater whole. In the larger family of the entire congregation, all the adults hold responsibility for the nurturing of all the children.

---

15. My use of the term *heroic* to describe Christian marriage comes from Stanley Hauerwas, "The Public Character of Sex: Marriage as a Heroic Institution," in *A Community of Character: Toward a Constructive Christian Social Ethic* (Notre Dame: University of Notre Dame Press, 1981), pp. 184-93. I extend his term to include single persons who are faithful to God's design for sexual chastity because that role is equally difficult in our society, characterized as it is by family breakdown and sexual idolatries.

This is a very practical matter for the Christian community to discuss and discern together. How many teenagers do we converse with on Sunday mornings? When we "pass the peace of God" to one another in worship, do we reach right over the heads of children to shake the hands only of other adults? (As a guest in all kinds of churches I've noticed that in both friendly gestures and liturgical actions the youngest members of the community are often ignored.) How could each of us instead deliberately nurture a few of our church's children so that they know they are the beloved of God and beloved members of the community in this place? How could we all take more seriously our calling to participate in raising all our parish's children in "the discipline and instruction of the Lord" (Ephesians 6:4)?[16]

If all the relationships in Ephesians 5:21–6:9 were lived as icons revealing God's love for us and the love of the community in which we enfold each other, what a tremendous gift it would be to our neighbors who long for such communal encircling. In a paradigm shift that at the time had national and international implications, churches once learned that Christ's love meant masters would treat their servants no longer as slaves, but as Christian brothers and sisters. What radical gifts could we bring to our neighbors in their struggles concerning relationships if churches could truly learn God's designs for marriages, parenting, single persons, families, and workplace relationships within the whole community of the beloved?

The Community's Vocation and Virtues

The strongest section in Ephesians on community building occurs in chapter 4. Here we find Paul begging the Christians in Ephesus to do exactly what put him in prison! Building on his great text of prayer and praise in 3:14-21, which invites them to know the fullness of

16. For reflections and discussion questions concerning our pastoral and parental heart for nurturing children in our churches, see my book *Is It a Lost Cause? Having the Heart of God for the Church's Children* (Grand Rapids: Wm. B. Eerdmans Publishing Co., 1997).

God's love by being a community ("together with all the saints"), he now earnestly entreats them to fulfill their calling.

> I, therefore, the prisoner in the Lord, earnestly ask you to "live a life that corresponds" (*SD* 66.6) to the calling with which you have been called . . .
>
> Ephesians 4:1

This is a paradigm shift critically important for our churches. People like to make their pastoral leaders feel necessary so that they can cop out of their responsibilities in the "priesthood of all believers." If we rediscover our pastoral call, however, we know that we are merely equippers, prodders, encouragers, and promoters of all the people so that each one fulfills his or her vocation in the Church. Then no one is any more "necessary" than any others, but all are set free to "be Church," to live in a way corresponding to the priesthood to which each Christian has been called.

This is especially important in an age when so many persons' occupations are threatened by the economic and political conglomerates that create such messes in our societies. As gaps between rich and poor get wider and wider throughout the world, as massive corporations pay their top executives exorbitant salaries while workers on the lower end of the spectrum are laid off, as college graduates face the fact that less than half of them will ever find a full-time and permanent job in their chosen fields, as world populations stretch beyond the limits of possibilities for human employment — all these factors and many more make this a rather awful world jobwise.

How refreshing it is, then, that we can make this paradigm shift and help all members in the Church know that their jobs are only secondary, that occupations are only one place where we engage in our *vocation,* which is to bear and display and bequeath the kingdom of God. As Paul explains in 2 Corinthians 5:17, if we are in Christ, *there is* a new creation — the old has passed away and everything has become new. We are made part of God's kingdom reign and thereby serve as ambassadors of it.

When the Gospels recorded the initial preaching of Jesus, the evangelists used the Greek perfect form of the verb, so that his message literally is, "the opportune time has come (and remains) here and the kingdom of God has come (and remains) near" (see, for example, Mark 1:14-15). In his incarnation Christ brought the new creation, the new aeon, into this one — and it remains instituted, so that we can participate in and pass on to others that kingdom now. We live in the meanwhile times, tasting the kingdom Jesus established, but not yet knowing its culmination. Someday, as Revelation 11 tells us, the seventh trumpet will sound and great voices in heaven will shout,

> The kingdom of the world has become the kingdom of our Lord
> and of his Messiah,
> and he will reign forever and ever.

Then all in heaven will fall on their faces before God and worship him, singing,

> We give you thanks, Lord God Almighty
> who are and who were,
> for you have taken your great power
> and begun to reign.
>
> Revelation 11:15, 17

That eschatological vision guides our communal vocation now. Because we know that Christ has inaugurated the kingdom, that it is currently here and functioning, and that someday it will triumph completely, we engage in its presence and purposes now and carry it wherever we go. Unceasingly and Joyfully we are priests of God's kingdom.

How can we who serve in pastoral ways equip all the saints in the community with vision and skills for their ministries as agents of the kingdom? How can we invite the people in our congregations to know that they are priests wherever they go, however they live, whatever they do in their regular employment? We never know how and where and when the kingdom of God might break through into this aeon.

Rediscovering our call leads us to invite our church communities constantly — in our preaching, singing, talking, praying — to receive

229

and rejoice in and revitalize their priesthood. We enfold the people in the lesson of the lamps (see Chapter 7) and set them free to shine. We revel with them in the ways in which God lights our lamps, sets us in our unique lampstand places, and brings people into our house and life. Most of all, we celebrate together the various ways each of us shines with the kingdom of God.

As St. Francis of Assisi once said, "Always share the gospel. When necessary, use words." Those of us with a pastoral call share the good news of the kingdom with skillful, practiced, theologically adept words. Meanwhile, we set others free to realize that they don't have to worry about how they will talk about the kingdom, since God promises to give us the words in our witnessing. Moreover, God uses all of our lives for his purposes if we are practicing his presence and carrying the kingdom wherever we go. What a delight it is that our calling as pastors is to equip the people in our communities with such a sense of their vocation.

The second verse of Ephesians 4 adds this set of virtues to its description of the priesthood of all the saints:

> . . . with all humility and gentleness, with emotional calm in the face of difficulties, being patient with one another in love . . .
>
> Ephesians 4:2

Remember our preludes in Chapter 2. To rediscover our call to equip the whole Christian community for its priesthood requires that we resist the glitz of our culture. We are equipping the saints not with glittering images, but with character — humble recognition that we aren't necessary, gentleness of attitude and behavior, the ability to suffer long and to forbear — so that we all can carry the kingdom by *who* we are in the world and for the world.

The Call to Preserve God's Unity

Here is another paradox critical to our call: on the one hand, God has already created the unity of the Church, so we are totally unnecessary;

on the other hand, we are challenged in the letter to the Ephesians to do all we can to preserve that unity. Humility and gentleness, patience and forbearance issue in

> . . . doing "your best to preserve the unity which the Spirit gives" (*SD* 68.63) in the bonds of peace.
>
> Ephesians 4:3

Maintaining unity requires constant attention and zealous effort since there are many powers working against it and sinful human desires and behaviors disrupting it. To continue participating in God's *shalom* demands the commitment of the whole community — all of us caring about it together, reconciling with each other, watching over one another, exhorting each other, being committed to one another over the long haul.

Robert Wuthnow, a wonderful Christian sociologist at Princeton, has discovered in his research on small groups in the United States that by and large most of them are not truly supportive in the truest sense of that word. Most groups become simply places to be coddled and to share feelings without objections. If people are rebuked or admonished by others in the group in order to be held accountable, they often leave for another group that is "more supportive."[17] To be unified in God's Spirit does not mean merely to pat each other on the back and continue with our own gluttonies and idolatries.

Truly to be unified is to be joined in common bonds, the *shalom* of God that brooks no false gods, including the god of comfort bought at the price of deception concerning, or dilution of, real disagreements. The Christian community measures its unity constantly against the scriptural narratives in order to discern the Spirit's true bonds, and members hold each other accountable when our unity is fractured by unbiblical attitudes, utterances, choices, or conduct.

In keeping with primary values in our culture, we have become a

---

17. See Robert Wuthnow, *Sharing the Journey* (New York: Free Press, 1994).

society of "church shoppers," with congregation members looking for the parish that "meets their needs" best, changing churches to "get more upbeat music," leaving a community if it holds them accountable, participating wherever they feel most comfortable. This is not what it means to "be Church." We are led astray by the vocabulary of marketing used with reference to churches; the sooner we can flush its ideas out of people's minds the better.

Discipleship is not something to be marketed, a commodity to buy. Churches are not "vendor[s] of religious goods and services" that cater to people's needs and whims, choices and tastes. Rather, the Church is commissioned to be "a body of people sent on a mission."[18] We therefore need to nurture a missional people who are in it together for the long haul and won't leave when the going gets tough. When conflicts or tensions, messes or problems erupt, these create a very good time to learn what it really means to be a community — provided we expend the energy required to process the situation thoroughly and biblically.

Celebrating Our Unity

The following three verses of Ephesians 4 are almost better danced than read. Each noun in the text is a deep symbol, carrying an entire ballet of many aspects of the Christian community's life together. God's unity in us is composed, first of all, of

> one body and one Spirit, just as also you were called into one hope of your calling.
>
> Ephesians 4:4

18. See George Hunsberger, "Sizing Up the Shape of the Church," in *The Church Between Gospel and Culture: The Emerging Mission in North America,* ed. George R. Hunsberger and Craig Van Gelder (Grand Rapids: Wm. B. Eerdmans Publishing Co., 1996), pp. 333-46. This book is the first in a series of resources from the Gospel and Our Culture Network for recovering "missional churches." Other resources from the Network include Darrell L. Guder, ed., *Missional Church: A Vision for the Sending of the Church in North America* (Grand Rapids: Wm. B. Eerdmans Publishing Co., 1998), and Craig Van Gelder, ed., *Confident Witness — Changing World* (see note 10 above). For information on the Network itself, contact Judy Bos, Administrator, or Dr. George R. Hunsberger, Coordinator, The Gospel and Our Culture Network, 101 E. 13th St., Holland, MI 49423-3622.

Imagine a triangle with each noun phrase at a corner. The one Spirit is too great, of course, for us to discuss thoroughly at this point, but let the name cause us to marvel at the Holy Spirit's wondrous works. For starters, how the Spirit can bring such an odd conglomeration of people together into one Body is certainly a divine mystery.

one Body   one Spirit

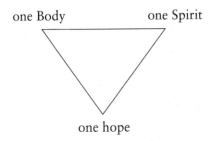

one hope

Some Christians have the mistaken notion that we ought all to like each other in our churches, but sometimes I think God purposely puts us together with people we can't stand to give us practice in learning to love our enemies. We are totally unnecessary for the creation of the Body of Christ; it is entirely the Spirit's work, despite our choices and machinations. One wonders what the Spirit might accomplish with our calling if we listened more closely to God's criteria before "choosing a church."

What might Paul mean here by the "one hope of [our] calling," a phrase he used also in 1:18? Again, we have to dance it because the New Testament is full of images to describe our eternal hope (beyond earthly hopes of rescue or companionship). We have hope in God (1 Peter 1:21), particularly in

> the hope of the gospel, which was preached (Colossians 1:23);
> the hope of righteousness by faith (Galatians 5:5);
> hope that God will not abandon us (Psalm 16, quoted in Acts 2);
> hope that God will instead keep his promises (Acts 26:6-7);
> hope that in nothing we will be ashamed, but that Christ will be magnified in our bodies, both in life and in death (Philippians 1:20);

hope for consolation in these meanwhile times (2 Corinthians
   1:7);

the hope of salvation (1 Thessalonians 5:8);

hope for resurrection (Acts 23:6; 24:15) because of Christ's resurrection (1 Peter 1:3);

hope unto the end (Hebrews 3:6; 6:11) and for grace then (1 Peter 1:13);

that blessed hope in the glorious appearing of the great God and
   our Savior Jesus Christ (Titus 2:13);

hope laid up in heaven (Colossians 1:5) and hope of eternal life
   (Titus 1:2; 3:7).

All of these are summed up in the truth that Jesus Christ is our
hope (1 Timothy 1:1) and that we have the hope of the glory of God
(Romans 5:2) because of Christ in us (Colossians 1:27). Everyone in
the Body is united by the Spirit's communication of this common hope,
that in Christ we participate in the fulfillment of all God's promises.

The second person of the Trinity offers us a second triad (imagine
it as another triangle), composed of

one Lord, one faith, one baptism.

Ephesians 4:5

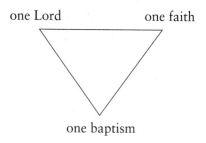

Our common faith is centered in the work that Jesus did on our behalf, in his revelation of all that the Triune God really is and does in relationship with us. We have entered into the community of those who believe in Jesus through our baptism, by which we drowned with Christ

and were raised to this new communal life in him and by his presence within us. As we dance with these deep symbols, we celebrate that our faith is in this one Lord Jesus Christ and that baptism puts him into us.

There are many ways in which we could explore the images in this song about Christian unity. The point is that each term represents entire doctrines concerning our life together. These verses give us all kinds of concepts by which we can be united and standards by which we can resist what would fracture the community.

We could indeed survey the range of biblical expressions for faith, as we did for hope, and we would find a diverse array of images, similes, and metaphors, centering in Jesus Christ and his work to bring us into relationship with the Triune God. Similarly, we could investigate various denominational understandings of baptism and the special contributions of each.

Instead, let us yearn for the day when our baptism into faith in Jesus Christ unites Christians throughout the globe, for truly we have all put off our old person by baptismal death with the same Jesus (Ephesians 4:22). We are being renewed daily by the same Spirit of Jesus and his Father (4:23). We are putting on the same new person by means of Christ living in and through us (4:24). All baptized Christians throughout time and space are part of the same community named Church. Jesus wants to lead us all into awareness of our one common faith and of our common way of life; he said that his work includes bringing together all the sheep from other folds so that there can be one flock following the voice of one shepherd (John 10:16).

We are instead abhorrently divided. At first the one, holy, catholic, apostolic Church separated into denominational differences, based on theological variations. Now we seem to be polarized more by moral choices and worship styles, and the splits often run through the middle of denominations.

We are called to preserve the unity that the Spirit gives in bonds of true peace. How can we learn to work together as much as possible across denominational lines to display the oneness that Jesus said would reveal to the world that his Father had sent him (John 17:21)? How can we learn to distinguish between disagreements that violate the faith and those that are less important, so that we are not so divided as to cause offense in our witness to the world? How can we learn to discuss all the complexities of our moral differences more thoroughly, gently, attentively, Spirit-inspiredly, biblically, compassionately, faithfully?

The final verse of this deep symbol dance presents an unusual triad of prepositions instead of nouns. The Christian community is knit together by

> one God and Father of all, the one above all and through all and in all.
>
> Ephesians 4:6

The Father is constantly creating the community, for he is above, through, and in everything to bring all together. We are able to keep pursuing community and maintaining it because in its genesis we are totally unnecessary. Mentioning the Father in this sixth verse completes the triangle of the Trinity, begun in verse 4.

More than twenty years ago I was struck by R. C. H. Lenski's observation that in Ephesians 4:4-6 Paul lists nine items (in an arresting way with no connectives or verbs, simply to point to facts that form the basis of our unity), but uses the word *one* seven times. Lenski stressed that both numbers did not seem to be accidental, for nine as a composite of 3 × 3 thoroughly underscores the Trinity as the basis for our unity in the Christian community. Furthermore, the seven (the Jewish number for perfection) combines three (the Trinity) with four (the number symbolizing the whole earth in Jewish thought), so it brings together God and his people in the most important unity of all.[19]

A few years later I developed the drawing at the top of the next page to illustrate this stunning celebration of the basis for our unity in the Trinity (represented by the three triangles) and of the joining of human beings with God (represented by the seven dots standing for each use of the word *one*).

---

19. R. C. H. Lenski, *The Interpretation of St. Paul's Epistles to the Galatians, Ephesians, and Philippians* (Minneapolis: Augsburg Publishing House, 1937), pp. 510-11.

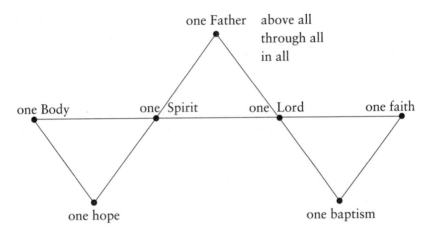

Again, remember that this dance through substantial symbols frees us from thinking we are necessary. The body, faith, hope, and baptismal life (the four dimensions of human unity) are already there in the unity of the Trinity. Harmony and partnership and congruence exist between the persons of the Triune God, who invites us into that intimacy and into what God is doing for us and in us, through us and beyond us. If we keep remembering that our unity already exists in God, then we can trust that as the Triune God expands his grace into and through his people, we are surely united in God's own unity.

The Gifts of the Community

This unity in the Body of Christ is supported by his gifting. Just as we begin to wonder how to participate in preserving the unity so wonderfully sketched in verses 4-6, we discover that this, too, depends on grace.

> But to each one of us has been given grace according to the measure of the gift of Christ. Therefore it says,
>
>> Having ascended on high, "he took many captives with him" [SD 55.24],
>>
>> he gave gifts to human beings.

(But what does "he ascended" mean if not that he also descended into the lower parts of the earth? He who descended is also the one having ascended far above all the heavens, in order that he might fill all things.) And he appointed some [to be] apostles, some [as] prophets, some evangelists, and some pastors and teachers . . .

Ephesians 4:7-11

What a glorious hymn of praise this section adds to the previous trinitarian dance over unity! The entire gospel of the incarnation, the triumph of Christ over the powers, the ascension, and the sending of the Spirit is sketched as the basis for the assurance that each of us in Christ's Body has been gifted with a fullness of his grace. Moreover, we never have to be jealous of others in the Body because each of us has received grace according to the measure of God's gift to us in Christ. I take that to mean that the measure is totally complete for each one because each baptized believer has Christ dwelling in him or her in all his plenitude.

What a spectacular result it is for the people of God that we can be set free from any envy of each other. If you have received the fullness of Christ and I have, too, then what does it matter if Christ is displayed in and through you by means of gifts that I don't have? Christ himself is the greatest gift, and we each have a fullness of him, no matter how that grace is present in, for, with, and through us.

I learned this from my friend Tim, with whom I had long talks (when we lived in the same town) while he was on his kidney dialysis runs. Once, many years ago, when I came back from a retreat and was pouring out all my excitement to him on the telephone, he listened kindly while I jabbered on and on. When I finally paused for breath, he said, "I am SO glad that we are in the community together." I asked, "Why?" and he replied, "Because all those things you said — I own them, too!"

What could happen if we would invite our churches into such genuine sharing (without envy), such mutual rejoicing and sincere celebration of the blessings others have received? How could we set each person free to use his or her own gifts without thought for how they compare with those of someone else? What would happen if our entire congregations were cognizant of the possibilities there could be if we all lived more grace-fully — that is, if each member displayed freely "the measure of the gift of Christ" that he or she possessed, if each person in the community knew that as grace is received, so it can be freely passed on for the sake of the rest of the community?[20]

To highlight the gifts of all the members of the community gracefully is not to treat people as their functions. Rather, it is to help Christians discover the supreme Joy of freely offering their spiritual gifts, of discovering more fully who they really are, of living more wholly as the people of God. The Scriptures convince us that life is the most fulfilling, the most delightful when we use our spiritual gifts and know the grace of God at work in and through us. Wouldn't it be glorious (refer to our discussion of "glory" in Chapter 2!) if all the people in our congregations knew that what we really want for them is that they truly enjoy being *themselves,* truly themselves as God has gifted them through the presence of Christ?

As I have been working on this Ephesians 4 text since the Regent conference that gave rise to this book, I have been more and more overwhelmed by the consummate appropriateness of the Psalm 68 quotation in this passage:

> Having ascended on high, "he took many captives with him"
> [SD 55.24],
> > he gave gifts to human beings.
> > > Psalm 68:18a, as quoted in Ephesians 4:8

The psalm itself is a troublesome one, as the commentators all insist. It contains several words that appear nowhere else in the First Testament, and it includes diverse materials that don't seem to belong together. Why would Paul choose to put this odd quotation (actually in a

---

20. This evoking and sharing of spiritual gifts is explored more thoroughly in my book *Truly the Community,* especially chapters 11-15 (pp. 92-138). The pastoral work of equipping the congregation for such gift-evoking will be delineated further in my *The Sense of the Call: Kingdom Shalom for Those Who Serve the Church* (Grand Rapids: Wm. B. Eerdmans Publishing Co., forthcoming).

form found only in the Aramaic Targum[21]) in the midst of a passage about gifts?

One very promising direction in interpretation is given by Robert Davidson's perception that

> however we divide the psalm, each section within it seems to focus in a variety of different ways on the triumph of God, past, present, and future. There is something of a watershed in the language used at the end of verse 18. In the first part of the psalm, the dominant note is that of the God who comes, with language such as, "Let God rise up" (v. 1), "God gives . . . leads" (v. 6), "went out . . . marched" (v. 7), "came from Sinai" (v. 17), and "ascended" (v. 18). After verse 18 the emphasis is more on the presence of God with his people, the God "who daily bears us up" (v. 19), the God who is "in his sanctuary" (vv. 24-25), "in the great congregation" (v. 26), and "in the temple at Jerusalem" (v. 29). (211)

For Psalm 68 these two parts hold together the complementary theological emphases of "the God who is on the march, ever active, going before his people, and the God who stays in their midst, meeting with his people in the beauty of holiness" (211).

Paul's reasons, then, could perhaps be to tie together the theological idea from which we just came — of the Triune God ever active in forming the Body in unity (vv. 4-6) — and the notion toward which we are going — that the Triune God stays in the midst of the people through the gifts he gives them according to the measure of Christ and by the anointing of the Holy Spirit for the Body to be upbuilt (vv. 7-16).

Whether such ideas were part of his reasons or not, we can be sure that Paul chose the passage for its emphasis on ascension, for by doing so he links the First Testament highlighting of God's triumphs, as accentuated by such poetic lines as Psalm 68:18 or "God has gone up with a shout" (Psalm 47:5), to the ascension of Christ as the crowning point of his entire salvific work (see Chapter 7).

---

21. Robert Davidson, *The Vitality of Worship: A Commentary on the Book of Psalms* (Grand Rapids: Wm. B. Eerdmans Publishing Co., 1998), p. 214. Page references to this book in the following paragraphs are given parenthetically in the text.

Paul delineates elements of that salvific work in his elaborate parenthetical comment,

> (But what does "he ascended" mean if not that he also descended into the lower parts of the earth? He who descended is also the one having ascended far above all the heavens, in order that he might fill all things.)
>
> Ephesians 4:9-10

By stating that Christ "descended into the lower parts of the earth," this passage seems primarily to be proclaiming the incarnation, but could Paul also or instead be connoting the descent to the dead (suggesting the extent of his suffering) or the descent into hell, to the "spirits in prison" of 1 Peter 3:19 (suggesting his total triumph over all the powers; see Chapter 5)? And is he implying the pouring out of the Spirit in noting the ascension "in order that he might fill all things"?

Perhaps I read too much into Paul's cryptic parenthetical remark, but it seems to hint at entire doctrines elaborated in comments elsewhere in his letters. However, the fact that verse 11 goes on with

> And he appointed some [to be] apostles, some [as] prophets, some evangelists, and some pastors and teachers . . .

seems to lead us into Pentecost, for those who followed Jesus heard him promise them just before he ascended that they would "receive power when the Holy Spirit has come upon you" (Acts 1:8). Prior to that, on the evening of his resurrection, Jesus had commanded them, "I am sending upon you what my Father promised; so stay here in the city until you have been clothed with power from on high" (Luke 24:49). Thus the fulfilling of their roles and ours in the Body is only possible because of his ascension and subsequent gifting.

Christ Gave You as a Gift to the Church

The final section we will consider begins with that appointment of the various leaders of the Church. The emphasis in verse 11 is not so much

241

on the *giving* of some to be this or that, but on the *one who gave* or *appointed* them. Because Christ gave pastors and teachers, you and I are gifts to the Church! What a wonderful encouragement this is — both a reminder that we are unnecessary and a way to rediscover our call!

First let me focus on its encouragement because some of you reading this book might be very dejected by the difficulties of your present call. How can I tell you how much I admire you? I served in two different parishes after finishing my M.A. in English and during/after earning my M.Div. — so I partially know in some ways how discouraging it can be. But the times are much harder now; the expectations seem to be more mistaken. Sometimes I wonder if I am called into the freelance ministry that I do because I'm not strong enough to do what you pastors are doing. You are there! And you're sticking it out, in spite of many false expectations and a culture quite inimical to genuine pastoring! Let me remind you that *you are a gift* to the church you serve!

Christ gave you, appointed you, as a gift to your church and the whole Church. Nobody can take away that divine call. When the gift of you is shoved aside, the pushers are not thrusting you away. They are rejecting the One who sent you. That might not help very much to make you feel any better, but it is true.

When the surface reality looks like a tangle of all the messes in the church, the truth underneath it is that God gave you as a gift. Knowing that you are Christ's gift can liberate you in a way. You might still be in a prison of muddled expectations, but your spirit can soar free in the confidence that God has not put you there fruitlessly, that your labor in the Lord is not in vain. Your freedom might be release from some principalities and powers that get you down; you might recognize enough truth to help you expose what is going on so that you can freely be the gift to God's people that God has called you to be.

The rest of the passage makes more clear what your role is as such a gift and the result for the people in the Body. Christ appointed some to be apostles, prophets, evangelists, pastors, and teachers

> [12]*in order to* prepare the saints fully *for* [their] work of service, *for* building up the body of Christ, [13]until we all attain to the unity of

the faith and of the full knowledge of the Son of God, to mature manhood, to the measure of the stature of the completeness of Christ, 14in order that we may no longer be children tossed to and fro by the waves and carried about by every wind of teaching, by people's trickery in deceitful scheming, 15but speaking the truth in love that we might grow in every way into him who is the head, [even] Christ, 16from whom the whole body, being joined together and knit together by every ligament with which it is supplied, according to the proper working of each part, causes the growth of the body for building itself up in love.

Ephesians 4:11-16

Verse 12 is one of the clearest descriptions of your pastoral role in all the Bible, but it is often confused because of the old King James translation, which rendered all three of the verse's prepositions with the word *for*. Newer versions use "in order to" for the Greek *pros* and "for" for the Greek *eis,* in order to distinguish between the pastoral work of equipping the saints and the saints' work of service or ministry *(ergon diakonias).* If what we do as pastors and teachers is to equip the saints or prepare them fully (SD 75.5), then primarily we are working ourselves out of a job.

This is one of the wisest things my father ever told me (and he is one of the greatest teachers I have ever had). The night before I began my first teaching job at the University of Idaho he told me over the telephone, "It is really dangerous if you think your role is to be indispensable. Your role is to equip people with skills so that they don't need you anymore."

As a pastor you train the people with skills for prayer, for studying the Bible and teaching it to their children, so that they can engage in spiritual practices in their homes. You prepare them to evangelize by giving them an ever larger vision of God. You enable them to fulfill their mission in the world by modeling your own sense of mission.

This call to equip the saints is one of the main reasons why I am troubled so deeply by the present confusion between worship and evangelism, for worship is a primary place where pastors equip the saints for *their work* of evangelism, of being Church to bring the gospel to their neighbors.[22] Just think how our churches would grow (deeper and perhaps, but not necessarily, larger) if all the saints fulfilled their ministries in building up the Body! We equip them for their work not only by leading in worship, but also in the classes we teach, the manner in which we are present with them, the practices in which we engage them, and the expressions we have for reminding them that they are saints, the beloved baptized of God, gifted persons created in God's image.

I saw a beautiful example of preparing someone for ministry at the concert I attended with some of the Regent conference participants. Pepe Romero, one of the world's most famous classical guitarists (and a member of the great Romero family of guitarists) played a duo concerto with Alexander Dunn, one of his students. Before the concert began, I had barely enough time to skim the descriptions of the two men's backgrounds, without looking at their pictures. Throughout their performance I had the two of them reversed in my mind because Alexander played the first part, and Pepe kept looking over at him with an expression that seemed to say, "Wow! I wish I could do that." It was Pepe, the teacher, affirming his student's skills and letting him shine. Only when Pepe played some encores after the concerto did I realize who he was and what an amazing guitarist he is.

The concert taught me a stupendous lesson in the way Pepe joyfully and fearlessly let the other person shine. Oh that we would be evokers and equippers like that! Oh that we could draw out the best in other people (without jealousy or feelings of threat) so that they could find their greatest Joy in doing the work of their ministry!

Verse 13 is frequently misunderstood. I have often heard people say something like, "I really have to work to come to that 'mature manhood in the faith.'" Such a comment ignores both that God is the one who makes us mature and that this is the goal for *y'all*, not just one person. Verse 13 is not about individual personhood. It is about the maturity of the whole Body, which is why I keep the word *manhood,* since it is Christ's Body and he is the measure of the Body's stat-

22. See especially chapter 9, "Don't Let the People Cop Out of Witnessing," and chapters 29-30, "Worship to Form a Missional Community" and "Always Be Ready to Give an Account," in *A Royal "Waste" of Time,* pp. 120-34 and 333-52.

ure. It is the unity of the faith, the true knowledge of the Son of God that will lead us all together into the mature completeness of Christ.

None of us reaches maturity by ourselves; it is the community that enfolds us and nourishes us, and the community becomes more unified when we learn this together. Paul accentuates this in verse 15 by underscoring the importance of our being truthful in everything in love toward each other so that the whole Body can grow toward its Head, Christ.

Verse 14 also underscores the importance of our pastoral and teacherly call to equip the saints, so that the Body becomes wise enough to be no longer "children tossed to and fro by the waves and carried about by every wind of teaching, by people's trickery in deceitful scheming." We live in an age with a wide variety of genres of waves and winds, of false (and sometimes satanically dangerous) teaching, of many sorts of dishonesties, hypocrisies, strategies, treacheries. Of course, all the members in the Body contribute to the wisdom that helps the community not to be childish, but pastors are especially trained and practiced in spiritual wisdom, so we must take seriously the importance of our equipping call to enable the Church's members to swim against the tides of streams inimical to the gospel.

Most of the verses in this last passage for our consideration here enable us to rediscover the pastoral call, but verse 16 primarily reminds us that ultimately we are no more necessary than anyone else in the Body. However, it took me a very long time to unravel this verse's riddle:

> . . . from whom the whole body, being joined together and knit together by every ligament with which it is supplied, according to the proper working of each part, causes the growth of the body for building itself up in love.

The problem with the text is this: What is the subject of the verb *causes?*

I shouldn't have had so much trouble with that question, but I resisted looking at any English translations because I wanted to unravel the complexities of Paul's Greek theological stacking. Finally I realized that the subject of the phrase "causes the growth of the body" is "the whole body" or "all [the parts of] the body." Though at first it seemed

I wasn't following the Greek right in deducing that the "body causes the growth of the body," I began to see that this does make sense — the cells of our own body cause the body to grow. Furthermore, this discovery leads us to a final mystery.

Once again we reach this paradox: we all cause the growth of the Body, but we are totally unnecessary. Think of your own body. Your cells produce more cells, but how are they able to do that? All the growth that comes inherently from the body's parts must ultimately be attributed to the Great Designer, the Creator of the universe who so fashioned us that we could exist and develop in this way.

Even so, Ephesians makes this clear in the connection of verses 15 and 16:

> . . . that we might grow in every way into *him who is the head, [even] Christ, from whom* the whole body, being joined together and knit together by every ligament with which it is supplied, according to the proper working of each part, causes the growth of the body for building itself up in love.

Every ligament does its knitting, every joint does its jointy thing, but everything depends on "him who is the head, Christ, from whom" the Body is able to function as a Body and grow.

We are back to where we started — with the need for this great paradigm shift: that every single person in our churches would know that she or he is absolutely essential for the well-being of the whole. That realization takes us even further back to the beginning of Ephesians with its doxology — that none of us is necessary, none of us can take credit for what is utterly dependent upon the Trinity's work for us and in us and through us.

You don't need me to tell you this, for we all know these things. But perhaps this reminder will encourage you to remember yourself and not to give up communicating these two truths to all of God's people:

Everything depends upon God, so we are unnecessary.
God nevertheless uses us, so let us each and together rediscover our call.

From Christ we receive the possibility of being parts of the Body. By his Spirit we are empowered to work properly according to the part of the Body that we are by the Father's call. But when we fulfill that call, we cause the growth of the Body. We all build the Body up in love. If this book evokes such ministry from you, the pastor or pastoral person, then you will evoke it from others. Praise be to God!

This dialectic is strengthened when we review these main themes we've sketched from Ephesians:

1. Doxology shows us that everything is grace, that we can't do ministry by ourselves, that we really are unnecessary.
2. The principalities and powers pull us away from our role, make us think that we are necessary, cause us to forget or confuse our call, and take what is good and stretch it beyond its proper functioning.
3. The biblical narratives show us how unnecessary we are to the culture around us, form us in that unnecessary role, and teach us and remind us of God's design for our call.
4. As a community, we discover even more that we are unnecessary, for everything depends on the One who is our Head, even Christ. Meanwhile, we also learn that each one of us matters supremely because we are part of the whole, the Body of Christ, and participants in its growth.

May these truths together lead to a revitalization of the various communities that make up the Church — a cosmic Body that is an alternative, parallel society offering the world exactly what it needs! Thanks be to God!

Let us pray: O Triune God, your Word is truth. Let us all continue in that Word together so that we may truly be your disciples and know your truth. May we be formed by your Word to live its truth freely, to be the Church and the Church's servants that you have designed and called us to be. We long for this. Give us the courage and hope never to give up on it. Amen.

For Further Reading

Balthasar, Hans Urs von. *Bernanos*. San Francisco: Ignatius Press, 1996.

———. *The Glory of God*, volume 3. San Francisco: Ignatius Press, 1986.

Banks, Robert. *Redeeming the Routines*. Grand Rapids: Baker Books, 1993.

———. *The Tyranny of Time: When 24 Hours Is Not Enough*. Eugene, OR: Wipf and Stock Publishers, 1997.

Barth, Karl. *The Christian Life: Church Dogmatics IV, 4 Lecture Fragments*. Translated by Geoffrey W. Bromiley. Grand Rapids: Wm. B. Eerdmans Publishing Co., 1981.

Braaten, Carl E., and Robert W. Jenson, eds. *Union with Christ: The New Finnish Interpretation of Luther*. Grand Rapids: Wm. B. Eerdmans Publishing Co., 1998.

Brueggemann, Walter. *Finally Comes the Poet: Daring Speech for Proclamation*. Minneapolis: Fortress Press, 1989.

———. *Theology of the Old Testament: Testimony, Dispute, Advocacy*. Minneapolis: Fortress Press, 1997.

Burrows, William. "Witness to the Gospel and Refounding the Church." In *Confident Witness — Changing World*, pp. 189-202. Edited by Craig Van Gelder. Grand Rapids: Wm. B. Eerdmans Publishing Co., 1999.

Clapp, Rodney. *A Peculiar People: The Church as Culture in a Post-Christian Society.* Downers Grove, IL: InterVarsity Press, 1996.

————, ed. *The Consuming Passion: Christianity and the Consumer Culture.* Downers Grove, IL: InterVarsity Press, 1998.

Coupland, Douglas. *Generation X: Tales for an Accelerated Culture.* New York: St. Martin's Press, 1991.

————. *Life after God.* New York: Simon and Schuster, 1994.

Covington, Denis. *Salvation on Sand Mountain.* New York: Addison-Wesley, 1995.

Davidson, Robert. *The Vitality of Worship: A Commentary on the Book of Psalms.* Grand Rapids: Wm. B. Eerdmans Publishing Co., 1998.

Dawn, Marva J. "The Concept of 'The Principalities and Powers' in the Works of Jacques Ellul." Ph.D. dissertation, University of Notre Dame, 1992.

————. "Hermeneutical Considerations for Biblical Texts." In *Different Voices/Shared Vision: Male and Female in the Trinitarian Community.* Edited by Paul Hinlicky. New Delhi, NY: American Lutheran Publicity Bureau, 1992.

————. *I'm Lonely, LORD — How Long? Meditations on the Psalms.* Revised edition. Grand Rapids: Wm. B. Eerdmans Publishing Co., 1998.

————. *Is It a Lost Cause? Having the Heart of God for the Church's Children.* Grand Rapids: Wm. B. Eerdmans Publishing Co., 1997.

————. *Joy in Our Weakness: A Gift of Hope from the Book of Revelation.* St. Louis: Concordia Publishing House, 1994.

————. *Keeping the Sabbath Wholly: Ceasing, Resting, Embracing, Feasting.* Grand Rapids: Wm. B. Eerdmans Publishing Co., 1989.

————. "I Timothy 2:8-15." In *Different Voices/Shared Vision: Male and Female in the Trinitarian Community.* Edited by Paul Hinlicky. Delhi, NY: American Lutheran Publicity Bureau, 1992.

————. *Reaching Out without Dumbing Down: A Theology of Worship for the Turn-of-the-Century Culture.* Grand Rapids: Wm. B. Eerdmans Publishing Co., 1995.

————. *A Royal "Waste" of Time: The Splendor of Worshiping God and Being Church for the World.* Grand Rapids: Wm. B. Eerdmans Publishing Co., 1999.

———. *The Sense of the Call: Kingdom Shalom for Those Who Serve the Church.* Grand Rapids: Wm. B. Eerdmans Publishing Co., forthcoming.

———. *Sexual Character: Beyond Technique to Intimacy.* Grand Rapids: Wm. B. Eerdmans Publishing Co., 1993.

———. *To Walk and Not Faint: A Month of Meditations on Isaiah 40.* Second edition. Grand Rapids: Wm. B. Eerdmans Publishing Co., 1997.

———. *Truly the Community: Romans 12 and How to Be the Church.* Grand Rapids: Wm. B. Eerdmans Publishing Co., 1992; reissued 1997.

Ellul, Jacques. *A Critique of the New Commonplaces.* Translated by Helen Weaver. New York: Alfred A. Knopf, 1968.

———. *The Ethics of Freedom.* Translated and edited by Geoffrey W. Bromiley. Grand Rapids: Wm. B. Eerdmans Publishing Co., 1976.

———. *The Humiliation of the Word.* Translated by Joyce Main Hanks. Grand Rapids: Wm. B. Eerdmans Publishing Co., 1985.

———. *Money and Power.* Translated by LaVonne Neff. Downers Grove, IL: InterVarsity Press, 1984.

———. *The New Demons.* Translated by C. Edward Hopkin. New York: Seabury Press, 1975.

———. *The Political Illusion.* Translated by Konrad Kellen. New York: Alfred A. Knopf, 1967.

———. *The Politics of God and the Politics of Man.* Translated by Geoffrey W. Bromiley. Grand Rapids: Wm. B. Eerdmans Publishing Co., 1972.

———. *The Presence of the Kingdom.* Translated by Olive Wyon. New York: Seabury Press, 1967.

———. *Propaganda: The Formation of Men's Attitudes.* Translated by Konrad Kellen and Jean Lerner. New York: Alfred A. Knopf, 1965.

———. *Sources and Trajectories: Eight Early Articles by Jacques Ellul*

That Set the Stage. Translated and edited by Marva J. Dawn. Grand Rapids: Wm. B. Eerdmans Publishing Co., 1997.

———. *The Subversion of Christianity.* Translated by Geoffrey W. Bromiley. Grand Rapids: Wm. B. Eerdmans Publishing Co., 1986.

———. *The Technological Bluff.* Translated by Joyce Main Hanks. Grand Rapids: Wm. B. Eerdmans Publishing Co., 1990.

———. *The Technological Society.* Translated by John Wilkinson. New York: Vintage Books, 1964.

———. *The Technological System.* Translated by Joachim Neugroschel. New York: Continuum Publishing Co., 1980.

Farley, Edward. *Deep Symbols: Their Postmodern Effacement and Reclamation.* Valley Forge, PA: Trinity Press International, 1996.

Fee, Gordon. *1 and 2 Timothy, Titus.* A Good News Commentary. San Francisco: Harper & Row, 1984.

Fore, William F. *Television and Religion: The Shaping of Faith, Values, and Culture.* Minneapolis: Augsburg, 1987.

Fretheim, Terrence. *The Suffering of God.* Minneapolis: Augsburg-Fortress, 1984.

Gaventa, Beverly R. "He Comes as One Unknown," in "The Challenge of Christmas: Two Views." *Christian Century* 110, no. 36 (15 Dec. 1993): 1270-80.

Greenberg, David. *The Construction of Homosexuality.* Chicago: University of Chicago Press, 1988.

Guder, Darrell L., ed. *Missional Church: A Vision for the Sending of the Church in North America.* Grand Rapids: Wm. B. Eerdmans Publishing Co., 1998.

Hall, Douglas John. "Metamorphosis: From Christendom to Diaspora." In *Confident Witness — Changing World,* pp. 67-79. Edited by Craig Van Gelder. Grand Rapids: Wm. B. Eerdmans Publishing Co., 1999.

Hansen, David. *The Art of Pastoring: Ministry* Without *All the Answers.* Downers Grove, IL: InterVarsity Press, 1994.

Hauerwas, Stanley. *A Community of Character: Toward a Constructive Christian Social Ethic.* Notre Dame: University of Notre Dame Press, 1981.

Havel, Miroslav Václav. *Living in Truth.* Edited by Jon Vladislav. London and Boston: Faber and Faber, 1989.

―――. *Open Letters: Selected Writings 1965-1990.* Edited by Paul Wilson. New York: Alfred A. Knopf, 1991.

Hays, Richard B. *The Moral Vision of the New Testament: A Contemporary Introduction to New Testament Ethics.* San Francisco: HarperSanFrancisco, 1996.

Healy, Jane M. *Endangered Minds: Why Our Children Don't Think.* New York: Simon and Schuster, 1990.

―――. *Failure to Connect: How Computers Affect Our Children's Minds — For Better and Worse.* New York: Simon and Schuster, 1998.

Hinlicky, Paul, ed. *Different Voices/Shared Vision: Male and Female in the Trinitarian Community.* Delhi, NY: American Lutheran Publicity Bureau, 1992.

Howatch, Susan. *Glittering Images.* New York: Alfred A. Knopf, 1987.

Hunsberger, George. "Sizing Up the Shape of the Church." In *The Church Between Gospel and Culture: The Emerging Mission in North America,* pp. 333-46. Edited by George R. Hunsberger and Craig Van Gelder. Grand Rapids: Wm. B. Eerdmans Publishing Co., 1996.

―――, and Craig Van Gelder, eds. *The Church Between Gospel and Culture: The Emerging Mission in North America.* Grand Rapids: Wm. B. Eerdmans Publishing Co., 1996.

Job, Rueben P., and Norman Shawchuck, eds. *A Guide to Prayer: For Ministers and Other Servants.* Nashville: The Upper Room, 1983.

Johnson, Luke Timothy. *Living Jesus: Learning the Heart of the Gospel.* San Francisco: HarperSanFrancisco, 1999.

―――. "The New Testament and the Examined Life: Thoughts on Teaching." *Christian Century* 112, no. 4 (1-8 February 1995): 108ff.

―――. *The Real Jesus Is the Christ of Faith.* San Francisco: HarperSanFrancisco, 1997.

Kelly, J. N. D. *A Commentary on the Pastoral Epistles*. London: Adam and Charles Black, 1963.

Kenneson, Philip, and James Street. *Selling Out the Church: The Dangers of Church Marketing*. Nashville: Abingdon Press, 1997.

Kroeger, Richard Clark, and Catherine Clark Kroeger. *I Suffer Not a Woman: Rethinking I Timothy 2:11-15 in Light of Ancient Evidence*. Grand Rapids: Baker Book House, 1992.

Leddy, Mary Jo. "The People of God as a Hermeneutic of the Gospel." In *Confident Witness — Changing World*, pp. 303-13. Edited by Craig Van Gelder. Grand Rapids: Wm. B. Eerdmans Publishing Co., 1999.

Lenski, R. C. H. *The Interpretation of St. Paul's Epistles to the Galatians, Ephesians, and Philippians*. Minneapolis: Augsburg Publishing House, 1937.

Lewis, C. S. *The Abolition of Man*. New York: Macmillan, 1947.

Lindbeck, George. *The Nature of Doctrine: Religion and Theology in a Postliberal Age*. Philadelphia: Westminster Press, 1984.

Louw, Johannes P., and Eugene A. Nida, eds. *Greek-English Lexicon of the New Testament Based on Semantic Domains*. New York: United Bible Societies, 1988.

Luther, Martin. "The Bondage of the Will." Translated by Philip S. Watson. In *The Career of the Reformer III*, edited by Philip S. Watson, volume 33 of *Luther's Works*, Helmut T. Lehmann, general editor. Philadelphia: Fortress Press, 1972.

Lutheran Book of Worship. Minneapolis: Augsburg Publishing House, 1978.

Middleton, J. Richard, and Brian J. Walsh. *Truth Is Stranger Than It Used to Be*. Downers Grove, IL: InterVarsity Press, 1995.

Norris, Kathleen. *The Cloister Walk*. New York: Riverhead Books, 1996.

Nouwen, Henri J. M. *In the Name of Jesus: Reflections on Christian Leadership*. New York: Crossroad Publishing Company, 1989.

Olsen, Charles M. *Transforming Church Boards into Communities of Spiritual Leaders*. Bethesda, MD: Alban Institute, 1995.

Pelikan, Jaroslav. *The Christian Intellectual*. London: Collins, 1996.

Peterson, Eugene H. *Answering God: The Psalms as Tools for Prayer.* San Francisco: Harper & Row, 1989.

————. *The Contemplative Pastor: Returning to the Art of Spiritual Direction.* Grand Rapids: Wm. B. Eerdmans Publishing Co., 1994.

————. *Five Smooth Stones for Pastoral Work.* Grand Rapids: Wm. B. Eerdmans Publishing Co., 1992.

————. *A Long Obedience in the Same Direction: Discipleship in an Instant Society.* Downers Grove, IL: InterVarsity Press, 1980.

————. *The Message: The New Testament in Contemporary Language.* Colorado Springs, CO: NavPress, 1994.

————. *The Message: The Wisdom Books.* Colorado Springs, CO: NavPress, 1996.

————. *Subversive Spirituality.* Edited by Jim Lyster, John Sharon, and Peter Santucci. Grand Rapids: Wm. B. Eerdmans Publishing Co., 1997.

————. *Take and Read: Spiritual Reading, An Annotated List.* Grand Rapids: Wm. B. Eerdmans Publishing Co., 1996.

————. *Under the Unpredictable Plant: An Exploration in Vocational Holiness.* Grand Rapids: Wm. B. Eerdmans Publishing Co., 1992.

————. *Where Your Treasure Is: Psalms That Summon You from Self to Community.* Grand Rapids: Wm. B. Eerdmans Publishing Co., 1985.

————. *Working the Angles: The Shape of Pastoral Integrity.* Grand Rapids: Wm. B. Eerdmans Publishing Co., 1987.

Phillips, Timothy R., and Dennis L. Okholm, eds. *The Nature of Confession: Evangelicals and Postliberals in Conversation.* Downers Grove, IL: InterVarsity Press, 1996.

Postman, Neil. *Amusing Ourselves to Death: Public Discourse in the Age of Show Business.* New York: Viking Penguin, 1985.

Schmidt, Thomas E. *Straight and Narrow? Compassion and Clarity in the Homosexuality Debate.* Downers Grove, IL: InterVarsity Press, 1995.

Schneiders, Sandra M. *The Revelatory Text.* New York: HarperSanFrancisco, 1991.

Sine, Tom. *The Mustard Seed Conspiracy.* Waco, TX: Word Books, 1981.

Tiede, David L. *Prophecy and History in Luke-Acts.* Philadelphia: Fortress Press, 1980.

Torvend, Samuel, and Lani Willis, eds. *Welcome to Christ: A Lutheran Catechetical Guide.* Minneapolis: Augsburg-Fortress, 1997.

———. *Welcome to Christ: A Lutheran Introduction to the Catechumenate.* Minneapolis: Augsburg-Fortress, 1997.

———. *Welcome to Christ: Lutheran Rites for the Catechumenate.* Minneapolis: Augsburg-Fortress, 1997.

Towner, Philip. *The Goal of Our Instruction.* Sheffield, Eng.: JSOT Press, 1989.

Van Gelder, Craig, ed. *Confident Witness — Changing World.* Grand Rapids: Wm. B. Eerdmans Publishing Co., 1999.

Walsh, David. *Selling Out America's Children.* Minneapolis: Fairview Press, 1995.

Wesche, Kenneth Paul. "Eastern Orthodox Spirituality." *Theology Today* 56, no. 1 (April 1999): 29-43.

Whitehead, Barbara Dafoe. *The Divorce Culture: Rethinking Our Commitments to Marriage and Family.* New York: Alfred Knopf, 1997.

Williams, Charles. *The Descent of the Dove.* Vancouver, BC: Regent Publishing, 1997.

Wink, Walter. *Naming the Powers: The Language of Power in the New Testament.* Philadelphia: Fortress Press, 1984.

Wright, N. T. *Jesus and the Victory of God.* Volume 2 of *Christian Origins and the Question of God.* Minneapolis: Fortress Press, 1996.

———. *The New Testament and the People of God.* Minneapolis: Fortress Press, 1992.

Wuthnow, Robert. *Sharing the Journey.* New York: Free Press, 1994.

Young, Frances M. *The Theology of the Pastoral Epistles.* New York: Cambridge University Press, 1994.